For the Zekaria family!

Best wishes,

Marina Sigh

London
April 2015

BEING INDIAN, BEING ISRAELI

BEING INDIAN, BEING ISRAELI
Migration, Ethnicity, and Gender in the Jewish Homeland

MAINA CHAWLA SINGH

MANOHAR
2014

First published 2009
Reprinted 2014

© Maina Chawla Singh, 2009

All rights reserved. No part of this publication may be reproduced or transmitted, in any form or by any means, without prior permission of the author and the publisher

ISBN 978-81-7304-839-5

Published by
Ajay Kumar Jain *for*
Manohar Publishers & Distributors
4753/23 Ansari Road, Daryaganj
New Delhi 110 002

Typeset by
Kohli Print
Delhi 110 051

Printed at
Salasar Imaging Systems
Delhi 110 035

*To Arun, my fellow-traveller
and my reason for going to Israel*

Contents

Foreword   9
Preface   15
Acknowledgements   21
Glossary   23

1. Migration, Diaspora and Indian Jews in Israel   27
2. Where Are the Indian Jews Today? Immigration and the Israeli Setting   65
3. Emigration from India: 'When We Came to the Land of Milk and Honey . . .'   90
4. Accountants as Watchmen and Clerks Digging Roads: Negotiating Work and Professions   119
5. Raising Jewish Families in Israel: Gender, Religious Practice and Life Cycle Rituals   153
6. Mediating Assimilation and Separation: Community Networks, National Politics and Indian-Israeli Identity   184
7. Epilogue   220

Appendices

1. Questionnarie   225
2. Map of India: Origins of Indian Jews   228
3. Map of Israel: Clusters of Indian Jews   229
4. Select List of Interviewees/Respondents who Participated in this Research   230

Bibliography   235
Index   243
Illustrations   bet. pp. 128–9

Author's Note to the 2014 Reprint

I write this five years after *Being Indian, Being Israeli* was first published in 2009. The experience of living and researching in Israel (2005-8) remains unforgettable. I remain in touch with many Indian Jews in Israel and the insights gleaned during this project continue to underpin my writing. In recent years, the Indian Jewish community has made strides in consolidating itself more cohesively. In September 2013, the first 'National Convention of Indian Jews in Israel' was held in Ramle, and in November 2013 'An Indian Weekend' was held in Jaffa, the scenic historic port adjacent to Tel Aviv. The Indian Jewish Heritage Center, Haifa, an entity long in abeyance, increasingly functions as a banner for community-wide mobilization. Enhanced visibility through conferences, bilateral exchanges and India-Israel scholarship is also reshaping the contours of community identity among the 'Indian Israelis'.

This book was written in Israel. Since then, I have lived in the United States, which has the second largest concentration of Jews in the world, after Israel. Today, I live in France, which has the third largest. An unexpected sequel to the publication of this book has been the journey of its dissemination and the curiosity this subject generated, which exceeded my expectations, by far. Numerous book-talks in Israel, India and the United States and interactions with hugely diverse audiences became a fascinating learning experience—a bonus I least expected.

As I prepare to speak at my first French-Jewish event in Paris this Spring, I pause for a moment and reflect on this experience.

To begin with, I learnt that the Indian Jewish story of migration seems to fascinate many diverse audiences especially in the US: academic and non-academic, Jewish and non-Jewish; university undergraduates interested in Indian diaspora or Hillel groups interested in the *Jewish* diaspora; retirees at Jewish community centers or synagogue members who come to Sunday-morning brunch-talks; even donor-members of pro-Israel groups who are invitees at events sponsored by the American Jewish Committee and AIPAC. The Indian diaspora in the US is perceived widely as a community of successful professionals, scientists and entrepreneurs and one that prioritizes 'family values'. In turn, many Indian Americans perceive the Jewish community as a model worth emulating. In fact, collaborative campus and community events have begun to happen between Indian and Jewish networks across America. Thus, the post-migration trajectory of Indian Jews interests *both* these groups, although many are 'surprised' that Indian Israelis, unlike Indian Americans have produced few world-class scientists, or hi-tech entrepreneurs. Yet, information-levels about the Indian Jewish communities remain low and even among well-informed American Jewry, 'I had no idea there were so many Indian Jews', was a recurring remark. Ironically, in the New York and Westchester area, most of my Ashkenazi audiences were unaware that there is a thriving Indian Jewish congregation in New York city! Many Indian Jews living in the US and Canada have narrated to me their experience of being asked by other Jewish folk: 'So, when did Indian Jews convert?' Given the 2000 year-old history of Jews in India, this is deeply offensive to Jews of Indian origin.

Further, while I was reasonably well-armed to respond to questions about Indian Jewish identities, I was less prepared for the personal question, 'Are you Jewish?' Puzzling at first, this frequently-asked-question, I came to understand, reflected genuine puzzlement that delving so deeply into ethnographies of Indian Jews was completely unconnected to my own religious identity. Jewish non-academic audiences were particularly fascinated that my deep engagement with Indian Jewish migration narratives or my easy familiarity with remote, less-known townships in Israel, could not be traced to some iota of Jewish heritage in me.

Today, as this book is poised for a 2014 reprint, it is only apt to express deep appreciation for my audiences at the Library of Congress, Washington DC, at universities including Yale, Georgetown, Brandeis, American University, Johns Hopkins, Penn State and the Universities of Miami and Michigan State; to the chapters of the American Jewish Committee in Florida, Seattle, Cleveland, Westchester and New York and many synagogue groups in Washington, Maryland, New Haven and New York who hosted these talks. In engaging with this book, they have deepened the sociological understandings of a non-Jewish, non-Israeli scholar about Jewish identities in and outside Israel, the influential role of Jewish organizations, the varied models of assimilation, and of course, complex notions of belonging, which remain embedded in our ever-shifting identities.

Paris
February 2014

MAINA CHAWLA SINGH

Foreword

It is indeed surprising that such a book was not written earlier. A few scholarly works have appeared on Indian Jews in Israel, but they are either dated or too narrow in their approach. There are so many specialists on international migration and theories about space and place abound in them, but somehow a rigorous socio-historical study of contemporary Indian Jews in Israel has escaped long-term diligent attention.

Fortunately, this lapse has been more than adequately corrected by Dr Maina Chawla Singh. This volume opens new veins for research on international migration. We need to understand the extent to which the arrival and presence of Indian Jews to Israel adds complexity to our notions of culture, identity and conflict between traditions. This volume draws our attention to these themes by enquiring into issues which most of us never seriously considered before. For instance, it is interesting to know the difference between migrating to a 'homeland', instead of leaving one, and the significance of adopting an identity when a large part of it is determined by politics.

Dr Singh was perhaps uniquely blessed in writing this book. She not only had access to Israel, but also an enquiring mind that allowed her to make the best of her advantage. There have been other Indians in Israel before, but nobody cared to delve into this theme with the same depth and rigour. Indian Jews may have been out of their sight for most of them as they generally live outside the big cities, but not by much. They may not be numerous in Tel Aviv, but they are hardly scarce 30–40 miles away in places like Ashdod, Ramla and Lod. But it needs more than sighting Indians. Dr Singh has systematically interviewed about 150 Jews of Indian descent in Israel and presented her findings by adroitly weaving in theory with anecdotal detail.

Interestingly, unlike other kinds of international migration, the

Indians who went to Israel in search of their homeland did not, in the main, go singly, but as a family. It is not as if families were not split by this migration (or *aliya*): that too happened, but the trend was in the other direction. To make matters more difficult, Indian Jews were lumped initially with those who were migrants from North Africa, or West Asia—the *Mizrahis*. Culturally, they had nothing in common with those from Arabic cultures, other than the fact that they were not *Ashkenazis*, or Jews of European descent.

In spite of this, or may be partly on account of this, Indian Jews in Israel clung to many of their so-called South Asian attributes. They participate in the Indian Republic Day and Independence Day celebrations; speak Hebrew but also Marathi, Malayalam and English. This depends largely on whether they are Bene Israelis from Mumbai, Cochinis from Kerala, or Baghdadis from Kolkata. These Jews also identified respect for parents and elders as valuable heritages of their South Asian descent. The Bene Israelis bear surnames like the rest in Maharashtra where the suffix 'kar' is appended to their place of origin. These names have survived along with the taste of *samosas* and *bhaji*. The Bene Israelis are most particular of all the Indian Jews, in abstaining from eating beef. Long years in Hindu Maharashtra have drilled this attitude deep in their aesthetics and dietary preferences. Of course, dating was not a good idea among them in India, but as the author comments, it is difficult to do 'moral policing' in Israel. Further, the Jewish Agency helped many single Indian Jewish women to migrate, but true to form, they nearly always went with a sibling or a cousin—hardly ever without a relative.

South Asia remains with Indian Jews in Israel in other ways too. Divorce rates are usually lower, Bene Israelis have a *mehendi* ceremony when the bride wears a traditional Indian dress, but over time, inter-community marriages are also taking place. In Nevatim the Cochini Jews have built a synagogue which is a replica of the one in Cochin. The young speak Hebrew and sing Hebrew songs, but they also swing as easily to Bollywood hits. The Bene Israelis also bring out *Mai Boli*, which is a Marathi language journal. On India's Independence or Republic Day

Indian Jews in large numbers attend the flag-hoisting receptions hosted by the Indian Ambassador and they sing the Indian national anthem! These Israeli Indians live in Israel, but India is a fond memory, yet it is never flogged for political attention. This is another major difference between Indians migrating to Israel and those to Europe and America. In Israel, politics is the politics of Israel. But Indians in USA or UK, leverage their cultural baggage to win minority recognition from the host countries. This is often done under the guise of 'multi-culturalism'.

So what took them to Israel? Dr Singh reminds us that Indian Jews did not leave the land of their birth for the 'Jewish Homeland' because they were persecuted. In fact, they often found it difficult to identify with tales and folklores of Jews from elsewhere. They chose Israel because of the draw of the 'homeland' of course, but also because of some straightforward this-worldly considerations. Educating their children, owning a house (especially if you were from a crowded city like Mumbai), and putting away tidy savings for the future, were some of the motivating factors for making *aliya*.

But it wasn't as if they entered the land of 'Milk and Honey' as soon as they landed on its shores. Many Cochini Jews who had never done agriculture before were sent to *Moshavs* and settled in clusters. In the early years, many who went to Israel in fact, gave up office jobs only to be given manual work with a spade in the desert. Only recently are there greater numbers of Indian Jewish migrants who walk straight into professional careers. Unlike other forms of international migration, this was a case where many migrants self-consciously took an economic hit and had to scale down their lifestyles. Yet they rarely complained.

What came to them as a shock however, is the colour discrimination they faced. Some girls looked 'too Indian' (read 'dark skinned') and were denied secretarial and office jobs. This kind of discrimination they were not ready for. In fact, the Bene Israelis had to also prove their Jewishness. This spurred off agitations and also bonded this community, but it was a very unwelcome aspect of their 'homecoming'.

Even so, politics inevitably played a major role in the making of Jewish culture in Israel. Learning Hebrew was compulsory and this was primarily to bond Jewish migrants from different parts of the world into a strong nation with one language. Teenage Indian migrants found this the most difficult, so did the older ones who at 50 were too advanced in years to pick up a new language. Yet they persevered and eventually succeeded in learning a totally foreign tongue. Another interesting detail reflecting the primacy of politics in Israeli culture relates to compulsory military service. Indian Jews like other Israelis, recall with pride their years of compulsory service in the army. This corrects a widespread impression that Indian Israelis are meek pen-pushers, easy to dominate and too eager to please. Today, it is the masculine, military role model that is looked up to in Israel. Gone is the earlier Jewish masculine ideal type of the Talmudic scholar, immersed in the holy texts, taking time off only to rub his eyes. Though Indians are generally present in less physically taxing occupations, they too partake of this role model and are proud to have played their role in the Israeli military. Politics and culture come together yet again when Indian Israelis identify strongly with the state in its condemnation and perennial suspicion of Arabs.

Dr Singh's treatment of changes at the family level, especially among women and the kind of work they perform, post-*aliya*, or migration to the homeland, is finely crafted and should interest scholars who work on family and gender. The domestic sexual division of labour in Israel is not quite what it is in India, but there are similarities. It should, however, be noted that many of these women had no extra-mural occupations in India, but in the Jewish Homeland they were out taming the desert, working in fields and doing some pretty rigourous jobs. Naturally, all of this affects the relation between sexes at home and the attitude towards children.

The richness of this study is undoubtedly on account of its novelty, but this new research also unveils many theoretical possibilities as it points towards new directions for future investigations. I believe that Dr Singh's treatment of gender, coupled with the Israeli idealization of the military model suggest some interesting leads about how younger 'Indian-Israelis' perceive themselves, and the kinds of political influences which colour their sense of being in the 'homeland'. This study also demonstrates how and under what conditions migrants submit to extraordinary hardship without complaining too much. An investigation such as this will not only enrich existing research in diaspora studies (as they are often called), but also interest policy-makers who are concerned with the re-settlement of internal migrants.

Professor　　　　　　　　　　　　　　　　　　DIPANKAR GUPTA
School of Social Sciences
Jawaharlal Nehru University
New Delhi

Preface

Between 2005 and 2008, I lived in Israel for long periods of time. An affiliation to Tel Aviv University (2006–7) and Haifa University (2007–8) provided a wonderful opportunity for research, student interactions and valuable exchanges with the faculty on areas of mutual interest. My husband's assignment with the Embassy of India, Tel Aviv exposed me to two almost parallel worlds. On the one hand was the world of the Israeli elites—politicians, policymakers, businessmen investing in Indian markets and military elites working along areas of bilateral defense projects. The other was the world of the Indian-origin Jews. Unlike other diasporic communities from India settled elsewhere in the world like the United Kingdom, the United States or Canada, the community in Israel comprises largely of Jews of Indian origin who are *permanently* settled in Israel, having been granted Israeli citizenship on the basis of religion *immediately* upon their landing in the Promised Land.[1]

The first group of Jewish emigrants came from India in 1949. As a result of subsequent waves of migration since the 1950s and natural population increase, today there are over 70,000 Indian Jews in Israel. Yet, when I remarked about this in my lectures at Israeli universities, or in social or diplomatic circles, it evoked a note of surprise, 'Are there so many?' As I straddled these two worlds, and became increasingly aware that the Indian Jews were absent from the higher ranks of bureaucracy, military or business elites, I searched elsewhere. In professions like medicine, academics or Information-Technology where Indian-origin communities have shone globally, they were hardly a presence in Israel. Scattered individual success stories raised questions about ethnicity, location and class stratification in Israeli society. As I travelled in Tel Aviv, Jerusalem and Haifa—the largest and busiest cities in Israel—Indians were hardly to be spotted. Yet, in Ashdod,

40 km from Tel Aviv, or in Ramla or Lod about 20–30 km from Tel Aviv, I saw lots of Indians. On a Friday they could be seen shopping at the Indian grocery store, or at the Indian 'take away' buying Indian *kosher* food for the Jewish Sabbath. Many of the men wore *kippas*, the Jewish traditional cap, but hearing phrases in Marathi on the streets was not uncommon. The cultural evenings organized by Indian associations, which I attended in Ramla and Lod in 2005–6, fascinated me. The programmes were typical Bollywood fare, of the latest film songs and dances from Hindi cinema put together by amateur groups. Young Indian Jewish girls dressed in bright, gaudy Indian clothes, swayed to the tune Indian pop and film music emoting to the seductive lyrics blaring on the music system, in Hindi—which many of the dancers and their audience did not even understand!

On the Indian Republic Day and Independence Day, the Ambassador of India to Israel traditionally hosts a reception for 'people of Indian origin'—an open house in which Indian Jews turn up in huge numbers. On 26 January 2006 there were about 400 and on 26 January 2007 there was an unprecedented 500 Jewish Indians! They had commuted long distances, some up to even 100 km to arrive by 8.30 a.m. to attend the unfurling of the Indian flag and hear the Indian Ambassador deliver excerpts from the speech of the President of India. When the Indian national anthem was being sung several Indian Jews joined in, recalling the words which they had learnt during their schooldays in India, as far back as forty years ago! Though Israeli citizens, they clearly felt no hesitation in singing the praises of a country that had once been their home for several centuries! Their enthusiasm was palpable. Many Indian-Jewish women had turned up in *saris*, while many men wore *kippas*. People lounging in the garden, chatting in groups and relishing Indian savouries like *jalebis* and *samosas* created an ambience within which the comments of Ben-Sion (one of my respondents) were so apt: 'You can take the Jew out of India, but you cannot take the Indian out of the Jew', he chuckled. Ben-Sion himself sported a Nehru jacket, an Indian-style white cap and a T-shirt with Gandhi's spectacles printed on it with a caption that said: *They don't make 'em like him any more!*

It was hard to imagine another Jewish immigrant group in Israel gathering voluntarily at an embassy-sponsored programme celebrating the national day of their 'country-of-origin', to which they do not even have dual citizenship rights.[2]

These are the Indian Jews—citizens of the Jewish State and native speakers of Hebrew, who emigrated on the basis of religion and worked physically to 'build' the nation of Israel, digging its roads, planting its trees and draining its swamps, alongside their other Jewish immigrant cousins, with whom they shared either a commitment to Zionism or at least a strong religious affiliation. Now six decades after the formation of the State of Israel (1948), it is important to ask questions about community identity—about social mobility, acculturation and assimilation pertaining to the Indian Jews. We need to raise questions about ethnicity and identity—both at the time of entry to the Promised Land, and in the new millennium when the first immigrants are in their late seventies, watching their grandchildren grow as Israelis. How did the markers of ethnicity create barriers to assimilation 50 years ago—from language access problems to dealing with stereotypes of Indians as coming from a 'backward', 'poor' country? And over time, how did Indian Jews negotiate/resist exclusions? Finally, in the context of today, what are the markers of 'Indian-ness' consciously retained—both in the *private sphere*, the life cycle rituals, food, everyday practices, gender relations and concept of family, as well as in the *public sphere* where Indian groups and organizations mobilize community members by invoking a shared 'Indian culture' through programmes of Indian dance and music mirroring the latest trends in popular music and fashion in contemporary India?

This project emerged out of these and related questions during my stay in Israel, lecturing and straddling two parallel worlds in Israeli society. After several meetings with the community of Indian Jews between 2005 and 2006, during which I visited many places in Israel having concentrations of Indian Jews, and attending numerous community programmes (organized both by community networks and the Embassy of India, Tel Aviv), I embarked on a systematic project of collecting qualitative data on Indian Jews in Israel—life-stories, early emigration narratives, issues of acculturation, assimilation and community self-perceptions today. Between February 2006 and January 2008, indepth interviews were conducted with about 100 individuals. Additional discussions with other individuals through focus group discussions would add up to over 150 respondents. Although interviews were conducted across a cross-section of age, this study mainly focuses on the first generation of Jewish immigrants now living in Israel—those who were born in India and came here either as children, adolescents or adults. The bulk of Jewish migration to Israel from India took place before the 1970s, and most of the interviews were conducted with those who came during this time. However, I have also included families who came later, because research revealed that individuals coming from India in the 1980s and 1990s were more educated which ensured their easy access into the Israeli job market, than had been the experience of their predecessors. This linkage between education, access to professional achievement and consequent social status figures as an important theme for discussion in subsequent chapters.

The response of the interviewees was overwhelming—both in terms of their willingness and in the openness with which they shared their experiences. Men and women shared their life-stories, immigration experiences, struggles, photographs and anecdotes. Many of the older respondents (now well over sixty) claimed that these interviews triggered memories of experiences long 'forgotten', and perhaps never recounted before. I visited Indian Jews spread across northern and southern Israel—sometimes over a 100 km from Tel Aviv. Individuals, couples and often their children were glad to share their stories, offering information and warm hospitality. Many of them offered comparative stories, of their own, of friends and relatives, with similar (or different) immigration experiences, of those who had come in different immigration 'waves': why some came later, and why some preferred to stay on in India, and still others who came to Israel, only to move on to the United Kingdom, the United States or

Canada because they found the immigrant challenges in Israel too daunting. Those I interviewed led me to other connections—enabling me to locate Indian Jews who do not reside in ethnic community neighbourhoods. Thus, I identified and interviewed Indians living in 'Indian neighbourhoods' as well as those who did not fit stereotypes, i.e. those who lived in wealthy neighbourhoods like Herzliya, the beach-side town near Tel Aviv, or the hilly picturesque Carmel in Haifa, or those who have chosen to live in a *kibbutz*—a rare choice of lifestyle among Indian Jews. The older generation of retirees, who now lead quiet lives, were particularly helpful—not only because they offered a storehouse of the early experiences of the 1950s–60s but also because as retirees with more time on their hands they maintained stronger intra-community links and could lead me to others of their generation, who live scattered across Israel. I thus, covered a wide range by way of age, year of arrival in Israel, profession, region of origin *in India*, as well as class and status *in Israel*.

Although some Indian Jews were aware that their communities had been the focus of some research,[3] almost all the respondents figuring in this study remarked that their experiences of migration and struggle had not been collected or documented. Also, the men and women, who were active in local associations, said that specific issues pertaining to ethnicity and identity of the Indian Jews remained mostly unnoticed within the larger cleavages within contemporary Israeli society, i.e. between *Ashkenazim* (Jews of European descent) and *Mizrahim* ('Oriental' Jews—broadly including all non-white Jews from West Asia and North Africa). Indian Jews widely remarked on how they felt 'culturally different' from the Moroccan, Iraqi or Algerian and other Jews who were grouped as *Mizrahim*. In their self-perception they were distinct—often more *dis*-similar than similar to other Jews of North African or West Asian origin, although they were commonly clubbed within the same broad classification of *Mizrahim*.

These specificities of identity, being 'Israeli'-'Jewish'-'Indian', are important underlying themes of this volume.

NOTES

1. For the same reason they are also distinct from other diasporic Indian communities settled in Mauritius, Surinam or East Africa.
2. For instance, there are large Jewish communities from Morocco and Iraq in Israel, but neither country has diplomatic relations with Israel. In the case of Jews from United States or Russia, both countries permit individuals to hold dual passports which many in fact, do retain. By contrast, the Indian government does not permit dual citizenship. Even though Government of India's Overseas Citizen of India (OCI) scheme gives certain benefits, the Indian Jews are have *only* Israeli citizenship. Their enthusiasm for the Indian Republic Day or Indian Independence Day is therefore, remarkable.
3. This was in the case of Indian Jews in Lod (from the Bene Israeli community) and in Nevatim (from the Cochini community).

Acknowledgements

This book was written during the last six months of my stay in Israel in 2008. The actual process of writing was fairly quick and personally very fulfilling. Upon re-visiting the drafts in later months, I felt there was little I wanted to change. I attribute this to the quality of my experience of living in Israel and the generosity of the many Jewish friends and colleagues who nourished my curiosity for their society as I researched this book.

My first thanks go to the Indian Jewish community—the men and women who opened their homes and shared their lives, trusting me to use their stories of joy and hardship with sensitivity, even as I sought to give visibility to their issues. Their excitement at the prospect of this book, their pride in their Indian homeland and their sheer affection for me were moving. Community leaders like Noah Massil (Jerusalem), Eliyahu Dekel (Rosh Pina), Eliyahu Bezalel (Moshav Shahaar), Moshe Pinchas (Kiryat Bialik), Elizabeth David (Shoham) and Moshe Binyamin (Dimona) supplied me ample local information. Among senior members I wish to acknowledge Uriella Solomon (*b.* 1927), Dvora Isaac Joseph (*b.* 1924), Diana Benjamin (*b.* 1928), Becky Issac, Ruth Sanker, Elizabeth Joseph and Bina Solomon for long interviews filled with anecdotal details about family immigration experiences of the 1950s–60s. Through community outreach I collected scores of photographs featuring family occasions and community programmes. I thank Ben Sion Benjamin, David Negrekar, David Israel, Dan Shishoren and also others who I was unable to locate individually for contributing to my photo collection.

While the fieldwork data was exciting, the academic inputs I received were equally enriching. Tel Aviv University, Bar-Ilan and University of Haifa provided me research affiliations, library resources and the opportunity for valuable faculty exchanges. Although I rued the fact that most seminars and classroom discussions at Israeli universities were in Hebrew, there were numerous Israeli academics who generously gave me time—brainstorming and commenting on what I was processing. For this, I wish to thank Henriette Dahan Kalev (Ben Gurion University), Moshe Shokeid, Noah Lewin-Epstein, and Yehouda Shenav (Tel Aviv University), Debbie Bernstein, Sammy Smooha, Oz Almog, Sharon Halevi (Haifa University).

I wish to acknowledge the support of many at the Embassy of India, Tel Aviv especially Sybil, Georgina, Rania and Beton. Shayela Israel assisted me cheerfully and tirelessly in tracking individuals and details as I edited the book—even after I had left Israel. At a personal level, in Tel Aviv and Herzilya I wish to acknowledge friends for stimulating conversations over Shabbat meals, Seder dinners, Succot evenings and walks by the Mediterranean: Orly and Nochi Dankner, Itzhak and Eti livni, Nili and Amiram Cohen, Baty, Ruth Kaddari, Ariella Zelouf and most of all, Katie Koren, my dear Calcutta-born Baghdadi friend whose warmth cushioned my 'expatriate' existence in special ways !

I am grateful to Mini Kapoor in Delhi and Prof. Dorothy O. Helly in New York for their 'long-distance' support and conversations as I revised the manuscript.

Emiko Pavini, I thank you for creative inputs in the jacket design—and for being my daughter! Arun, your support and unfailing patience as my in-house discussant, commentator and 'proofreader' was invaluable!

My special thanks to Rebecca Yehezkiel for granting permission to use her painting on the jacket of this book and to Michal Yehezkiel for the photographic imaging.

My special gratitude to Prof. S. Ilan Troen, Prof. Noah Lewin-Epstein, Prof. Dipankar Gupta and Prof. Andre Beteille for engaging with this manuscript despite many pressing demands on their schedules. Finally, it was a pleasure to work with Siddharth Chowdhury and Ramesh Jain at Manohar Publishers & Distributors. I appreciated their patience and support.

June 2009 MAINA CHAWLA SINGH

Glossary

Note: This glossary goes beyond literal meanings to offer explanatory contexts which may help non-Israeli/non-Jewish readers to understand words/concepts used in this book which are drawn from Israeli society or Indian Jewish culture.

Aliya: Literally meaning 'ascent'; refers to making committed migration to the Jewish Homeland. Making *aliya* is a basic tenet of Zionism and it is a loaded term because the Hebrew word used to describe emigration *from* Israel is termed as *yerida* (or descent).

Ashkenazi: Jews of Eastern European origin primarily from Germany, Poland, and Russia.

KAMAG/Kamaag: The official Hebrew acronym for Negev Nuclear Research Center (known colloquially as the Dimona reactor). This is Israel's largest and most significant Israeli nuclear facility and a highly guarded area. KAMAG is located in the Negev desert about 12 km south of Dimona.

Kashruth/kashrut: From the Hebrew root *Kaf-Shin-Reish*, meaning fit, proper or correct. Used to describe Jewish laws especially relating to food—which foods are *kosher* and how those foods must be prepared and consumed.

Khazan/Hazzan: Literally means 'messenger on behalf of the public/congregation'. In practice it is someone who may lead the prayers in a Jewish congregation. (Not to be confused with a *Rabbi* who has religious authority invested in him.)

Kiryat/Qiryat: A village. Many places in Israel have that prefix: Kiryat Gat; Kiryat Ata, Kiryat Yam.

Kibbutz (plural *kibbutzim*): A collective community in Israel traditionally based on agriculture; a form of communal living that combines socialism and Zionism. In Hebrew, *kibbutzim* also refers to the communities who live on the *kibbutz*.

Kosher: Basically means something that follows all the Jewish guidelines. *Kosher* food can be any food that adheres to Jewish dietary laws.

Kupat Holim: The health organization of workers in Israel which was begun at the 2nd Convention of Jewish Agricultural Workers (Judea, December 1911) before the formation of Israel. It is a functioning health care organization in Israel.

Ma'baara (plural: *Ma'baarot*): Derived from the Hebrew word *ma'avar* meaning transit. *Ma'abarot* were transit camps offering very basic housing (even sheds) widely built in Israel in the 1950s to accommodate the vast influx of new *olim* (Jewish immigrants) to Israel. Most *ma'abarot* were inhabited by immigrants of *Mizrahi* origin from North Africa or West Asia which reinforced certain negative stereotypes of *Mizrahis*.

Malida: A ceremonial offering accompanied by an invocation for the presence and blessings of the Prophet Elijah. This ceremony is also known as the *Eliyahoo Ha-Navi* ceremony—essentially a Bene Israeli tradition.

Mizrahi/Mizrachi (plural *Mizrahim*): Jews of Middle Eastern, North African, and Asian descent. Other terms like Eastern/Oriental/Arab Jews are sometimes used synonymously. *Mizrahi* Jews sometimes refer to themselves as *Sephardi*.

Moshav (plural *moshavim*): A cooperative Israeli village or agricultural community comprising of small farms, generally based on the principle of private ownership of land, avoidance of hired labour, and communal marketing. This represents an intermediate stage between privately owned settlements and the complete communal living of the *kibbutz*. *Moshavim* are built on land belonging to the Jewish National Fund or the state. In Hebrew, *Moshavim* also refers to the communities who live on the *moshav*.

Olim: Special term for those immigrants who have made *aliya* to Israel. The feminine form is '*olah* (feminine) or *olot* (masculine)'.

Often *olim* is used together with the word *chadashim* which means 'new'.

Pesakh/Pesach: The Passover festival; a Jewish and Samaritan holy day and festival commemorating the escape of Jews from enslavement in Egypt. Passover begins on the 14th day of the month of Nisan (usually March/April).

Rosh Ha Shana: Jewish New Year and the first day of the High Holidays observed in the autumn each year. This is also to be a 'day of rest' like the weekly Jewish *Shabbat*. All Jewish festivals follow the lunisolar calendar and the dates change each year accordingly.

Sabra: A term used to describe a Jew born in Israel. Being a *sabra* is a matter of pride for Israelis—it distinguishes those who were born in the Jewish Homeland from those who came as *olim chadashim* (new immigrants)—denoting a higher status for the *sabra*.

Sephardic/Sephardi: Literally meaning Jewish population primarily of Spanish origin or from certain parts of Italy. In broad contemporary usage it refers to *all* Jews of non-European origin including those from North Africa.

Shabbat: The Jewish Sabbath (extending from time of sunset on Friday to sunset on Saturday). A 'period of rest' prescribed by Jewish law, *Shabbat* is observed to varying degrees of strictness in Israel. Orthodox Jews begin the *Shabbat* evening by lighting candles and reciting prayers before breaking the special *Challah* bread (white egg bread reserved for the *Shabbat*) over the *Shabbat* dinner. They refrain from watching television, using telephones or travelling in automobiles/elevators during *Shabbat*. The Israeli state observes a Friday–Saturday weekend and Sunday is a regular working day. For 'secular Israelis, *Shabbat* is simply the 'weekend' involving family-visiting and fun. *Shabbat* Friday dinners are a very special part of Israeli family culture. People drive long distances to assemble in parental homes. Elaborately prepared meals are the norm on *Shabbat*, although they may or may not be *kosher* depending on the levels to which a family is observant.

Sukkot/Succot: Feast of Booths or Feast of Tabernacles. A Biblical pilgrimage festival that occurs in autumn on the 15th day of the month of *Tishrei* (late September to late October). The holiday lasts seven days. This was a celebration of gratitude and praise to God for the harvest.

TsarKhaniya (tsarkhani'ya): A neighbourhood grocery store selling basic necessities.

Ulpan: An intensive language immersion programme (extending over a few months) primarily offered in Israel to those who are new *olim*.

Yeshiva (plural *yeshivot*): Generic name for any school that teaches Jewish scriptures, Torah, Mishnah and Talmud to any age group. In practice these are usually post-high school institutions or rabbinical schools catering to young Jewish aspirants of serious religious education—open to males only.

Yom Kippur: The Day of Atonement; this is the most solemn and important of the Jewish holidays. Its central themes are atonement and repentance. Jews traditionally observe this holy day with a 25-hour period of fasting and intensive prayer, often spending most of the day in synagogue services. On *Yom Kippur*, life comes to a halt in Israel and roads are empty of traffic.

Youth Aliya: A project promoting the immigration of Jewish youth (usually groups of teenagers) from different countries to Israel. These were sponsored projects executed through a collaboration between organizations like the Jewish Agency and local Jewish communities in different countries.

CHAPTER 1

Migration, Diaspora and Indian Jews in Israel

Overseas Indians attract considerable attention today. Indian diasporic communities in a transnational world and the ambivalent connections between their 'ancestral homelands' and their 'new belongings' have triggered much scholarship in Migration Studies as scholars seek to understand how 'Indian' identities have been mutated through migration since India's Independence in 1947. The importance of historical and political imperatives has been underlined and interlinkages between empire and migration have been offered as important underpinnings shaping the migrations of post-colonial Indian communities to United States, United Kingdom, Canada and elsewhere.[1] Scholars argue that the Indian diaspora has become 'a contact zone' for various formations of identity and that diasporic sensibilities are produced in complex ways, not simply as an 'outgrowth of the nation-state'.[2] The impact of migration on the cultural and religious lives of communities is also widely recognized as an important factor as scholars seek to understand post-colonial Indian subjectivities in transnational locations.[3]

But in the loud narrative of 'the Indian abroad', be it the Indian entrepreneur in 'Silicon Valley' in the United States or the manual labour in the 'Gulf countries' in West Asia, the story of the Indian Jewish community is inaudible. The migration of Indian Jews has not been studied. Indian Jews barely find notice as *Indians* who migrated out of India or as *Jews* who migrated from different parts of the world to the Jewish Homeland. The historical and political configurations that shaped Indian Jewish migration and subsequent acculturation in their new homeland remain uninvestigated. Yet, the migration of Indian Jews to Israel, the Jewish

Homeland is rich with analytical possibilities. It raises multiple and wide-ranging questions pertaining to motivation, acculturation, identity and assimilation. As a model it is unique. Yet, the case of Indian-Jewish migration to Israel remains mostly unmapped. Is this because when Indian Jews migrated to Israel they were perceived as '*returning* home' to the 'Jewish Homeland' rather than '*leaving* home' where they and their ancestors were born? Is it because unlike a more common pattern of migration (as individuals or as families), Jewish migration to Israel was often in groups, sometimes planeloads of Indian Jews who flew together from Bombay to Israel, often without requiring passports? Is it because there was a distinct sense of 'finality' about this migration perceived in Israeli nationalist discourses as the 'end of Jewish exile'? Finally, do the ideological underpinnings associated with Jewish emigration from India distract scholars of South Asia from this investigation? Perhaps, it is all of the above.

But surely, such simplistic assumptions gloss over important complexities. Surely migrating from the 'Indian homeland' to the 'Jewish homeland' was neither simply linear nor uncomplicated —spatially, socially and psychologically. The relationship between the notion of a 'homeland' and of 'diaspora' is always fluid and problematic and not indelible. When one distinguishes between the definitional and the operative levels, this association is in fact, far more tenuous and complex. The assumption that all Jews migrated from India because they felt impelled by religion or Zionism is an assumption that bears serious scrutiny. Two simple facts may be enough to re-open this trajectory of investigation. First, that although the first group of Indian Jews left for Israel in 1949, a year after Israel was established, the bulk of Indian Jews came in the 1960s and 1970s. This reflects that as a community they were in no rush to emigrate—either as Jews or as Zionists. Secondly, even today, there are over 5,000 Jews living in India— mostly in the Bombay region. These are Jews who have chosen to *stay on* as a minority in India, where they and their forefathers were born. Almost *all* Jews in India have some relatives in Israel— siblings, cousins, uncles, aunts or even parents. Their transnational linkages with their relatives in Israel, UK, USA or Canada are akin to those of other Indians who have family members in the diaspora. There is, however, an obvious difference: Indian Jews are aware that they can emigrate at will to Israel, claim Israeli citizenship and all the preferential benefits automatically bestowed on *all* Jews upon arrival in Israel. Indian Jewish migration to Israel is therefore *unique*. It bears analysis—both as a sociological project in *dis*-location and *re*-location. This migration is an important phenomenon of recent history affecting both India as the country-of-origin, and Israel as the 'Jewish homeland'.[4]

As a study exploring migration, ethnicity, gender and diasporic identities, this book is poised on two important premises. First, that for an analysis of ethnicity, migration relating to the Indian diaspora, the case of Israel is *unique*. This uniqueness needs to be investigated and underlined since it shaped the 'push' factors for emigration, as well as the 'homecoming' and reception that the new immigrants received at the end of their journey. Indian Jews who left India for Israel were *migrants with a difference*—their motivations were shaped by the fact of their Jewish-ness, which was a pre-requisite for this migration. This also meant that entire families or groups of families could plan migration *together*. Apart from these features, the emigration of Indian Jews to Israel was notably unique because of the circumstances at the port of arrival. Given that Israel was/is ideologically and institutionally committed to welcoming *all* Jews from all over the world, it creates a special configuration for new immigrants. According to the Law of Return (1950) and the Law of Nationality (1952), every Jew has the right to settle in Israel and citizenship is automatically conferred upon arrival. Potential immigrants are wooed through outreach programmes of organizations such as the Jewish Agency, and invited to emigrate. Following this, state commitment to the successful integration of its (Jewish) immigrants into society is borne out by the generous governmental support to the new immigrants and the efforts of state authorities and voluntary organizations to facilitate easy settlement. Financial support, language classes are all included.[5] Israelis use a special word for a Jew who emigrates. He/she is making *aliya* (literally meaning 'ascent'). Making *aliya* is special because the act brings 'back' the Jew to the 'homeland' (as opposed to being in 'exile'). In this sense, for an Indian Jew to be migrating to Israel would be very different from migrating to any other country like Britain or Canada, because in coming to Israel an immigrant could legitimately have expectations from the State, to ensure basic well-being from the very outset. The second premise is that within this configuration of multi-ethnic Jewish migration from all over the world, after the establishment of the State of Israel as a Jewish homeland, the Indian Jews are a community marked by distinct characteristics which remain understudied.

A DISTINCT COMMUNITY

Indian Jews in contemporary Israel are drawn from different regions of India. There are three main Jewish communities with Indian origins: the Bene Israeli, the Kerala Jews, and the Baghdadis from Iraq.[6] Each group practised important elements of Judaism. The *Sephardic* rites broadly predominated among Indian Jews while they were settled in India although local rituals had variations. Bene Israelis (literally, 'Sons of Israel') are the largest community and they were broadly from western India, the Bombay region and a few scattered in Ahmedabad, Delhi and Karachi. They spoke Marathi, Hindi or Gujarati. Cochini Jews from southern India spoke Malayalam. The Calcutta Jews were mostly of Baghdadi origin, so that while the earlier generations spoke Arabic, they acquired English through education and spoke street versions of Hindi or Hindustani while communicating with the outside world.[7] In Israel, Indian Jews live alongside other Jews who came from Europe (Germany, Russia, Poland, Romania, Bulgaria and so forth), and from North Africa or parts of the Middle East (Morocco, Tunisia, Algeria, Turkey, Yemen and so on). Israeli sociologists and social scientists today deal with two major 'blocs' in Israeli Jewish society broadly stratified along lines of class and privilege—the *Ashkenazis* and the *Mizrahis*—terms which were coined to denote those who came from Europe (and are predominantly white), and those who came from North Africa (and are non-white). When these are deployed as sociological categories, the *Mizrahis* supposedly share a common 'Oriental' culture, customs, modes of prayer, language and food habits that emanate from that common heritage.[8] Indians, comparatively a smaller community, than for instance the Moroccans or the Iraqis, are subsumed into this *Mizrahi* bloc.

A key objective of this book is to argue that culturally and linguistically Indian Jews may share little with those who come from broadly Arabic cultures. In fact, even among the Baghdadi Jews who had settled in Calcutta, Arabic had rarely been passed on in the family, so that the Baghdadi-Indian Jews, who migrated from India, mostly used English and different versions of conversational Hindi to communicate, rather than Arabic. Thus, when Indians are unquestioningly grouped with the North Africans or others from West Asia, it suggests a categorization by colour (non-western/non-white) than by shared civilizational heritage. This book seeks to make a space for the Indian Jewish community as a *distinct* community, within the Israeli multi-ethnic mosaic consisting of Jews from other parts of the world. The distinctiveness of these Indian-Israelis has some important underpinnings which merit discussion. A key aspect that needs to be underlined in understanding Indian Jews in Israel is that their life experiences as Jews *before* migration and *before* the formation of the state of Israel was, in many ways, unique. The most important fact that distinguishes Jews of Indian origin from Jews elsewhere in the world is: Jews in India did not experience religious persecution. Jews who came to Israel from India therefore, were *not* refugees. They came of their own free will and they came from settled homes in different parts of India. They had only a distant intellectual understanding of Jewish suffering in Eastern Europe and the larger meta-historical drama involving the persecution of Jews over the centuries. Jewish communities in India were not under pressure to live in ghettos or segregated communities. Pogroms, for the Indian Jews, were what they had read in textbooks. Indeed, during the interviews many Indian Jews now living in Israel claimed that they had not even heard of the holocaust while they grew up in various parts of India in the 1940s! Histories of Jewish martyrology did not resonate with their experience of life in India, where

Jewish families could have lived in Calcutta or Bombay in completely mixed neighbourhoods next to Hindus, Muslims and Christians, or as in Cochin where 'Jew Town' was merely a descriptive term—not a discriminatory one. In India, Jewish communities had lived and practised Judaism for centuries. They had established their own relationship to time, to history, to 'home' and to the linguistic, religious and cultural pluralism of India— under British colonialism and beyond.[9] Therefore, the rhetoric of 'saving' Jewish life did not apply to the Indian case and documentation of pogroms for the political purpose of building the case for Jewish national rights did not touch the personal experiences of Indian Jews. Those who come from educated families or lived in big cities had access to media or international news, read about Jewish persecution. But they had no experience of it.

This distinction is a key factor. Just as persecution looms large in Jewish history, and in analyses of Jewish migration and identity, so the *absence* of religious persecution must also be borne in mind as we seek to understand issues of identity, motives for migration and attitudes to assimilation among Indian Jews in Israel. It is in this context that we can understand how the Jewish Agency outreach in India was premised on offering attractive economic prospects to potential immigrants. Indeed, the narratives of the first generation of Indian Jewish immigrants, interviewed for this research, revealed that for that generation it had been a heart-rending experience to leave settled lives, friends and extended networks of which they were an integral part, wherever they lived. In fact, upon coming to Israel, many of the older immigrants experienced severe cultural displacement and have chosen to remain in neighbourhoods close to each other even today, speaking Marathi or Malayalam, although the next generation has moved to bigger cities for better economic prospects. Most of the Bene Israeli Jews who were living in the Bombay region were perfectly acculturated in the only home they had known, and their decision to emigrate *en famile* was a sentimental tearing away. Many of the older women respondents recalled tearful farewells from friendly neighbours who voiced deep concerns about the children of their

Jewish friends and the future they would face in a country widely perceived as 'war-torn'.

Thus, the case of Indian Jews complicates the narratives of 'persecution' and of a 'homeland'. When Indian Jews emigrated from India, they in fact left stable homes, to become part of the larger project of a Jewish Homeland. Although, they were enthusiastic about the Jewish Homeland, for many, emigration from India created a huge disruption socially, culturally and psychologically. For thousands of them, their disrupted education could never be resumed in Israel—given the language problem and severe economic struggles faced in the early decades. In the 1950s and 1960s, hundreds of teenaged children who belonged to modest backgrounds and whose parents had little education, were compelled to join the workforce on low-paid jobs, in remotely situated immigrant towns in Israel. In the 'Promised Land', they had no choice but to become what I term 'circumstantial drop-outs'. Migration caused a huge upheaval and an extended sense of displacement in many lives—although the severity of it varied, depending upon the age, socio-economic class, and the skill-levels/education they *came* with.

Today, the community of Indian Jews in Israel is marked by significant class variations. Even as some Indian Jews are successful businessmen, physicians or managers, a vast majority remain confined to middle-level and modestly paid jobs, living in 'peripheral' regions of Israel, preferring close-knit Indian communities, and the familiarity and comfort of worshipping in exclusive Indian synagogues. Among the high-end business circles or the political or military elites in Israel, Indians remain invisible. Among those who are second-generation (born in Israel), university-level education is less common than their counterparts in India today. What are the configurations that shape such stratification? What are the issues of class, location, access to resources and education? These are important questions. To understand these questions, we must contextualize them within the broader framework of sociological research, which examines ethnicity, pluralism, and stratification in Israeli society. Thus, this book addresses not only the historical and anthropological scholarship on Jews in India, but also current sociological research in Israel, a rich body of scholarship (in Hebrew and English) which extensively analyses issues relating to immigration, identity, ethnicity, class stratification and the related issues of access to resources, education, intergenerational and social mobility within this pluralistic society, where religion and Jewishness occupy a pivotal position.

UNDERSTANDING INDIAN-ISRAELI IDENTITY: SOME KEY OBJECTIVES

This study lies at the cusp of history and ethnography. I focus on the community of Indian Jews in Israel, now scattered across the Jewish Homeland, living alongside their brethren drawn from other Jewish diasporic communities—European as well as non-European/'Oriental'. In a sense, this research begins where much of the existing historical and anthropological scholarship on Indian Jews ends. It begins where scholarly 'requiems' stop. A primary objective of this book is to interrogate this 'closure' of the story at the point when the Jews arrived 'home' to the 'Promised Land' and to suggest reopening the narratives to see the continuities, fractures, accommodations in the cultural identity of the Indian diasporic community in Israel. I seek to retrieve the narrative of the Indian Jews from a historical time-freeze, and to restore a continuity through which we may go beyond a preoccupation with Jewish identities as they existed in nineteenth and twentieth centuries in India, to understand Indian-Jewish identities, as they exist in Israel today—in the twenty-first century. It is important to bring the narrative forward, and to examine the history of the Indian Jews in Israel since the establishment of the Jewish Homeland in 1948. It is time to shift the focus and to carry forward the scholarship from the history of the Indian Jews to the sociology of that emigration—from the moment of departure to the uprooting, the displacement, the arrival and the struggles of adaptation and the points of acculturation. In short, I believe, it is time to move beyond the 'Jews-of-India' model of ethnographic studies, focusing predominantly on life cycle rituals, religious practices or narrowly focused region-specific aspects of Jewish-ness, and to raise broader issues of identity, by linking acculturation and assimilation to the early life-experiences of new immigrants. Sixty years after Israel's formation, it is important to recover the processes which drastically changed the lives of the Indian immigrants in the new Jewish Homeland. In short, it is time to move beyond issues of Indian-Jewish identity to turn the spotlight on 'Indian-Israeli' identity—its formation and its articulations. Thus, two broad questions that frame this research are:

- What were the 'push' and 'pull' factors that shaped the emigration of Indian Jews from India?
- What followed in subsequent decades as Indian Jews acculturated themselves within a Jewish majoritarian society as 'new immigrants' in the process of becoming Indian-Israelis?

It is also worth asking how this historical event of the formation of a Jewish state attracted Indian Jewry and how the metaphors of 'home' and 'homecoming' played out in their lives *after* they arrived in Israel. In fact, 'home' and 'homeland' are key concepts that guide this investigation. There are important reasons for this. 'Homeland' and 'diaspora' are categories which frame scholarship in Jewish History in important ways. In these discourses, Jewish communities outside of the Jewish Homeland are all living 'in exile'. In this book, I use the Indian Jewish experience to subject these notions of 'home', 'exile' and 'diaspora' to scrutiny. I wish to argue that these concepts cannot be used seamlessly. They need to be re-examined in the light of specificities and the lived realities of Jewish communities. For instance, this research revealed that for the Indian Jews, India was widely experienced as a 'home' because civilizationally it embraced their Jewish-ness and enabled them to practice their faith without affecting their opportunities in the wider social, educational, commercial and professional world. While in their prayers Jews living in India dreamt of a homeland for the Jews, their everyday lives or the family histories of their forefathers did not re-inforce their self-image as one of Jewish 'exile'. For most Indian Jewish families, India was the only home they knew in living memory. Thus, for most Indian Jews their 'home' (India) and the 'Jewish Homeland' (Israel) were not binaries which generated tensions of identity. These are key ideas that frame the discussions in this book. These theoretical discussions however need to be contextualized. Thus, we need to pose some specific questions such as the following:

- What was the sense of community Indian Jews shared with their Jewish brethren when they contemplated emigration? What notions of 'imagined community' did they nurture when they looked at the future of their children in Israel?
- Was 'homecoming' a shared referential trope for the Indian Jews, who had not faced religious persecution?
- How did this collide with what they actually confronted upon arrival? What was the 'homecoming' like for these new immigrants in the Israeli nation?
- How did their placement in remote arid agricultural areas, or in new 'development towns' far away from the more prosperous areas in central Israel, shape their struggles for employment and resources?
- How did this politics of location shape the next few decades of their lives and the future prospects for their children?
- How did emigration affect the personal sphere—in restructuring gender relations, family systems, conjugal relations, language, food and community life?
- What were the pressures to reject language/food and other markers of 'Indian' culture in order to 'fit in' with the broader universalistic model of being 'Israeli'?
- In contemporary Israel, what do the community activities, religious practices and life cycle rituals of Indian Jews reveal about understandings of gender, class and community? How does all this texture our understanding of ethnicity and hybridized diasporic identities in the Jewish society of Israel?
- And finally, in this mosaic of ethnicities in Israeli society, *where* are the Indians today? Given that India's trade with Israel today amounts to 3.3 billion US dollars (2007), what is the relationship of Indian Jews to the India of the twenty-first century?

These are some of the questions that this study seeks to address. I may add that this study does not include the Bnei Menashe group in the analyses. The Bnei Menashe (Children of Menasseh) are a group of more than 8,000 people from Manipur and Mizoram in north-eastern India, who claim descent from one of the Lost Tribes of Israel.[10] In the past two decades, some 1,300 Bnei Menashe have moved to Israel. However, the migration of this group is too recent to fall within the framework of this research.[11]

EXISTING SCHOLARSHIP ON INDIAN JEWS

In spite of compelling questions that await exploration, Indian Jews as a community have received little scholarly attention. They have been studied from a historical perspective, mostly as the Jewish diaspora in India. Given that an important cornerstone of Jewish studies has been documentation about Jewish diasporic communities in various locations and cultures worldwide, this is not surprising. Scholars of Jewish studies have enthusiastically researched the history of the Jews in India—by region and community, as three distinct groups—the Bene Israelis (mostly in Maharashtra), the Cochinis (from Cochin in south India) and the Baghdadis (predominantly in Calcutta but also in Bombay).[12] At another level, there is some scholarship from the 'family history' perspective. Such scholarship (mostly inspired by the author's own community affiliation) offers vivid details of family lives and networks as they existed in a specific Jewish community in the twentieth century. The works of Elias Cooper and Jael Silliman are examples of such scholarship.[13] Silliman, a Baghdadi Jew who was born to a Baghdadi Jewish family settled in Calcutta and who did her early schooling at a Catholic convent school in Calcutta, explores the lives of her foremothers—Baghdadi Jewish women widely dispersed across Asia in the nineteenth and twentieth centuries. From the story of Farah, Silliman's great-grandmother who moved from Basra (Iraq) to Calcutta, the author weaves in issues of gender and community across four generations of Jewish Baghdadi women. In that, this book adds a dimension that is rare in scholarship on Indian Jews—a gender-sensitive approach which recognizes the distinctness of women's experiences and highlights it to nuance our understandings of migration, religion and community identity.

The personal stories capture a range of experiences which make the narrative compelling.

Along another scholarly terrain anthropological approaches have long displayed a tendency to exoticize the non-Western Jewish communities, and Jews of India have been attractive models for such approaches. Jews of Cochin were studied under this rubric in Strizower's *Exotic Jewish Communities* (1962).[14] One of the few published works on the Indian Jews in Israel is an anthropological study by Gilbert Kushner, who studied a section of the Cochini community which was settled by the government at a *moshav* (agricultural village) near Jerusalem.[15] Kushner's field study is based on the situation in 1961–2—soon after the bulk of Cochini immigration to Israel took place (between 1949 and 1955). Kushner examines the ways in which this community becomes an 'administered community' subjected to highly controlled patterns of state planning and closely monitored development. His broad thesis is that subjected to a 'process of directed change' the community 'cannot evolve into an autonomous community, despite the planners' conception of an administered community as a transitional form that is supposed to evolve'.[16] Kushner's analysis does have some value in illustrating how a highly controlled state-sponsored development could have a crippling effect on community participation, and stilt autonomous and 'organic' community growth in the long-run. However, Kushner's study is problematic. First, it is based on the experience of American Indians (native American)—a model which I believe is inappropriate to study Indian Jewish communities such as the Cochinis. We may also note that Kushner's fieldwork engaged with only a section of the Cochini community (which, in turn, is only *one* of the three major communities that constitute Jews of Indian origin). In any case, Kushner's data was collected almost 45 years ago. In the process of searching at Israeli university libraries, I located a doctoral thesis on Indian Jews done in the 1970s. This study focused on a section of the Bene Israeli community living in the city of Lod. The subtitle of the dissertation reflects the scholar's perceptions about what she calls the 'The Persistence of Ethnicity' among the Indian community.[17] The choice of words reveals the analytical lens. 'Persistence' is a loaded term. It strongly suggests 'drawbacks' or 'inabilities' of a community to acculturate to a mainstream culture, to erase its ethnic markers and practices. Such scholarship reflects an evaluative lens rather than an investigation which is culturally sensitive. In fact, the strand of scholarship which focuses on aspects of Indian Jewish cultural heritage—discussing Jewish synagogue architecture in India, and detailed analyses of religious practices, food, dress and life cycle rituals of Jews in India, is richer as it makes a valuable contribution through providing some original visual material about the Cochinis, Baghdadis and the Bene Israelis.[18]

Broadly speaking, as projects in 'recovery', such studies capture the flavour of a bygone era, before India's Independence and before the formation of Israel. Since then, the majority of Indian Jews have migrated to Israel—and thousands of them have spent 40 years in the Jewish Homeland. Yet, much of existing scholarship seems to linger in what I believe is a 'nostalgia mode'—singing a 'requiem' to the story of Indian Jews, as a story which ostensibly 'ended' when they emigrated from India. For instance, Nathan Katz states that his book on Cochini Jews 'is intended as an affectionate requiem for the Cochin Jews'.[19] Such studies, mostly done by Western historians or anthropologists treat the Indian Jewish communities as models of 'exotic' Jewish diasporas disconnected from each other—entities in the past. Most such scholarly interest trails away at the historical juncture of Jewish emigration from India. Such a preoccupation with the historical, and little attention to examine continuities or interconnectedness, can fracture community identities. I believe re-search cannot neglect to examine how community identities are mutated by tides of change, and how they co-opt and resist those tides. A wide array of questions about acculturation and assimilation of Indian Jews remain unanswered. It is time to address these questions.

Margaret Abraham has examined post-migration issues of the Indian Jewish community to some extent but her essays are based on a limited sample of some 40 Indian Jewish informants in Israel and the fieldwork was done over two decades ago.[20]

BEYOND THE 'THREE-COMMUNITY' MODEL

Here is another methodological issue: it has been customary to study the three communities of Indian Jews as Cochini, Baghdadi (or Calcutta Jews), and the Bene Israelis. Geographically these were communities dispersed across long distances. Indeed, they were separated from each other not only physically, but they also followed different variants of Jewish injunctions resulting from centuries of adaptation. They had also partaken of the local regional influences and differed considerably in their food habits, and the languages they called their own. Living thousands of miles away from each other, even inter-marriage was rare. They shared some life cycle rituals but practised others which were unique to their group. Yet, in this project, I study issues relating to all three communities—going beyond those lines of separation—searching for connections without homogenizing their distinct features. Why study them together? For several reasons: first, while not disregarding the heterogeneity in language, food and culture, I believe we need to study Jews of Indian origin as a *category*—holistically. I wish to argue this holistic approach for the following reasons:

- Living for centuries in India, regardless of whether they lived in Calcutta, Bombay or Cochin, Indian Jews were shaped by the broader civilizational context of South Asia: the politics and culture of the region, and the pluralistic traditions where Hindus, Muslims, Christians and Jews lived among each other and their children commonly played and went to school together.
- We must note that while settled in India, Cochinis, Baghdadis and Bene Israelis all identified their religious practices as 'Jewish' and this 'Jewish-ness'(defined in different ways) was their common reason for emigration from India.
- This shared Jewish-ness constituted their entitlement as Jews and facilitated their entry into Israel—as the homeland for all Jews. Thus, religion and ethnicity remain deeply intertwined in their emigration—whether they were from Cochin, Calcutta or Bombay.
- Consequent upon the above, in Israel today, Jews from India share the country-of-origin and collectively constitute the

'Indian-Jewish diaspora'. Hundreds of Indian Jews attend the Indian Independence Day and the Republic Day celebrations held annually in August and January and hosted by the Indian Embassy in Tel Aviv. Bene Israeli and Cochinis attend with those of Baghdadi-Indian origin—and the medley of languages that can be heard (Hebrew, Marathi, English and Malayalam) reflects a scene common to an Indian diasporic gathering anywhere in the world today, where overseas Indians speak many different vernacular languages among themselves!

Thus, from the perspective of migration scholarship or Indian diaspora studies, the intra-community cultural and linguistic differences among Indian Jews are no more pronounced than within other Indian diasporic communities in the UK or US, or even between Hindus and Muslims living in India who may be from Cochin or Calcutta or elsewhere in multi-lingual, multi-cultural India. Indeed, the Government of India offers Indian-Israelis the same options and privileges of being 'Overseas Citizens of India' (OCI) as it does to other Indians abroad.

CONTEMPORARY ISRAELI SCHOLARSHIP: ETHNICITY, PLURALISM AND CLASS

It was important to place this research on Indian Jews within current frameworks in Israeli sociology. Although Indian Jewish culture and identity remain unexplored in contemporary Israeli scholarship, the analysis presented in this book has benefited from the work of several Israeli scholars. The scholarship relevant to this study of ethnicity and the immigrant experience (which also paid attention to gender) led me to identify three parallel but related trajectories in Israeli sociology. First was the literature on migration and immigrant absorption in Israel; second, the recent studies on inequalities and cleavages within Israeli society—highlighting stratification, class and ethnicity and so forth; and finally, the scholarship on gender in Israeli society which focused on the immigrant experiences of Jewish women who did not come from Europe or America. These trajectories are interlinked and provided important frameworks for my own research on Indian Jews as I investigated issues of acculturation, stratification, status attainment and social mobility, within an overarching framework of ethnicity, class and gender. A brief overview below illustrates how existing studies opened the space for this research, suggesting new avenues of investigation.

Following from the early sociologists like S.N. Eisenstadt, who were concerned with immigrant absorption and broad demographic changes since the 1950s, I examined the work of subsequent scholars who studied immigrant integration into the emerging social structure in Israel. Studies of immigrant absorption in the *moshavim* (cooperative agricultural settlements), *kibbutzim* and the huge national project of creating 'new towns' or 'development towns' in the peripheral regions of Israel, set an important context for me to understand what the repercussions could be when Indian Jews in the 1950s and 1960s were taken in busloads from the airport and settled in *moshavs* like Nevatim and Kfar Yuval, or 'new towns' like Dimona, Yarukham or Kiryat Shmona. It textured my understandings of how complex inter-community dynamics emerged 'after the ingathering' (to use Alex Weingrod's phrase), and the complexities that emerged when different ethnic groups were settled in state-designated urban or rural spaces which were chosen for 'population dispersal'.[21] Parallel to these were the strong critiques provided by Sammy Smooha, Ela Shohat and Henriette Dahan Kalev which served as intellectual frames for me to understand issues relating to identity and the struggle from the 'margins'.[22] Such scholarship resonated with my own ethnographic data when, for instance, I interviewed Indians living in peripheral areas in northern Israel like Kiryat Yam and Kiryat Ata, which remain mostly untouched by Israel's economic growth even today.

In recent decades, ethnicity and class have been the focus of much research in Israel—both in relation to access to education, resources and professional opportunities. Although official discourses are mostly silent about the interlinkages between ethnicity and the social and economic inequalities in contemporary Israeli society, within Israeli sociological discourses the acknowledgement of social and cultural divides is unequivocal. Sociologists have widely written about the divides in Israeli society arguing that given Israel's ideological position as 'homeland for the Jewish people', the political system aims at the realization of Jewish national interests and aspirations. Such challenging critiques argue that resources allocated to Jewish populations are far greater than to the Muslim and Christian minorities.[23] This in turn shapes the access to occupational and educational opportunities. However, given that Jewish population itself is far from homogeneous, socio-economic inequalities within the Jewish population, have also been a major focus of sociological research. Although Jews may broadly be *Ashkenazim* (those of European or American origin), or *Sephardim/Mizrahim* (Jews of Middle-Eastern/West Asian or North African descent), in contemporary Israel a Jew is also 'Russian', 'Moroccan', 'Iraqi', 'Polish', 'German', 'Ethiopian' and so forth. Sociologists have argued that important socio-economic and class differences exist between the *Ashkenazim* and *Sephardim*, with the *Ashkenazim* being more privileged and over-represented in positions of political power and in the professions.[24] Further, educational levels tend to be lower among the *Sephardim* who typically become concentrated in lower white-collar and skilled blue-collar occupations.[25] These socio-economic disadvantages can get further compounded by the 'peripheral' location of certain communities.[26] In fact, contemporary Israeli sociology reflects a growing interest in analysing ethnicity as a key variable to understand class and social inequalities.[27] More radical critiques about how ethnicity and race determine levels of access and 'acceptability' in Israeli society figure in the work of Yehouda Shenhav and Henriette Dahan Kalev, both of whom maintain that being *Ashkenazi* or *Mizrahi* in Israeli society continues to be a key marker of identity and an underlying factor for discrimination against the non-white *Mizrahi* segments of the population—however masked those attempts at exclusion may be. We may note that some significant scholarship is published only in Hebrew and remains unavailable to international audiences. In general, within this scholarship on ethnicity and class, gender remains a neglected terrain. Although some excellent gender-based critiques exist in relation to women and religion, and women and the military, only scattered essays forcefully investigate the linkages between gender, ethnicity and inequality.[28]

Some recent critiques were particularly useful for this research. For instance, work of Swirski and Safir who radically challenged existing frameworks through their book *Calling the Equality Bluff* (1991). Swirski offered a Marxist class analysis to argue that structural underpinnings in Israeli social organization kept *Mizrahi* Jews from higher status attainment levels, and that their so-called 'ineptness' was a direct result of institutional arrangements and discriminatory policies.[29] This meshed with my own analysis of identity, Indian-ness and ethnic stereotypes. More recent is the work of Aziza Khazoom who seriously questions the genesis of 'segregation' beginning in the 1950s. Khazoom asks whether in the placing of Jewish immigrants in 'development towns' 'did the Israeli state engineer segregation?'[30] Focusing on the early period of Israeli statehood Khazoom examines how the European Jewish founders treated Middle Eastern Jewish immigrants and argues that *Ashkenazim* were shaped by their own unique encounter with European colonialism, and were intent on producing Israel in the image of the West. Middle Eastern Jews as new immigrants threatened this goal of westernization and had to confront exclusions and discrimination.

Such scholarship provides valuable framework for this study of Indian Jews at two levels. First, it serves as a parallel context to map the ways in which Indian immigrants (who were also overwhelmingly dispersed into remote development towns, struggled as a community. Second, by highlighting certain specificities which distinguish Indian Jews from Middle Eastern or North African Jews, I wish to interrogate the homogenizing rubric which in fact, erases distinct identities of Indian Jews within a blur of *Mizrahim*. As the interviews for this research revealed, Indian Jews had experienced British imperialism (read: white supremacy) as a benign rule which employed Jews widely in civil and military services and enabled their businesses to thrive. They did not know racism at the hands of the white colonizer. In fact, large numbers of Indian Jews were the beneficiaries of an 'English' education—

an asset which they brought to Israel as new immigrants. This, in turn, facilitated the entry of many Indian Jewish immigrants into Israel who brought professional qualifications in English which Israel needed and valued in the 1950s and 1960s. They brought no wealth but had human capital which state authorities were shrewd to identify—issues I examine in subsequent chapters.

It is evident from the above review that Israeli scholarship on pluralism and ethnicity has taken little notice of Indian Jews as a community.[31] In scholarly discourses on migration and ethnicity in Israel, Indian Jews are lost among the blur of ethnicities homogenized as *Sephardic* or *Mizrahi*, on the basis of shared colour (non-white), although culturally they may share little with Jews from Arab societies. An important objective of this book is to problematize this homogenizing category of 'Oriental Jews' to place the Indian Jews with their specific markers of identity—not only as 'non-white' but also 'non-Arab'. This book seeks to insert the Indian Jews as a community into the Israeli scholarly discourses at two levels. At the first level, I seek to document ethnicity-related issues from the time of emigration (from a non-persecution driven situation) to acculturation as Indian Jews—as manifested in family organization, life cycle rituals, community networks and so forth. At a more important level, I wish to interrogate the ways in which Indians are situated within the racial *Ashkenazi-Mizrahi* divide. Although Indian-Jewish religious prayers fall within a broadly *Sephardic* pattern, I wish to argue that their South Asian origins make the Indian Jews civilizationally distinct from other Jews broadly categorized as *Sephardic*, mostly West Asian and North African. Sixty years since the establishment of the homeland for the Jews and close to fifty years since the first Indian Jews began to come to Israel, it is important to pose these questions. It is important also to deploy a multi-disciplinary approach in which histories of migration can inform the sociology of community life, so that we can trace the process of acculturation and highlight immigrant negotiations with issues of ethnicity, gender and class.

By highlighting the specificities that marked the immigrant experiences of Indian Jews, and shaped their struggles to mediate their individual and community identities, this study offers a critique which complicates current examinations of stratification and ethnicity in Israeli sociology and makes a space for the examination of the Indian-Israelis and their distinct immigrant experiences which merit further research.

RESEARCH METHODOLOGY

In order to systematically examine issues of religion, emigration and ethnicity and their impact on issues of identity, status and gender, I deployed multiple approaches. In-depth interviews (lasting 2–3 hours) with Indian Jews have been a core resource for this research and in the explication of the major themes of this study. I have offset this with current sociological research about ethnicity, migration and class in Israeli society. Attending community programmes, religious services and collecting documents of community programmes were all methods used for this research. Thus, information-gathering was done in three ways:

Interviews[32]

Although I had a large sample comprising of over 100 respondents, in keeping with the aims of this book, I adopted a qualitative approach. My questionnaire was designed accordingly. Although questionnaires were important many of my respondents were only moderately educated. Not only were interviews crucial but the structure and sequence of questions was also crucial. Recalling early immigration experiences first was a successful strategy. The language, and a 'comfort zone' in terms of location were also important for the first meeting (subsequent conversations on the phone were much easier). In conducting interviews, I have been mindful of these issues. While quoting individuals in the text of this book, I have used fictitious names, so as to protect their privacy. I do, however, provide the year of birth, because I believe it enhances our understandings of how age affected education, employment or cultural assimilation.

As an appendix I provide a select list of Indian Jews who

participated in this study either by answering the questionnaire or being interviewed for 2–3 hours. This table provides the place of birth, the year of migration and the place where the individuals were residing when I interviewed them in 2007–8. Some details have been omitted as was the wish of some respondents.

(a) *Covering a wide range of locations* was the first aspect of interview-planning, and extensive travel was essential—to locate and visit the Indian Jews where they *were*—spatial locations being important indicators of economic and social locations. Thus, in order to gather information and interview Indians, I travelled extensively across Israel from areas in the north bordering Lebanon, to the southern tip where the Gulf of Accaba washes the waters of Israel at Eilat, a small but trendy resort-city from where the Egyptian border is a mere 2 km and the Jordanian flag is visible 200 metres away. Eilat is a city of tourism and Indians work in large numbers in the tourist industry and in the many luxury hotels. I made visits to the cities of Indian immigrant concentration like Ashdod, Ramla and Lod where many Indians were settled in the 1970s. My search for the narratives of the oldest among the Indian Jews led me to some remote areas, Kiryat Ata (north Israel), *moshav* Sha'haar and Dimona (in the south), yielding fascinating interviews with men and women like Dvora (*b.* 1924 in Maharashtra), Diana (*b.* 1928 in Karachi), Rachel (*b.* 1930 in Calcutta), Ruth Sankar (*b.* 1939 in Bombay), Eliyahu (*b.* 1930 in Jew Town, Cochin). I visited *moshavs*, originally dry tracts of barren land which were turned into functioning agricultural economies by the early Indian Jews of the 1950s. Each family gave me references of other individuals they knew, so I could cover a wide range by age, year of arrival in Israel, profession and region of origin in India (Cochin, Bombay, or Calcutta). I made several day-long trips to Nevatim and Sha'haar —*moshavs* where Indian Cochini Jews have lived since the early 1950s, and to Dimona, a small town where planeloads of Bene Israelis were settled in early 1960s when Dimona was little more than a dot on the map—with neither housing nor roads. All these are in the arid infertile southern Negev region and Indian Jews *literally* built these townships—digging access roads, laying water and sewage pipes, planting the first trees.

While I made multiple visits to the cities which have large concentrations of Indians (Ashdod, Ramla, and Lod) and to *moshavs* and small towns (Dimona and Nevatim), I did not restrict myself by location. It was my endeavour also to locate Indians who were not living in 'Indian' neighbourhoods, those who had done well economically, professionally and were now living in more privileged neighbourhoods, in central Israel, in cities and neighbourhoods (bordering Tel Aviv) like Ra'naana and Herzliya which are predominantly 'western/white' and wealthy.

(b) *Highlighting heterogeneity among the focus community*: The respondents selected varied across age and socio-economic class. Their experiences related to education, work, conjugality and parenting were wide-ranging, as were their levels of current socio-economic status in Israeli society. For instance, some first-generation immigrants are also families who came after the 1980s, with higher levels of education and professional degrees acquired from Indian universities. These individuals/families have been absorbed smoothly into well-paid jobs and privileged Israeli neighbourhoods. But these are too few and far between, and for this research it was important to seek the older generation of Indians who came in the 1950s and 1960s. This was important for several reasons. First, most of these individuals came as children, adolescents or young adults, either alone or in groups of youngsters brought in by the Jewish Agency or with their parents. They could recall an Israel in the throes of 'becoming'—when townships were being planned and immigrants were coming in planeloads and being packed off in hundreds to occupy either towns which had been abandoned by Arab communities fleeing war and violence, or development towns which existed as spots on a map—tracts of land conceived as towns which were to be 'built-up' by the physical labour of the new immigrants. In about 10 cases, I also did family history interviews (with two generations together) so as to encourage intergenerational discussions on issues of ethnicity and identity.

Finally, I interviewed community leaders to understand group initiatives, the difficulties of mobilization and collective aspirations. I wished to incorporate their perspectives on the challenges of assimilation.

ATTENDING COMMUNITY PROGRAMMES:
SYNAGOGUE SERVICES, LIFE CYCLE RITUALS

I was fortunate to have a sustained and wide-ranging exposure to the Indian Jewish community. My location among the Indian Embassy community provided some initial access after which my personal connections with Indian Jewish femilies grew rapidly between 2006–8. The exposure to Indian community get-togethers was important to observe groups at a social level. Attending Jewish religious functions was also useful. I visited Indian synagogues in Ramla and Lod. Public celebrations and community programmes offered fascinating insights into group dynamics and community mobilization. Between 2006–8 I attended Indian Independence Day celebrations, arranged both by the Indian Embassy in Tel Aviv and also by the Indian Jewish community in Ashdod (both held in August to mark Indian Independence Day on 15 August). The annual cultural festival *Hodu-yada* held traditionally at the resort beach-city of Eilat, and attended by over 2,000 Indian Jews, provided me with some excellent new contacts in 2005 and 2006.

EXISTING SOCIOLOGICAL RESEARCH

While interviews and narratives provided important insights which enabled me to map community practices, I also drew upon scholarship which conceptualized issues of race and class in this pluralistic society. It was important to place my understandings of the Indian community—alongside existing analyses of class stratification by colour and race in Israeli-Jewish society. My colleagues at Tel Aviv, Haifa and Ben Gurion universities sharpened my understandings of ethnic identities in Israeli society and guided me towards the excellent sociological research on Israeli pluralism, the *Ashkenazi-Mizrahi* issues, and stratification in modern Israeli society. Such scholarship paved the way for my analyses of the Indian Jews as a community whose issues await insertion into the Israeli discourse on religion, race, ethnicity.[33]

A NOTE ON LANGUAGE AND SPELLINGS

Language was, and is, an important issue for diasporas. Though less obvious than skin-colour or dress, it is an important marker of identity. Language, however, can be manipulated more easily by state control and policy. When a language is institutionalized through the education system, and supported by administrative and legal use, it can take firm roots. Dress, on the other hand, is a 'personal' matter, allowing more room for choice. Although the social pressure to 'blend in' influences dress codes and choices, language can be controlled by external dictates—by the state or the established workplace culture. Language can also be the first and often the most painful barrier to inclusion for new immigrants, whose sense of 'otherness' and marginality is painfully felt in communication disability. By the same token, a common language can go along way in connecting people from diverse ethnic, religious backgrounds. In short, language is an important tool in the hands of a state both to homogenize—and hegemonize.

The issue of language is key to understanding migration in the Israeli context. State institutionalization of Hebrew was a critical choice made by the state at the juncture of nation-building.[34] Israel made Hebrew mandatory, so as to make language the connecting thread between heterogeneous populations of Jews that came from locations as diverse as Poland and Yemen or Germany and Morocco. It was to bridge diversity across the Jewish brotherhood/sisterhood and for this the state put extensive language training programmes in place which were to cater to the new immigrant. This policy of the Israeli State, in fact, reached well beyond Hebrew to promote 'Jewish-ness', and its widespread deployment has given the Hebrew language a firm footing. Today, almost 60 years after the establishment of the Israeli State, for a non-Hebrew speaking person, it is possible to walk through the main streets and shopping centres in central Tel Aviv, Jerusalem and Beersheva without being able to read much more than the names of the streets in English. The signs outside shops, the labels and descriptions on products in supermarkets, are overwhelmingly in Hebrew. At ordinary restaurants the menu is in Hebrew (although if you look sufficiently lost, they will produce a menu in English). Young Israelis study English in school as a subject. To enter the more prestigious universities in Israel, you need to pass an English proficiency test, but all the humanities and social sciences subjects are taught in Hebrew.[35]

Given this scenario, all Indian Jews like their fellow Israelis, are Hebrew speakers. But language also had a generational twist. During the interviews it became obvious that among those who had come as children/adolescents in the 1950s and 1960s, many retained the Hindi, Marathi or English they had studied or spoken in India. The Baghdadis from Calcutta spoke fluent English with a British accent (usually learnt at missionary schools), the Bene Israelis from Bombay spoke Hindi and Marathi and those with better schooling spoke English as well. Among the Cochinis of the older generation, they spoke Malayalam among themselves. But Hebrew became the language that their children learnt. Many parents improved their Hebrew skills through their children. I wish to also note that language is the medium through which immigrant communities often wish to preserve their ethnic identity. Among many Bene Israeli families I noticed continued use of Marathi, whereby second and third generations also understand the language of their Indian grandparents. For this research, I communicated in English, Hindi and a mix of Hindi with Marathi words. Most of my respondents who had acquired some collegiate education in India prior to migration, were well-equipped with at least two languages—a regional language Malyalam, Marathi or Hindi and some English. I used a Hebrew-speaking interpreter rarely and when I did, I chose a person of Indian origin, so as not to miss the nuances of the responses. Language, in fact, posed no barrier in this research, less perhaps than if I had been conducting similar research in say south or north-east of India where the vernacular would be unfamiliar to me.

While writing this book I also had other language-related

concerns. Although this research is anchored in rigorous fieldwork and engages with key theoretical categories like ethnicity, gender and class to understand migration experiences, I also wish to reach out to a readership beyond those with a scholarly interest in such questions. Thus, to make this book more accessible to a wider readership, I have been mindful of elements like language, spelling and even the manner of citing my sources. With this in mind, I have minimized the number of endnotes by offering references and citations in clusters, so as to maintain a flow in the textual narrative. Similarly, I have organized the Bibliography into sections which may facilitate further reading for readers with varied interests. Thus sources are listed in sections relating to 'Israel Studies', 'Indian Jews', and 'Migration Studies/Indian Diaspora'. These are broad organizational divisions and I am aware that there would be overlaps.

In the use of language, I have preserved some phrases in Hindi/Marathi that my interviewees used (to which I provide some broad translations). I also refer to the erstwhile names of places (Bombay and Calcutta rather than Mumbai and Kolkata) because those were the names that the respondents associated with in their pre-migration lives in India. Similarly, I have retained some Hebrew words that emerged commonly in conversations in Israel. For instance, the Jewish Sabbath or end-of-the week cannot be translated as Friday or Saturday (because it begins on Friday at sunset and ends on Saturday, also at sunset). Thus, in this book words like *Shabbat, Ashkenazi, ulpan, ma'baarot* and so forth have been retained to preserve the local flavour. Spellings, however, posed a problem. I noticed that the English spellings of Hebrew words and of Israeli names varied in different contexts. Thus, Herzliya was sometimes spelt 'Herzliyya' or Beersheva was spelt as 'Be'er Sheva'. I found that people used Ramla/Ramle and Kiryat Shmona/Kiryat Shmone interchangeably. Although the Academy of Hebrew Language offers some standardization (<http://hebrew-academy.huji.ac.il>), some words were particularly tricky like 'Mizrahi/Mizrachi' or 'Pesakh/Pesach'. While many standardized texts in Israel used the latter versions, I found this confusing. As an English-speaking person I read 'ch' (as in 'chat'). This was phonetically incorrect! Thus, in this book, while I provide the different versions in the Glossary, I am mindful that there may be many non-Hebrew-speaking readers like myself. I have therefore, taken the liberty to use the more phonetic versions in the text using 'h' or 'kh' which are much closer to the Hebrew pronunciation.

Finally, this book on Indian Jews is really about identities and hybridities ... about ethnicity and *Indian-ness*. ... In what ways (and what extent) do Indian Jews perceive themselves as Indians/Jews/or Indian Jews? What are the markers in the private sphere: gender dynamics, connections between food and ethnicity, and language and ethnicity? What is 'Indian' about a Jewish-Indian wedding? How do the domestic ideologies which govern family structures, reveal inherited cultural patterns? And how have gender relations and family expectations been transformed (or mutated?) by pressures of acculturation? Are parental expectations different in an Indian Jewish family compared to the surrounding culture? How do Indian Jews experience class markers in the wider Israeli multi-ethnic mosaic (in which they are non-European and non-white)? Do racial/ethnic identities get blurred through status accumulation, through professions or through inter-racial marriage? What are the changes in self-perceptions of community identity since the first immigrants came in the 1950s and 1960s? Has India's economic rise and global image influenced the self-image of the Indian-Jewish community? What is the role of global politics, in terms of Indo-Israeli trade and defence collaborations in 'boosting' the image of India? Is there a co-relation between enhanced travel to India by Indian Jews since the 1990s, and the endorsement of destination-India by the dominant/privileged groups in Israeli society? Is there a causal link between India's international image and the increased tourism that takes Indian Jews 'back' to the 'homeland' they left?

These 'smaller' questions are critical to our understanding, because together they constitute the 'bigger' picture as we seek to understand Indian Jews in Israel, and raise questions which remain virtually unexplored.

STRUCTURE

In Chapter 2, entitled 'Where Are the Indian Jews Today? Immigration and the Israeli Setting', I place the Indian-Jewish community in the context of modern Israel. I begin by discussing Israeli society, its multi-ethnicity resulting from the waves of immigrants who came to the Jewish Homeland after it was established in 1948. After a discussion of this multi-ethnic mosaic of society in Israel, I place the Indian community, briefly discussing the historical origins of the three different communities of Indian Jews that came to Israel—the Baghdadis, the Bene Israelis, and Jews from Kerala or 'Cochinis'. The final section of this chapter locates these Indian immigrants in Israel in the cities and towns where they now live and where I found them for this research. A description of some of the main cities with a concentration of Indian Jews serves to provide an important backdrop to our subsequent analysis. Alongside brief descriptions of the main cities of Israel: Tel Aviv, Haifa, Jerusalem and Beersheva, I offer some comments on cities, towns and agricultural villages, where large groups of Indian immigrants were settled like Ashdod, Ramla and Lod, which are closer to Tel Aviv, and the remote 'new towns' like Dimona in the south and Kiryat Ata in the north, which were planned immigrant towns also known as 'development towns', where vast numbers of immigrants were settled as a strategy for what sociologists have called 'population dispersal'. To understand the community issues, I also provide information about the numerical strength of the Indian-Jewish community in these cities, the number of Indian synagogues and so forth. This section also explains other important categories of urban planning like *moshavs* and 'development towns' which are unique to Israel as a part of its process of nation-building since 1950. Given that many first-generation Indians are still living in the *moshavs* and development towns where they were allotted houses by the government upon arrival, this contextual and spatial dimension needs to be understood before we proceed to examine issues of immigrant assimilation and acculturation.

Chapter 3, 'Emigration from India: When We Came to the Land of Milk and Honey' is based on the early narratives of immigration.

The source material for this were the earliest immigrants who came from India almost immediately following the end of British rule in India and the formation of the Israeli State in 1948. The situation in Israel in the early 1950s was one of flux. There was barely any infrastructure and hardly any urban planning and yet planeloads of Jews had begun to 'return' to their 'homeland'. This chapter draws upon the experiences of some of the oldest surviving immigrants (both men and women) of the Indian community. Most of those who were articulate and actively able to participate in this project were in their late-seventies—they were children or young adults when they had arrived in Israel. My oldest respondents were born in the 1920s. Their descriptions and narratives of the early years, their hardships in settling and surviving economic and cultural challenges, all these were extremely important for this research. These early immigration stories set a background to understand the Indian community in Israel. These narratives are also an important project in recovery. This is an important objective of this book—to capture the early stories and through them to reconstruct portraits—both of individual lives, as well as of the new Homeland they helped to build— literally with manual labour—as many of them dug the first roads in the Negev desert and planted the trees on Mount Carmel in the north.

Following this, Chapter 4 is about 'Accountants as Watchmen and Clerks Digging Roads: Negotiating Work and Professions'. This is an important chapter because work is closely linked to status attainment, which in turn, is a crucial avenue for social mobility especially of immigrant communities. Thus, understanding access to work and professions is key to assess class and social stratification both at community and individual levels. This chapter discusses issues of work by presenting profiles of several individual men and women who came as new immigrants at different ages, and in different phases beginning in the 1950s. This methodology enables me to present a wide range of individual experiences which reflect the professional challenges, disappointments and successes that Indian Jews faced. This chapter argues that the age at which an individual immigrated into Israeli society, was an important factor which shaped his/her future professional life. For instance, if they came as young children with their families, they were thrown into a new educational system and an unfamiliar social context at an early age, and learnt to swim with the tide. Similarly, those who had completed their education in India and had skills to offer were easily absorbed as 'productive' members in the emerging Israeli economy. However, those who migrated as teenagers faced immense disruption and rarely managed to get integrated into a new Hebrew-based curriculum. The economic hardships of the early years compelled most youth of such age to join the workforce early, and to begin supplementing the family income. Ironically, the parents of such children, who were often in their late-forties or older were equally challenged by a new ethos and a difficult language. They had left behind salaried jobs but were too old to begin all over again and got stuck in manual or very low-paid work. Many claimed that they faced a 'colour-bias' as 'dark-skinned' Indians who came from a 'poor', 'undeveloped' country. This chapter pays special attention to gender, highlighting the occupations Indian Jewish women were able to find in the 1960s and 1970s. I discuss women professionals who have had successful careers, as well as the many more who retired from low-paying semi-skilled jobs in which they got stuck for two decades or more. This section contains profiles of struggle as well as success. Through these narratives of work experience, this chapter demonstrates the correlation between education, access and social mobility on one hand, and ethnicity, professions and 'work-place stereotypes' on the other.

After this, Chapter 5 'Raising Jewish Families in Israel: Gender, Religious Practice and Life Cycle Rituals' discusses issues of kinship and family organization, as well as life cycle rituals and Jewish observances among the Indian community. This discussion draws upon the responses of interviewees to questions that were posed relating to family structures and issues of 'values' and 'culture' in the home. For instance, how were women and family environments affected by the huge churning that took place as a result of migration and displacement? How was Jewish-ness affected in the Jewish Homeland? Did families become more observant after they left their pluralistic mixed neighbourhoods in India? Or did living in a Jewish society reduce the emotional need to assert their religious identity as Jews? Indian Jews have some distinct rituals and observances in their life cycle rituals which are unique to them. This chapter discusses the *mehndi* ceremony for the bride and the *malida* (thanksgiving ceremony) as examples of this 'Indian-Jewish-ness'. This chapter also examines what happened to family life as language, food and the community ethos were all drastically altered. Were family dynamics re-shaped? Were gender ideologies transformed for those first-generation women who had always borne the entire brunt of the domestic work but now also felt compelled to join the workforce in Israel, although they had little education and no prior experience? This chapter discusses how many respondents identified certain behaviour patterns of 'politeness' and 'respectful behaviour towards elders' as 'Indian' traits they wished to preserve in their homes, which they claimed were not insisted upon in the Israeli schools their children went to. Thus, in discussing issues of gender, marriage and family in this chapter, I explore linkages between ethnicity and parenting to ask how parental expectations reflect certain preferences in family spaces. As this chapter incorporates responses to how respondents defined self-perceptions of 'Indian-ness' in the private sphere, it prepares the ground for a discussion of community self-perceptions and community networks in the next chapter.

Finally, Chapter 6, 'Mediating Assimilation and Separation: Community Networks, National Politics and Indian-Israeli Identity', picks up on the discussions of 'Indian-ness' from the earlier chapter and explores issues of community identity. This is especially complex since Indians came to Israel from three different communities, which had traditionally maintained significant degrees of 'separateness' from each other. Inter-racial marriages in Israel further complicate this discussion. Unlike earlier chapters where history underlies much of the sociological discussion, this chapter focuses on a scenario which is sociological and 'current'. Here I present associational activities, and community programmes including cultural concerts, newsletters and felicitation ceremonies which document the range of community initiatives. In the past three or four years there is a heightened visibility of Indian community cultural programmes in Israel, which are also attracting media attention. In this chapter I have two objectives. First, I wish to present an assessment of community mobilization efforts based on the success of the programmes that are organized across Israel—many of which I attended. For instance, the annual *Mai Boli* (which means 'Mother-tongue') programme, usually held in Lod (to celebrate the Marathi language), and the *Hodu-yada* annual song and dance bonanza event in Eilat which is attended by over 2,000 Indian Jews. The associational networks like the Central Organization of Indian Jews and the Indian Women's Organization which has chapters in many cities like Lod, Ramla, Dimona and Beersheva are also discussed. But I wish to go beyond this documentation of activities to ask how such initiatives reflect how a community handles issues of separation and assimilation. I wish to raise important questions about the relationship of Indian Jews, who are Israeli citizens, to India and their connections with the 5,000 Indian Jews who have chosen to remain in India. Further, I wish to examine the levels at which Indian Jews who are 'Israeli' and 'Indian' connect to India through the Indian Embassy in Israel, which was established only in 1992—almost 40 years after the first Jews migrated to India. What are the ambivalences in that connection and how do we understand the enthusiasm of Indian Jews to collaborate and seek the support of the Indian Embassy and to participate in large numbers in programmes which celebrate a nation of which they ceased to be citizens several years ago?

I conclude this book by deliberating on these issues in a broader light. These deliberations are based on my observations in Israel between 2005 and 2008. We cannot disregard the importance of Indo-Israeli cooperation which has grown immensely in the last decade, not only in defence but also in trade and high-tech. India's perception in Israeli society has further been mediated by the 40,000 young Israeli backpackers who visit India on almost year-long tours every year. Indian restaurants are emerging rapidly in this country where not long ago immigrants were mocked for the 'curry smells' that floated out of their apartments. How have all these factors transformed the image of India in Israel? How has the image of a globalizing India re-shaped images of the Indian in Israel? In overt and subtle ways 'external' factors which have re-shaped the constructions of India are, I believe, also forcefully re-shaping community self-perceptions to newer levels of ethnic pride even as hybridized identities mediate between 'Jewish'-*ness,* 'Indian'-*ness* and 'Israeli'-*ness.*

NOTES

1. Crispin Bates (ed.), *Community, Empire and Migration: South Asians in the Diaspora,* New Delhi: Orient Longman, 2003.
2. Sandhya Shukla, *India Abroad: Diasporic Cultures of Postwar America and England,* New Delhi: Orient Longman, 2004.
3. For a broad range of scholarship on this subject see Prakash C. Jain (ed.), *Indian Diaspora in West Asia,* New Delhi: Manohar, 2007; Ravindra K. Jain, *Indian Communities Abroad: Themes and Literature,* New Delhi: Manohar, 1993; Deepika Bahri and Mary Vasudeva (eds.), *Between the Lines: South Asians and Postcoloniality,* Philadelphia, PA: Temple University Press, 1996; Sunaina Maira and Rajini Srikanth (eds.), *Contours of the Heart: South Asians Map North America,* New York: Asian American Writers' Workshop, 1996; Jennifer Lee and Min Zhou (eds.), *Asian American Youth: Culture, Identity, and Ethnicity,* New York: Routledge, 2004; Judith M. Brown, *Global South Asians: Introducing the Modern Diaspora,* Cambridge: Cambridge University Press, 2006; Karen I. Leonard, *Making Ethnic Choices: California's Punjabi Mexican Americans,* Philadelphia: Temple University Press, 1994; T.M. Luhrman, *The Good Parsi: The Fate of a Colonial Elite in a Postcolonial Society,* Cambridge, Mass.: Harvard University Press, 1996; Darshan S. Tatla, *The Sikh Diaspora: The Search for Statehood,* London, University College, London, 1999; Mia Tuan (1999), 'Neither Real Americans nor Real Asians: Multigenerational Asian Ethnics Navigating the Terrain of Authenticity', *Qualitative Sociology,* 22 (2):105–25; Carla Petievich (ed.), *The Expanding Landscape: South Asian and the Diaspora,* New Delhi: Manohar, 1999; Madhavi Thampi, *Indians in China (1800–1949),* New Delhi: Manohar, 2005.
4. Throughout this book I use the concept of 'Jewish Homeland' and 'exile' as it is deployed in mainstream Israeli discourses. My own analysis in this book reveals that these concepts are problematic and cannot be used uncritically.

5. By contrast to Jewish immigrants, Israel makes it extremely difficult, almost impossible, for non-Jews to become Israeli citizens, or even permanent residents.
6. A much smaller group are also the *Sephardic* Jews from Europe, who were a small community of white Jews among the Cochinis, and came to be called White Cochini Jews. I discuss this in Chapter 2.
7. Indeed, as the titles of two recent studies on Baghdadi Jews indicate, this transnational community of Jews not only spoke English but also widely aspired to an 'English' identity. See, Ruth Fredman Carnea, *Almost Englishmen: Baghdadi Jews in British Burma*, Lanham: Lexington Books, 2007 and Betta Chiara, 'From Oriental to Imagined Britons: Baghdadi Jews in Shanghai', *Modern Asian Studies*, 37: 4 (2003), 999–1023.
8. An argument has also been made to differentiate 'Balkan Jews' (for instance, those from Greece, Turkey and Bulgaria) from this simplistic Ashkenazi-Mizrahi categorization. See Walter F. Weiker, *The Unseen Israelis: The Jews from Turkey in Israel*, Jerusalem: The Jerusalem Centre for Public Affairs/Centre for Jewish Community Studies, 1988.
9. See Joan G. Roland, *Jews in British India: Identity in a Colonial Era*, Hanover and London: University Press of New England, 1989.
10. Ethnically and linguistically, they are Tibeto-Burmans and belong to the Mizo, Kuki and Chin peoples (the terms are sometimes used interchangeably). On 31 March 2005 Sephardic Rabbi Shlomo Amar, one of Israel's two chief rabbis, accepted the Bnei Menashe's claim to be accepted in Israel as Jews.
11. The migration of the Bnei Menashe has become enmeshed in some controversies centering around their mass conversions to Judaism conducted by Israeli rabbis in India.
12. See Shirley Isenberg, *India's Bene Israel: A Comprehensive Inquiry and Sourcebook*, Bombay: Popular Prakashan; Berkeley: Judah L. Magnes Museum, 1988; Nathan Katz and Ellen S. Goldberg, *The Last Jews of Cochin: Jewish Identity in Hindu India*, Columbia: University of South Carolina Press, 1993; Cooper Elias, *The Jews of Calcutta: The Autobiography of a Community*, Calcutta: The Jewish Association of Calcutta, 1974; Dalia Ray, *The Jewish Heritage of Calcutta*, Calcutta: Minerva Associates, 2001; Ezekiel N. Musleah, *On the Banks of the Ganga: The Sojourn of the Jews in Calcutta*, North Quincy, MA: Christopher Publishing House, 1975.
13. Cooper Elias, *The Jews of Calcutta: The Autobiography of a Community*,

Calcutta: The Jewish Association of Calcutta, 1974; Jael Silliman, *Jewish Portraits, Indian Frames': Women's Narratives from a Diaspora of Hope*, Calcutta: Seagull Books, 2001.
14. Schifra Strizower, *Exotic Jewish Communities*, London: Thomas Yoseloff, 1962.
15. Although Kushner uses the pseudonym 'Bet Avi', I did in fact, visit a *moshav* near Jerusalem which is overwhelmingly Cochini, and may have been the model for Kushner's study.
16. Kushner, Preface: xv-xvi.
17. Shalva (Vail) Weil, 'Bene Israel Indian Jews in Lod, Israel: A Study in the Persistence of Ethnicity and Ethnic Identity' (unpublished Ph.D. thesis, 1977, available at Haifa University, Israel).
18. Shalva Weil, *Jewish Heritage of India*.
19. Esmond David Ezra, *Turning Back the Pages: A Chronicle of Calcutta Jewry*, vols. I and II, London: Brookside Press, 1986; R.A. Schermerhorn, 'Jews: A Disappearing Minority', in *Ethnic Plurality in India*, Tucson: University of Arizona Press, 1978; Fiona Hallegua, 'The Jewish Community of Cochin: Its Twilight Years', M.A. thesis, University of Kerala, St. Theresa's College, Ernakulam, 1984; for the reference to 'requiem' see Nathan Katz, and Ellen S. Goldberg, 'Kashrut, Caste and Kabbalah', in *The Religious Life of the Jews of Cochin*, New Delhi: Manohar, 2005, p. xxiv.
20. See Margaret Abraham (1995), 'Ethnicity and Marginality: A Study of Indian Jewish Immigrants in Israel', in Prakash C. Jain (ed.), *Indian Diaspora in West Asia*, New Delhi: Manohar. A recent study explores the image of Jews in India in the nineteenth and twentieth centuries, looking at the Indian attitudes towards Jewish communities. See Yulia Ergova, *Jews and India*, London: Routeledge, 2006.
21. Dorothy Willner, D. Weintraub, M. Lissak and Y. Atzmon, *Moshava, Kibbutz and Moshav: Patterns of Jewish Rural Settlement and Development in Palestine*, Ithaca and London: Cornell University Press, 1969; D. Weintraub, *Immigration and Social Change: Agricultural Settlements of New Immigrants in Israel*, Manchester: Manchester University Press, 1971; Alex Weingrod, *Reluctant Pioneers: Village Development in Israel*, Ithaca: Cornell University Press, 1966; Alex Weingrod (ed.), *Studies in Israeli Society: After the Ingathering*, New York; London: Gordon and Breach Science Publishers, 1985; Erika Spiegal, *New Towns in Israel*, Stuttgart: Karl Kramer Verlag, 1966; Matras, Judah, 'Israel's New Frontiers: The Urban Periphery', in M. Curtis and M.S. Chertoff (eds.), *Israel: Social Structure and Social Change*, New Brunswick, NJ: Transaction Publishers, 1973, pp. 3–14.

22. Sammy Smooha, *Israel: Pluralism and Conflict*, London: Routledge and Kegan Paul, 1978; Ella Shohat, 'Rupture and Return: The Shaping of Mizrahi Epistemology', *Hagar*, 1978, 2 (1): 61–92.
23. M. Al-Haj and H. Rosenfeld, *Arab Local Government in Israel*, Tel Aviv: International Center for Peace in the Middle East, 1988; Moshe Semyonov and Noah Lewin-Epstein (eds.), *Stratification in Israel Class, Ethnicity, and Gender*, New Brunswick: Transaction Publishers, 2004.
24. Sammy Smooha, *Israel: Pluralism and Conflict*, London: Routledge and Kegan Paul, 1978; Moshe Semyonov, 'On the Cost of Being an Immigrant in Israel: The Effects of Tenure, Origin and Gender', *Research in Social Stratification and Mobility*, 1997, 15: 115–31; Moshe Semyonov and Noah Lewin-Epstein (eds.), *Stratification in Israel: Studies of Israeli Society*, vol. 10; U. Rebhun and C. Waxman (eds.), *Jews in Israel: Contemporary Social and Cultural Patterns*, Lebanon, NH: University Press of New England/Brandeis University Press, 2004; E. Ben-Zadok (1993), 'Oriental Jews in the Development Towns: Ethnicity, Economic Development, Budgets and Politics', in E. Ben-Zadok (ed.), *Local Communities and the Israeli Polity: Conflict of Values and Interests*, New York: SUNY Press, pp. 91–122.
25. Rebeca Raijman and Moshe Semyonov, 'Modes of Labor Market Incorporation and Occupational Cost Among New Immigrants to Israel', *International Migration Review*, 1995, 29: 375-93; Semyonov, Moshe and Tamar Lerenthal, 'Country of Origin, Gender, and the Attainment of Socioeconomic Status: A Study of Stratification in the Jewish Population of Israel', *Research in Social Stratification and Mobility*, 1991, 10: 327–45.
26. Judas Matras, 'Israel's New Frontiers: The Urban Periphery', in M. Curtis and M.S. Chertoff (eds.), *Israel: Social Structure and Social Change*, New Brunswick: Transaction Publishers, 1973, pp. 3–14. Also, Erika Spiegel, 1976; C. Spilerman and J. Habib, 'Development Town in Israel: The Role of Community in Creating Ethnic Disparities in Labor Force Characteristics', *American Journal of Sociology*, 1976, 81: 781–812.
27. N. Lewin-Epstein, and M. Semyonov, 'Ethnic Group Mobility in the Israeli Labor Market', *American Sociological Review*, 1986, 51: 342–51; Nili Mark, 'Ethnic Gaps in Earnings and Consumption in Israel', *Economic Quarterly*, 1994, 41 (1): 55–77 (Hebrew); Moshe Semyonov and Noah Lewin-Epstein (eds.), *Stratification in Israel: Class, Ethnicity, and Gender*, New Brunswick: Transaction Publishers, 2004; N. Lewin-Epstein and M. Semyonov, 'Community of Residence, Community of Em-

ployment and Income Returns', *Israel Social Science Research*, 1992, 7: 15–27.
28. Although there is significant activist work for/among *Mizrahi* women, scholarship is scarce. See Pnina Motzafi-Haller, 'Scholarship, Identity, and Power: Mizrahi Women in Israel', *Signs*, 2001, 26: 697–734; Henriette Dahan Kalev (2001), 'You Are So Pretty, You Don't Look Moroccan', *Israeli Studies*, vol. 6: 1–14.
29. B. Swirski, and M. Safir (eds.), *Calling the Equality Bluff*, New York: Pergamon Press, 1991. For research on gender issues see Yael Azon and Dafna N. Izraeli, *Women in Israel*, New Brunswick: Transaction Publishers, 1993; Henriette Dahan Kalev (2001), 'Tensions in Israeli Feminism: The Mizrahi Ashkenazi Rift', *Women's Studies International Forum*, vol. 24: 1–16.
30. Aziza Khazzoom, 'Did the Israeli State Engineer Segregation? On the Placement of Jewish Immigrants in Development Towns in the 1950s'. *Social Forces*, 2005, 84: 1, 115–34, Aziza Khazzoom, *Shifting Ethnic Boundaries and Inequality in Israel*, Stanford: Stanford University Press, 2008. The counter-argument to this claims that *Ashkenazis* were also sent to 'development towns', but were able to out-migrate to economically better-off cities more quickly (possibly due of higher skill/education levels, smaller family sizes and so forth).
31. There are community-specific studies on some other communities. See Shlomo Deshen and Moshe Shokeid, *The Predicament of Homecoming: Cultural and Social Life of North African Immigrants in Israel*, London, Ithaca: Cornell University Press, 1974; Michael Ashkenazi and Alex Weingrod (eds.), *Ethiopian Jews and Israel*, 1987; Alex Weingrod, 'Reciprocal Change: A Case Study of a Moroccan Immigrant Village in Israel', *American Anthropologist*, vol. 64, no. 1, pp. 115–31; Walter F. Weiker, *The Unseen Israelis: The Jews from Turkey in Israel*, Jerusalem: The Jerusalem Centre for Public Affairs/Centre for Jewish Community Studies, 1988.
32. Throughout the book fictitious names have been used to ensure confidentiality for the respondents.
33. I consulted published research in English. Although Hebrew publications remained inaccessible to me, I benefitted immensely from university seminars and personal discussions with some leading sociologists at the universities of Tel Aviv, Haifa and Ben Gurion who generously explicated issues in Israeli society.
34. The Indian case serves as an interesting contrast. India evolved a

language policy to complement religious and regional pluralism which has enabled over 18 official languages to thrive in different parts of India today.

35. Although at Tel Aviv and Haifa universities, I lectured in English, it was obvious that courses offered in English make departments nervous about low enrolments, assuming that most students would be scared off by the requirements of course readings and term papers written in English.

CHAPTER 2

Where Are the Indian Jews Today? Immigration and the Israeli Setting

As I wrote this book in 2008, speaking about it in conversations with colleagues in Israel and later at lectures at American universities, I discovered high levels of curiosity about Indian Jews. However, the numbers always evinced surprise, '70,000? Are there really so many Indian Jews in Israel?' This recurring question revealed that the size and issues relating to the Indian Jewish community were outside the common awareness levels of even Israelis who lived an hour's drive away from Indian clusters. As a researcher, this question convinced me of the need to discuss location and space. It was key to analyse how the politics of location had long-term implications on the lives of Indian Jewish immigrants. Was location and space related to visibility, access and eventually, class mobility? These were important questions. More importantly, this analysis of space had to *precede* discussions of ethnicity, migration experiences and class because it was key to our understanding of the broader issues of community and identity discussed in this book.

This chapter then, is about contexts. It is about where the Jews were in India and where they are in Israel. Although this book is mainly concerned with the contemporary issues of identity and the processes by which Indian Jews became 'Indian-Israelis', to understand ethnicity and community identity we need to bear in mind both the pre-migration and post-migration scenarios. Thus, it becomes important to map not only recent histories but also take cognizance of older pre-migration civilizational and cultural contexts in which Indian Jews lived among other religious groups in India—a land still fondly remembered in collective Jewish memory. Beyond the mapping of contexts, this chapter is also about analysing the linkages between spatial location, access to resources and social stratification. Bearing these wider themes in mind, the specific objectives of this chapter are first to place the Indian Jews within India where they had lived for generations, and secondly in the Jewish Homeland to which they came and re-settled, alongside millions of other Jewish communities from Europe, West Asia and North Africa.

The discussion below is divided into three sections. The first section, Jews of India introduces the Indian context, mapping the scenarios within which Jews lived and practised their faith in the pluralistic society in India. Individual communities of Indian Jews have attracted much scholarly attention. Historians and anthropologists have keenly researched the three communities (Bene Israelis, the Cochinis and the Baghdadis) to cull out details about their respective histories, religious practices and social structures. For this section, I draw upon existing historical and anthropological research to sketch a descriptive map which will nuance our discussion of Indian-origin Jews in Israel. Existing literature is cited in the endnotes for readers with a deeper interest in histories of Jewish communities in India. The next section, which shifts the focus to the Israeli context, 'Immigrant Waves and the Israeli Setting', begins with a short overview of the waves of Jewish immigration which make Israel the multi-ethnic society that it is, in which Jews are the dominant, but by no means the only religious group. For the reader with a limited exposure to the complexities that make up Israeli society, I wish to underscore the diversity within Israel's *Jewish* population—by colour and country of origin. After 1948, in order, to cope with the massive influx of Jewish communities into Israel, the State and its agencies followed certain plans to settle new immigrants. These were large-scale state-controlled settlement plans which bear description. Hence, the following section on 'Urban and Rural Landscapes', describes how those new immigrants, who were mostly non-European and came from North Africa and West Asia, were settled in *moshavs* and 'new towns' in the 1950s and 1960s. This section leads up to our discussion of Indian Jews who migrated to Israel and how they were placed within this multi-ethnic scenario in the Jewish Homeland. One of the broader aims of this book is to highlight issues of location and to examine the consequences of that location. That is, to ask 'where are the Indian Jews in Israel today?'—both socially and spatially. This is not a matter of coincidence. Indian immigrants, like other new immigrants from elsewhere, were settled by the State in specifically chosen locations when they arrived in planeloads or shiploads. Highly qualified professionals or those who had special skills, were valued immigrants and could negotiate with State authorities. For most, the choice of city or township was rare. Once allotted a house, moving from the remote and poorly developed townships was difficult for all, and impossible for most. Immigrants could be allocated to a *kibbutz*, *moshav*, 'development town' or an emerging city. Many of these categories of urban planning are specific to Israel and deserve explanation. Thus, the section on, 'Cities, Towns and *Moshavs*' describes some of the major Israeli cities, drawing attention to the towns and *moshavs* which have concentrations or clusters of Indian Jews. Although Indian Jews are scattered across Israel, there are some locations where they have a significant presence, visible cluster of neighbourhoods or just an active cultural presence. I chose the most prominent among these and collected information about the community presence in those towns. The Map of Israel shows the location of these towns and *moshavs*, illustrating the spatial differences between central Israel and other less-developed regions constituting the 'periphery'. (See Appendix: Map of Israel.)

THE JEWS OF INDIA

Beginning with brief historical mappings, it is important to note that the 'Jews of India' has been a favoured subject of historical and anthropological scholarship, and several books trace the histories, traditions and religious practices of Jews in India. There is also some amount of disagreement in the literature regarding precise dates, social divisions and exact origins of the three main Jewish communities.[1] For this study, the histories of how the Jews *came* to India or the contestations around chronology are less important than to understand the sociology of their lives as settled communities in India *prior* to their migration to Israel. What is relevant is to understand how Jews in India lived their social, religious and cultural lives either mingled with, or in close proximity to, other segments of the Indian population—Hindus, Muslims, Christians, Sikhs, Jains or Buddhists. We need to understand the varying levels of acculturation which were reflected in the practices and community identities of Jewish groups in India. In the sections below the brief descriptions about the Jewish communities living in India, are not intended to be exhaustive.

There are several studies which deal with each of the three communities. My intention here is to map a pre-migration-context and to familiarize the reader with the Jewish groups as they existed in India. More importantly, since in this book I seek to study Indian Jewish communities holistically, I wish to make some comments on intra-community dynamics, an aspect which is neglected in much of the existing scholarship on individual Jewish communities. I wish to point out that intra-community dynamics between for instance, the Bene Israelis and the Baghdadis, or the Baghdadis and the Cochinis, reflected the varying levels to which the community identified (or did *not* identify) with the broader Indian ethos. This in turn, can help us to understand the different patterns and timings of emigration out of India. For instance, Cochinis moved in large numbers soon after Israel was established whereas, the bulk of Bene Israeli families came in the 1960s or later. Although there were some families from all three communities who chose early migration, broad patterns among individual groups are suggestive. I believe, the time of migration was shaped by many factors. While individual circumstance played a part, what was also important was the degree to which a Jewish community felt *connected* to the Indian ethos, without feeling compromised in their Jewish-ness or the degree to which they identified with the British colonial administration as 'better', than the prospects of self-rule.

'Cochinis': The Jews from Kerala[2]

The historical narrative of the Jews of Kerala claims that they came to Cranganore (south-west coast of India) after the destruction of the Temple in 70 CE. For many centuries they had their own principality. After a dispute within the rulers of the community broke out in the fifteenth century, sparking off hostility with neighbouring princes, the Jews of Cranganore left for Cochin. Henceforth, under the protection of the Hindu Raja, they lived in their own neighbourhood, which came to be called 'Jew Town'— merely a descriptive term, with no resemblance to the Jewish ghettos that existed in Europe. The Kerala Jews were spread across towns like Parur, Chendamanglam, Mattencherry and Cochin. The latter remained an important centre and has become a point of reference, thus Kerala Jews widely refer to themselves as 'Cochini'. In this book, I use the terms interchangeably. Cochinis claimed having had contacts with foreign Jewry through European Jewish merchants (from countries like Holland), who would spend time in Cochin and would send back prayer books and Jewish ritual items for the community.[3] In colonial India, under Portuguese occupation Kerala Jews experienced some persecution, but the Dutch Protestants who displaced the Portuguese in 1660 were more tolerant. From the nineteenth century, under the British, Jews lived in various parts of Kerala—Cochin, Ernakulam and Parur. In 1949, a small group of a few families left Cochin for Israel. Between 1952 and 1954, a few hundred children between 12 and 16 were brought to Israel through Youth Aliya, a Jewish Agency initiative to enhance youth immigration. It was hoped that if the children settled first, they would be 'guides' to the older people when they arrived. The bulk of the Cochini community (about 2,000 people) arrived between 1953 and 1955. Most had never been outside coastal Kerala, so this was the result of aggressive Jewish Agency efforts in the region. By 1968, only a few hundred Cochini Jews remained in Kerala. Many were white Jews.[4] Most of Cochin's Jews emigrated out of India and mostly to Israel. Only a few now remain in Kerala. Interestingly, the few Jews left in Kerala attract much attention of Western Jewry and

Western scholars studying Jewish diaspora. Jewish tourists to India flock eagerly to check out the Jewish areas around Cochin and travelogues written in a nostalgic vein rue the small numbers left in Kerala. Given that Cochini Jews were actively wooed by visiting Zionist emissaries and Jewish Agency representatives to migrate to the Promised Land, and indeed, their migration was applauded, to rue dwindling numbers or sparsely filled synagogues poses an interesting irony.

JEWS OF BAGHDADI ORIGIN OR 'CALCUTTA JEWS'[5]

The Baghdadis were Middle Eastern Jews from Iraq. They were largely a business community, and towards the end of the eighteenth century, through trade with India, they established a network which extended across parts of Asia, all the way in the far East to Kobe in Japan. Trading and travel routes of Baghdadi merchants went from Aleppo to Baghdad to Basra (in Iraq), Surat, Bombay and Calcutta (in India) to Rangoon, Singapore and beyond that to Hong Kong. Baghdadi traders and merchants had close family ties and community bonds with other Baghdadi families living in Asian cities along the trade routes. In India, Calcutta had a concentration of the Baghdadi Jews, although Bombay also had a smaller Baghdadi community—most prominently represented by the Sasoon family which owned large businesses in the shipping trade. Shalom Aharon Ovadiah Ha-Cohen is believed to be the founder of the Calcutta community. Born in Aleppo in 1762, he left in 1789, arriving at Surat in 1792, where he initially settled down. His trade extended up to Zanzibar. He moved to Calcutta in 1798. In 1805 his nephew, Moses Simon Duek Ha-Cohen, joined him. Thereafter, others migrated and a sizeable community of Baghdadis emerged in Calcutta. Culturally, Baghdadis retained their own language and lifestyle. Baghdadis (men and women) wore the long robe-like clothing, their food was Iraqi in origin, but over time was influenced by local Indian cuisine and became spicy. The first generation of Calcutta Jews spoke Judeo-Arabic at home, but by the 1890s, English was widely adopted by the

Baghdadis. During the years of British colonialism, Baghdadis prospered, growing in numbers and amassing wealth through trade across South-East Asian countries. This aspect has been widely studied by scholars of Baghdadi Jewish history.[6]

Politically, under British rule, the Jews of India did well—both in terms of wealth and in numbers. This was especially true of the Baghdadi community which traded all along the cities of the far-east and elsewhere in the world. The 'Calcutta Jews', as the Baghdadis in Calcutta were commonly called, felt completely at home in Calcutta although they lived in community enclaves and socialized little with local Hindu or Muslim Bengali residents of the city. Their numbers reached a peak of about 5,000 during World War II when they were swelled by refugees fleeing the Japanese advance into Burma. By the late 1940s, the Baghdadi Jewish community widely identified with the British rule. By local Indians, the Baghdadis were perceived as 'anglicized'. They preferred Western education and European dress. In Calcutta of the 1940s and 1950s, Jewish Baghdadi women dressed in Western clothes, did not blend easily with the regional Indian communities which may have been Hindu or Muslim. They could be more easily be identified with the Anglo-Indian community or the Indian Christian community, both of which had patronized Western-style dressing for their women. These choices were important markers of identity and difference from the majority of Indian Hindus and Muslims who still preferred their daughters to dress in Indian clothes. The Baghdadi Jewish community was small and most families knew of others. Intermarriages between Jewish and Hindu or Christian young men and women were highly disapproved of (but happened often enough for parents to be anxious about the marriages of their children).[7] These social structures were disrupted in the 1940s after World War II. As nationalist sentiments swept across India, Baghdadi Jews felt less comfortable in the new anti-colonial climate of the 1940s and families began to emigrate out of India. The Baghdadi emigration out of India was more individualistic. Many of the educated and qualified Baghdadis in fact, chose to go to the UK, USA and Canada.[8] They also had an advantage over other migrating Indian

Jews. Some of them had parents who had been born outside India and had remained British subjects. Such individuals and their children were permitted to remain 'British subjects' if they chose to be so. Thus taking advantage of this facility many exercised this option to migrate for better prospects in Western countries instead of Israel.[9]

THE BENE ISRAELIS FROM MAHARASHTRA, GUJARAT AND KARACHI[10]

The Bene Israel community, the largest community of Jews settled in India, trace their origins to some time before the destruction of the Second Temple, when it is believed that fourteen survivors from a shipwrecked commercial vessel sailing from Israel to India were washed off near the Konkan coast of western India. These fourteen survivors (seven men and seven women) are considered to be the 'forefathers' of the community which eventually settled in the villages of west Maharashtra near the Konkan coast. Agriculture and oil-pressing were the economic activities of the rural Bene Israeli community, which observed their unique Saturday regimen of not working on *Shabbat*. In time, they came to be popularly known as the *shanwar-telis* (*shanwar* meaning Saturday and *teli*—oil-presser). Other practices which distinguished them from other religious communities in the region were that they circumcised male babies on the eighth day after birth, and refrained from eating fish which didn't have fins and scales. Both traditions are dominant markers of Judaism. Although endogamy was important, the Bene Israelis had no scholars of Judaism. Religious teachers from Baghdad and Cochin taught them mainstream Judaism in the eighteenth and nineteenth centuries. Most Bene Israeli forms of community worship were overseen by individual members who commanded respect in the community. Rabbis were usually those who were visiting from elsewhere, not Bene Israelis.

Migration to cities began in the nineteenth century, and by the middle of the twentieth century Bene Israelis were predominantly an urban community spread not only in and around the industrial port city of Bombay but also in cities like Ahmedabad, Poona, Jabalpur and Karachi (later Pakistan). Large numbers worked in the British Indian Army, Indian Railways and in airlines like BOAC and Air India. Being urbanized, the Bene Israelis had adapted linguistically and culturally to the Marathi, Gujarati, or Hindi ethos depending on the region of India in which they lived. In fact, of all the Jewish communities living in India, Bene Israelis were the best acculturated to their surroundings. Bene Israeli women wore *saris* and traditional Indian jewellery. Interestingly, many wore the *mangalsutra* (a necklace of black beads on a gold chain widely considered auspicious for married women and worn by thousands of Maharashtrian Hindu women). These Bene Israeli women clearly saw no conflict between an accessory worn by their Hindu sisters and their own Judaism. Embracing cultural symbols did not threaten their Jewish identity or pose a problem to the cultural symbols drawn from their own Jewish faith. Bene Israelis spoke local languages, modified Jewish food with local flavours and spices without compromising Jewish *kosher* requirements. They imbibed some practices from the surrounding culture like abstaining from beef-eating—a Hindu practice and widely observed in India. Their Jewish festivals acquired Indian names, and apart from *Hannukah*, other Jewish festivals were less widely observed. During the research for this book, many Bene Israeli Jews recalled growing up among their Hindu school-mates and neighbours and joining in the festivities on *Diwali* and *Ganesh-chaturthi* which are widely celebrated in India. Bene Israelis often carried family names which were 'Indian'—in fact, the names indicated the village of their origin in Maharashtra to which a suffix 'kar' or 'ker' was added. Thus, Bene Israeli Jews from Roha, Pen, Pali, Ashtam or Naogaon, became Rohekar, Penkar, Palkar, Ashtamkar and Naogaonkar.[11]

Bene Israelis began emigrating in the 1950s but the major wave of emigration took place in the 1960s and early 1970s. Clearly, leaving strong social and cultural networks and emigrating to an unseen homeland was more difficult for a community like the Bene Israelis who were comfortable in their Jewish-ness within the multi-religious culture of India—both under British rule and in independent India. Even during the peak of the Bene Israeli migrations in the 1960s, it was common in families to have a branch of the family, through a sibling, cousin or uncle, who had no interest in migrating to Israel. Even today, the largest Jewish community living in India are the Bene Israelis. About 5,000 live in the Mumbai region.

INTRA-COMMUNITY DYNAMICS

Historically, these three communities lived in different parts of India, and like other Indians they spoke the languages of the region and partook of the surrounding culture to different degrees. However, links between the different Jewish communities were at best sporadic. The pervasive Westernization among the Calcutta community kept them relatively aloof, not only from Indians in general, but also other Jewish communities—the Bene Israelis and the Kerala Jews. Between the Baghdadis and the Kerala Jews there had been some degree of contact historically, through visiting rabbis who brought Jewish prayer books and so forth. The Bene Israelis were relatively isolated from other Jewish communities. We may note, however, that the Bene Israelis were a large community in themselves, and well-adjusted into their surrounding regional and linguistic culture.[12] Inter-marriages between the Jewish communities were rare and different pecking orders existed. In the 1930s and 1940s, for a Baghdadi to marry a non-Baghdadi Jew was also an issue. *Ashkenazim*, some of whom came to India after World War II, were considered less orthodox by the Baghdadi community. The Bene Israelis were considered too assimilated. White Cochin Jews were accepted but not 'Black' Cochini Jews. The following story is suggestive. In the 1940s, the secretary of a Calcutta synagogue objected to performing a marriage between a Baghdadi boy and a Bene Israeli girl. The Bene Israelis married in a *sari* and the Baghdadis in European-style dresses. The groom argued, 'What difference does it make . . . English clothes are not Jewish clothes and we accept them as Jewish . . . so long as she is a Jewish girl.'[13] The secretary finally relented. After the 1940s, mixed marriages became more common for many reasons. World War II brought in soldiers from Western countries who had served in Japan and elsewhere in the region. Refugees from Nazi persecutions also came and many Calcutta Jewish girls began to marry Western refugees or Jewish soldiers. Some young people began to marry non-Jews. Although frowned upon, some of the marriages were eventually accepted.[14]

It is clear that Jewish communities, spread out far from each other in India, existed in their own 'orbits'. Their levels of 'Westernization' and 'Indianization' differed. The Baghdadis were business-oriented and anglicized. The Cochinis remained isolated from other Indian communities even within Kerala, living in villages or small townships close to synagogues and to other Jews. Most were small merchants and levels of education in the community were low. Although the Bene Israelis were not anglicized, by the 1940s, education levels were high among the upper middle-class Bene Israelis. As a community they were highly urbanized, preferred salaried jobs and many held white-collar jobs in the railways, the British Indian Armed forces and commercial airlines. These distinctions and disparities need to be understood because when Jews emigrated from India, some of these groupings remained. For instance, in Israel also, they were settled as separate groups. The Cochinis were settled mostly in agricultural *moshavs*, the Bene Israelis were predominantly sent to 'development towns'. They were rarely neighbours. In that sense, the procedures of the absorption authorities in Israel hardened the boundaries between the communities. Living in India, the Cochinis, Calcutta Jews or the Bene Israelis may have had strong regional affiliations—as many regional communities in India have. However, when they migrated to Israel, they shared something important. In Israel, since all immigrants came from *somewhere*—the Polish from Poland and the Moroccans from Morocco, therefore the Cochinis, Calcutta Jews and the Bene Israelis *all* shared a common country of origin. In the multi-ethnic society in Israel, the ethnicity of Indian Jewish communities is broadly common despite some internal cultural variations. Thus, I consider investigating the different Indian groups as 'Indian Jews' as a valid framework of analysis for this study.

IMMIGRANT WAVES AND THE ISRAELI SETTING

The Israeli State, as the Homeland for Jews is ideologically committed to welcoming all Jews and to support their process of assimilation. According to the Law of Return (1950) and the Law of Nationality (1952) every Jew has the right to settle in Israel and citizenship is conferred upon arrival. Yet, Israeli Jews are not homogeneous and contemporary Israeli society is multi-ethnic, demographically varied by colour, region of origin and time of immigration. In order to understand this multi-ethnic mosaic it is important to briefly recall the process by which waves of immigrants arrived, each adding a layer to this mosaic. Although small-scale and sporadic migrations of European and Middle Eastern Jews to the 'Holy Land' had carried on over the centuries, what is pertinent here is to highlight the nationalist migration and the birth of modern Zionism which enables us to better understand the modern origins of the Jewish State.[15]

Before Israel was declared a State, the Jewish immigrants who came to Palestine were predominantly of European origin (mostly from East and Central European countries). These groups or individuals were strongly ideological and creating a Jewish Homeland was their driving ambition. When the State was established, these groups became the 'veteran immigrants' and moved into becoming the social and cultural elites, occupying the more lucrative and prestigious leadership positions in government, businesses and so forth. From the late 1940s, immigration swelled the population of Israel, and within the first five years of statehood Israel's Jewish population is said to have doubled. Immigrants were transnational. Some were survivors of the holocaust but there were also entire Jewish communities from the Middle East (i.e. Iraq, Yemen and Syria). From the mid-1950s came large Jewish communities uprooted from Morocco, Libya, Algeria and Tunisia. They were all Jews but other than that they had little in common across the spectrum. The languages they spoke were different and the cultural lives they were accustomed to were vastly different: the food they ate, the climates they were accustomed to and the dress they wore. There was great unevenness in their levels of education. The *Ashkenazim* were more highly educated. Some had professional education, were economically better-off and had even managed to transfer their assets to Israel. Unlike these however, most 'Oriental Jews' or *Mizrahim* from non-European countries came with lower levels of education, were less well-off and soon enough began to fill subordinate positions in relation to the *Ashkenazim*. Although access to resources for new imigrants has many complex dimensions this in simple terms, was the scenario in Israeli society in the 1950s and 1960s whereby, layers of class and hierarchies of power became deeply entrenched in Israeli society.

There was also the politics of location. Large groups of new immigrants who came in shiploads from North Africa or West Asia needed to be provided for. The Immigration Absorption authorities and allied organizations in Israel set-up ambitious plans by creating agricultural villages and new townships at strategically chosen locations. The locations were usually in remote regions and it was hoped that industrial structures and employment opportunities would follow. From the 1950s, such was the Israeli setting into which came new immigrants—not only from North Africa and West Asia, but also from India. It is important to understand these Israeli models used for settling new communities and creating a unique rural and urban landscape. Analytically, for this study, it is important to understand these rural and urban models because this is a salient point of distinction making the Indian Jewish experience of migration to Israel different from that of Indian origin communities who may have migrated elsewhere. For instance, those who migrated to the US, UK, Canada or even to West Asia would not have encountered a state machinery which took the decisions about the city or town in which they had to live. In Israel, the state did. Hence, the features of these Israeli cities, towns and agricultural villages sensitize us to what new immigrants confronted upon arrival. Below I discuss some Israeli cities, towns and villages to which new immigrants were sent. The descriptions are by no means exhaustive and my choice is selective. In keeping with my objectives, I have chosen to focus on locations where Indian Jews were settled in significant numbers.

URBAN AND RURAL LANDSCAPES: CITIES, TOWNS AND *MOSHAVS*[16]

This section provides a context and focuses on spatial dimensions—the rural and urban models that were used in Israel from the 1950s. The models created by the Israeli State and its agencies were quite unique as they addressed the influx of population groups. This distinct urban and rural landscape in Israel bears some description, as we seek to contextualize Indian Jews and their social and spatial location in Israel. The four major cities in Israel are Jerusalem, Tel Aviv, Beersheva and Haifa. Each of these cities is distinct in terrain, topography and demographic character. From the other cities some are newly established, while others have older histories from the time of the Ottoman Empire (or even earlier). The older cities have intermingled histories of Jewish and Arab heritage and some were predominantly Arab cities in 1948. However, when Israel was established as a home for Jews, and vast numbers of Arabs fled the increasing violence, the cities 'emptied' out and Jewish immigrants who were pouring into Israel were settled in those areas, the towns were in a sense 're-populated' and acquired a new character after 1948. This would be the case for Ramla and Lod (near Tel Aviv).[17] Apart from such towns where housing became available as Arab communities fled, there are numerous other Israeli towns which were created on specific locations. These were called 'new towns' or 'development towns' which were strategically planned on locations in the 'peripheral regions' (Tel Aviv and its surrounding area being the 'centre'—spatially and in terms of development).

'Development towns' were conceived as townships on spaces which were carefully chosen by the State for urbanization. The choice of location was usually shaped by a combination of many factors. A key purpose of the 'development towns' was 'population dispersal', so as to avoid further over-crowding in the Tel Aviv region. Further, environmentally, for a nation which had arid regions and vast stretches of land that could not be cultivated, it was important to plan the new urban areas away from the fertile tracts which needed to be preserved for agriculture. Finally, there were also strategic considerations. For the Israeli State, territorial anxieties have been a critical issue since its establishment. Thus, it was envisaged that arid, empty stretches of its territory would become more secure by enhancing human settlement, and creating townships with their civic paraphernalia—houses, schools, utilities, offices, shopping centres and in due course, attracting industries to use the human capital available.[18] In addition to the cities and towns, other models of settling communities designed by the Israeli State to cope with the masses of immigrants from different countries around the 1950s, were the *kibbutz* and the *moshav*. While the *kibbutz* as a 'commune', with a cooperative economy which is sustained by the labour of its members, is widely known, the *moshav* is less well known outside of Israel. Unlike the *kibbutz*, the *moshav* has a community which is bound together only by certain common commitments to the upkeep and governance of the *moshav*. They may do cooperative marketing of produce and so forth, but there is immense flexibility for the members to work on jobs outside the *moshav*, run businesses from home and so forth. In contemporary Israel, the model of *kibbutz* life has generated some serious ambivalences and most *kibbutzim* are undergoing restructuring, giving more scope to individual enterprise. *Moshavs* continue to draw families—sometimes new families join existing communities by applying and obtaining approval of the original *moshav* members to buy land and build a house on the compound of the *moshav*. Many young families with small children prefer the open environs and security of *moshav* life over city-life.[19]

In search of these locales, during 2006–7, I travelled extensively in Israel. It was important to conduct research in the 'periphery',[20] to evolve a better understanding of the processes by which immigrants had acculturated and how their identities had been 'hybridized' over time.[21] As I attended over 50 Indian community programmes at different locations across Israel, I interviewed individuals in far-flung locations where they had lived for the past

30 or 40 years—mostly unable to afford relocation to more prosperous areas. The linkages between spatial location, access to resources and social stratification became stark. It is this understanding that I wish to communicate through this section.

The towns, cities and *moshavs,* listed below, have been selected because over time, they came to have clusters of Indian community. It may be noted that in a *moshav* even 35 families would be a significant presence, whereas in a city it might be a thousand families. These were the locations where Indian Jews were originally settled and where over time, they have mobilized as community groups.

The Centre and the 'Periphery'

Small in size as Israel is, sociologically and economically there are deep and significant variations in the levels of development and the consequent availability of economic opportunities. To be living in central Israel or in the 'periphery' shapes an individual's opportunities for access to education and employment and can delay or diminish a family's opportunities towards upward mobility, sometimes into the next generation. The two main cities, Jerusalem and Tel Aviv, are considered the 'centre', marked off from the 'periphery'—the Northern District and the Southern District. Jerusalem and Tel Aviv complement each other in ethos and are serviced by one international airport in Lod, almost equidistant from both. Stunningly beautiful, green and hilly, Jerusalem is replete with history intertwining Judaism, Islam and Christianity—which shapes its complex politics as well as demography. It is the official seat of government, where the President lives, where the Knesset (Israeli parliament) convenes and where most Israeli bureaucracy and ministries operate out of.[22] Tel Aviv, settled along the long stretch of the Mediterranean, remains the financial capital—a city of businesses, bustle and opportunity. Jerusalem has a large population of religious Jews and a significant population of Muslims.[23]

Tel Aviv on the other hand, has a population which is predominantly secular-Jewish and far less observant. This shapes urban lifestyles in both cities.[24] Haifa in the north and Beersheva in the south are the other two major cities, both situated between 100 and 115 km from Tel Aviv. Haifa's location as a busy port and its proximity to many Arab towns and villages shapes its culture and demography. It has areas with Arab and Russian Jewish concentration. Tel Aviv, Jerusalem and Haifa remain sought after as cities to live in and have high real estate prices—Haifa, less than the others. Indian Jews in any of the three cities mentioned are few and scattered. Although many *work* in or near these big cities, yet few actually live there, although more in Haifa than in Tel Aviv. Indians started coming to Jerusalem from 1954—not in any systematic way but isolated individual cases who found jobs.[25] Over time 60 Indian Jewish families moved to Jerusalem in the early decades and they were from different groups—Cochini, Baghdadi and Bene Israeli. In the carefully planned, expensive, elegant housing in the municipalities surrounding Tel Aviv like Ramat Aviv and Herzliya which are located on the Mediterranean, there were no new immigrants from India. These were mostly *Ashkenazi*-dominated areas and the Indian Jews who moved there had usually married into wealthy families.[26]

It is in the cities of Beersheva, Ashdod, Ramla, Lod, Dimona, Yarukham that Indian Jews were settled in large numbers. They were also sent to populate *moshavs* at Nevatim and Sha'haar (Southern District) and Rosh Pina, Yesod Hama'alah, and Kfar Yuval (Northern District), on Israel's border with Lebanon. Brief remarks on these locations provide a context for subsequent discussions.

Southern District

Beersheva[27] is the central and largest city of the South District of Israel. It is the administrative, cultural and industrial capital of the Negev. Home to Ben Gurion University of the Negev, a centre for science and the humanities, it also contains the internationally recognized Jacob Blaustein Institute for Desert Research. Beersheva was one of the major absorption centres for the Jews from India.

Kiryat Gat, a city enroute to Beersheva, was established in 1954, on the land of the Arab village of Iraq al-Manshiyya, and it has expanded from there to reach al-Faluja, Sha'haar and Noga. The Polgat textile factory, the main employer, shut down in the 1990s. Today, Kiryat Gat is home to an Intel plant which manufactures Pentium 4 chips and flash drives. Although as part of state efforts to develop the 'periphery' and generate regional employment, incentives of $525 million were given to set up the plant, few employees in the hi-tech plant are from its neighbourhood. All these areas are unemployment black spots.

Nevatim,[28] between Beersheva and Dimona is only marginally less remote than the latter. The nearest settlements are the Bedouin settlements Tel Sheva and Shaqib-al-Salam (to the north and south respectively). Further in the north-east is the Nevatim Air base. In the early 1950s, Cochini Jews founded Moshav Nevatim. Of the estimated 600 people at Nevatim, almost all are Cochini, except for mixed-marriages or some new entrants into the *moshav*. It is important to note that Jews from Kerala were not the first settlers. Nevatim had been settled previously by Iraqi Jews and later by Jews from Eastern Europe. Its barren tracts proved challenging to earlier groups and the *moshav* didn't grow. Indian Jews from Cochin, who came in 1954, were the first group who stayed on and whose grit and sheer hard labour created agricultural success on this land. Although these Jews were mostly merchants and not farmers, with their determination and hard work they converted this tract in the Negev into farming land and their home. By the 1980s, through innovative experiments in agriculture Cochini Jews had created a successful and highly profit-making business in greenhouse flowers exported widely to Europe.

Dimona was conceived as a 'development town' in 1953, and settled in 1955, mostly by new immigrants from Morocco who, in fact, began the construction of the first houses and roads. Indians (Bene Israelis) arrived in Dimona from the early 1960s. The region around is arid, bare and isolated with vast stretches of desert. Economically, Dimona did not attract the industrial investment that the state hoped it would. Sources for employment are few. The Dead Sea Chemical Works is a major employer of Dimona's working population. That too was situated at Sedom, almost 50 km away. Not far away, is Israel's largest Nuclear Research Centre which also employs local residents. Two textile mills generate other employment—mostly low-skilled and poorly paid.

NORTHERN DISTRICT

Rosh Pina and Surrounding Areas

Rosh Pina dates back to the nineteenth century as an agricultural colony where in December 1882, the new Jewish settlers first ploughed the land. However, in early days, when under the patronage of Baron Rothschild, Rosh Pina concentrated in producing wine and silk. Today Rosh Pina and its surrounding areas are primarily agriculture-dependant and Indian Jews from Cochin settled in this region in large numbers from the early 1950s. Yesod Hama'alah,[29] is about 15 km away from Rosh Pina and Kfar Yuval is a *moshav* 45 km away from Rosh Pina. All these saw Jewish settlers from Kerala.

About 12 km north of Haifa is a small, poorly developed group of suburban towns collectively called the Krayot, located on the Mediterranean coast. These collectively consist of the Kiryat Ata, Kiryat Haim, Kiryat Bialik, Kiryat Motzkin and Kiryat Yam. Many immigrant groups, particularly those with low levels of education, were settled in the Krayot. Groups of Indian families were scattered in this region and have small local networks.

ON THE FRINGES OF CENTRAL ISRAEL

Be'er Ya'aqov is situated in central Israel, east of Ramla and south of the old main Jaffa-Jerusalem road. It was established in 1907. Lod and Ramla are towns situated in Israel's central plain, a little more than 50 km from Jerusalem and about 25 km from Tel Aviv. All three cities have a visible Indian presence predominantly consisting of Bene Israelis. Ramla and Lod are in close proximity and unlike immigrant towns which were planned and began from scratch, these have ancient histories. Lod's ancient history is supported by references in the Bible—in the book of Genesis and Ezra. In Roman times, Julius Ceasar restored the privileges of the Jews and the town of Lod was an important trading and religious centre for the Jews. After the Romans suppressed a Jewish revolt, Lod became predominantly Christian. Although, at the beginning of the twentieth century Lod was a small town with a few hundred Arab families, under the British mandate it became an important communications centre. Lod was captured by the Israeli forces in 1948, during the Israeli-British clashes. Following this, the state began an aggressive programme to direct Jewish populations to settle there which had dramatic results in altering its demography.[30] The Jewish immigrants settled in Lod were mainly of African and Asian descent. Although many Arabs fled the violence, many stayed back and even today both Ramla and Lod have a significant Arab presence, compared to many other Israeli towns like Dimona which are overwhelmingly Jewish. Many Arab Israeli women can be seen in the shopping areas in headscarves or stricter *hijab* covering which may involve wearing long traditional robes and veiling of the face. There are functioning mosques which make the skyline of Ramla and Lod very different from development towns like Dimona or Kiryat Gat which are overwhelmingly if not entirely Jewish.

Ramla is located in the coastal area in the centre of the country, on important road and rail crossroads on the main route between Tel Aviv and Jerusalem (which is also the main route connecting north and south). In 1954, the first two families arrived in Ramla from India. Between the years 1968 and 1973, majority of immigrants from India, mainly from Bombay, arrived in Ramla and made it their hometown. Lod and Ramla began to emerge as significant areas for Indian immigrants, mostly from Bombay, Gujarat and Karachi. Israel's only international airport, which after 1975 came to be known as Ben Gurion Airport, is in Lod, only about 4–5 km away from the town itself. The Israeli Aircraft Industry (IAI, or Bedek, as it is called in Hebrew) is also in the vicinity. The proximity of Lod to Ben Gurion Airport and the Bedek is one of the reasons why Indians began to prefer these cities—because in time both these establishments employed large numbers of Indian Jews.

Ashdod is situated on the sea shore, 27 km south of Tel Aviv and is the main port of the area. As a modern Israeli city, Ashdod was founded in 1956 and is among the 'new towns'. Thousands of Indian immigrants were settled in Ashdod and its economy began to grow because of its port status. Ashdod is perhaps the most successful example of a development town. Its opportunities and bustle make it an exception that no other immigrant town has been able to rival. Indian Jews have flocked to Ashdod from more remote locations like Kiryat Gat or Dimona, although the transition is not an easily affordable option for most.

CONCLUSION

Development towns and *moshavs* did not witness the economic growth that was expected. Even today, Ashdod is an exception in the economic boost it experienced on account of its location as a port. Other development towns remain peripheral to the industrial and technological growth visible in the regions of central Israel. Among the second generation, growing up in the 1980s, there has been massive out-migration to more prosperous, industrialized areas in search of employment opportunities. It may be noted that some individuals and families interviewed for this research, did not live in any of the above clusters but miles away from other Indian families. This could be for many reasons—either because they chose to stay on in the same area, although the next generation moved further away, or they had not been able to better their initial allotments of 30 or 40 years ago, and move to more prosperous neighbourhoods. In some cases, it was the reverse: there were a few successful professionals who were living in privileged areas with other upper-class Israelis, mostly *Ashkenazi*. These however, constitute exceptions. Relocation involved paying huge sums of money to the municipality for the original immigrant housing, and also raising additional money to buy new homes in the better developed regions. It has been simpler to stay on and retire where many came as young couples in their twenties.

In general, location and contexts were important in shaping community struggles for upward mobility. Over time, living in ethnic clusters in development towns also created negative stereotypes of *Mizrahi* communities since a majority were in modestly paid jobs. For many first generation Indian Jews it has been difficult to transcend these barriers and the resultant stereotypes. Following this discussion of contexts and spatial locations which shaped the Indian Jewish experience in the Israeli setting, in the following chapter I turn to some key thematic concerns of this book.

How do we understand Jewish emigration from India, considering that Indian Jews were not escaping religious persecution or cultural discrimination and were in no rush to emigrate? Also, when they did migrate, how did they experience their 'homecoming' in the Jewish Homeland? What did they see *visually*, what did they confront *socially* and *culturally*, and what did they experience *administratively* upon arrival, when the Israeli Immigrant Absorption authorities took control of their lives deciding where they would live, the jobs they would do and who their neighbours were to be?

These are the questions addressed in the next chapter.

NOTES

1. For example, about when exactly the Bene Israelis came to India or how precisely can we understand the segments within Cochini Jewish community—the 'Paradesi' or 'White' Jews and the 'Black' Jews and so forth.
2. For historical and anthropological work on the Cochini Jews see David G. Mandelbaum, 'The Jewish Way of Life in Cochin', *Jewish Social Studies*, vol. 1, no 4, pp. 423–60, New York, 1939; Nathan Katz and Ellen S. Goldberg, *The Last Jews of Cochin: Jewish Identity in Hindu India*, Columbia: University of South Carolina Press, 1993; Fiona Hallegua, 'The Jewish Community of Cochin: Its Twilight Years', M.A. thesis, University of Kerala, St. Theresa's College, Ernakulam, 1984; Nathan Katz and Ellen S. Goldberg, *Kashrut, Caste and Kabbalah: The Religious Life of the Jews of Cochin*, New Delhi: Manohar, 2005, pp. 169–78.
3. David G. Mandelbaum, 'The Jewish Way of Life in Cochin', p. 434.
4. Kushner, p. 23.

5. For the history of the Baghdadi Jews in India see Ezekiel N. Musleah, *On the Banks of the Ganga: The Sojourn of the Jews in Calcutta*, North Quincy, MA: Christopher Publishing House, 1975; Nisith Ranjan Ray, *Calcutta: The Profile of a City*, Calcutta: K.P. Bagchi & Co., 1986; Dalia Ray, *The Jewish Heritage of Calcutta*, Calcutta: Minerva Associates, 2001; Elias Cooper, *The Jews of Calcutta: The Autobiography of a Community*, Calcutta: The Jewish Association of Calcutta, 1974; Stanley Jackson, *The Sassoons*, NewYork: E.P. Dutton & Co. Inc., 1968.
6. For Jewish identity during the British colonial period in India see Joan G. Roland, *Jews in British India: Identity in a Colonial Era*, Hanover and London: University Press of New England, published for Brandeis University Press, 1989; Mavis Hyman, *Jews of the Raj*, London: Hyman Publishers, 1995.
7. Several Baghdadi women I interviewed who had been of young marriageable age in Calcutta narrated that although they had lived in mixed neighbourhoods and went to Christian missionary schools, they had almost no friends who were Anglo-Indians, other Christians, Hindu or Muslim. They were strongly encouraged to socialize with Jewish youth. Their male cousins, had more freedom, although they too were expected to marry Jewish women.
8. I discuss such examples in greater detail in Chapters 3 and 4.
9. Baghdadi Jews who migrated from India to Israel and were interviewed for this research, commonly spoke of siblings and cousins settled in Britain and Canada who visit back and forth.
10. For a comprehensive history of the Bene Israelis see Shirley Isenberg, *India's Bene Israel: A Comprehensive Inquiry and Sourcebook*, Bombay: Popular Prakashan; Berkeley: Judah L. Magnes Museum, 1988.
11. In Israel, some dropped their Indian family names and took on Jewish or more neutral names to 'blend-in'. Thus, Ashtemkar became 'Ashton' and Kolatker or Koletkar became 'Kollett'. However, many Bene Israelis have retained their last names. I came across Chincholkar, Bamnulkar, Penkar, Sugaokar, Koletkar, Ashtemkar and so on.
12. The Bene Israeli gentleman who narrated this to me remarked that the Westernized and 'anglicized' Baghdadis considered themselves 'superior' to the more 'Indianized' Bene Israelis!
13. Elias Flower and Judith Elias Cooper, *The Jews of Calcutta: The Autobiography of a Community*, Calcutta: The Jewish Association of Calcutta 1974, p. 49.
14. Many of my interviewees mentioned a sibling or an aunt or uncle who in the 1940s or 1950s had married a non-Jewish person. After the initial hostilities, most families accepted the relationship.

15. Alex Weingrod, *Israel: Group Relations in New Society*, New York: Frederick A. Praeger, 1965.
16. For this section I have drawn upon several studies: Dorothy Willner, D. Weintraub, M. Lissak, and Y. Atzmon, *Moshava, Kibbutz and Moshav: Patterns of Jewish Rural Settlement and Development in Palestine*, Ithaca and London: Cornell University Press, 1969; D. Weintraub, *Immigration and Social Change: Agricultural Settlements of New Immigrants in Israel*, Manchester: Manchester University Press, 1971; Alex Weingrod, *Reluctant Pioneers: Village Development in Israel*, Ithaca: Cornell University Press, 1966; Alex Weingrod (ed.), *Studies in Israeli Society: After the Ingathering*, New York; London: Gordon and Breach Science Publishers, 1985; Erika Spiegal, *New Towns in Israel*, Stuttgart: Karl Kramer Verlag, 1966; Judah Matras, 'Israel's New Frontiers: The Urban Periphery', in M. Curtis and M.S. Chertoff (eds.), *Israel: Social Structure and Social Change*, New Brunswick: Transaction Publishers, 1973, pp. 3–14.
17. In radical critiques, Ramla and Lod have been referred to as the 'depopulated' cities into which newly arrived Jewish communities replaced the Arab or mixed populations.
18. Much research has been done on Israel's 'development towns' and the immigrant populations who grew up there since the 1950s. See, Spiegel, 1966; Judah Matras, 1973.
19. Some families return to a *moshav* where one of the spouses grew up, so that their children grow up close to their grandparents. In 2007, I saw a new section of 'young families' and newly-built houses which has emerged in Moshav Sha'haar in the Negev. The original houses in the *moshav* are over 40 years old.
20. 'Periphery' also included areas too close to Israeli borders, which the state believed needed to be developed and 'populated' for strategic reasons. Thus, large communities were directed to the 'peripheries'.
21. As an expatriate I lived in a privileged sea-side neighbourhood near Tel Aviv, very much in the 'centre'. Yet, early on in this project it became clear that this research would require several visits to remote towns and agricultural villages across Israel.
22. Interestingly, while ministries like the Foreign Ministry, Agriculture Ministry and so on are located in Jerusalem, the all-important Defense Ministry operates from the heart of Tel Aviv.
23. East Jerusalem which came under Israeli control in 1967, is almost entirely Muslim, whereas, its neighbouring Mea Sharim is entirely Jewish, mostly orthodox and ultra-orthodox Jews. Spatially almost

Where Are the Indian Jews Today? 89

adjacent, there are two different worlds separated by deep mistrust and antagonism.

24. On the Jewish *Shabaat* for instance, when much of Jerusalem shuts down, many more commercial establishments are open in Tel Aviv. In general, Tel Aviv is the beach city with a café culture and a night life to rival that of New York, Paris or Bangkok. Indeed, it is nicknamed the 'New York of Israel'!
25. Information provided by Noah Massil, Chairman, Central Organisation of Indian Jews in Israel (COIJI).
26. From Herzliya and Ra'naana, where many expatriates and diplomats live alongside wealthy Israelis, I met eight of my Indian Jewish respondents. Seven out of eight had 'mixed' marriages. They were married to *Ashkenazi* men or women who were Israeli-born, *not* first-generation immigrants.
27. Information gathered from the Embassy of India and Reuben Raymond, a resident-representative from Beersheva to the Central Organization of the Jews from India.
28. Information provided by Shahaf Nehemia, Director of River Authority and an active member of the Indian community.
29. Information gathered from interviews. I am grateful to Eliahu Dekel, a Cochini Jew whose parents came to the Rosh Pinna area in 1950. Dekel continues to live in this area. He is a member of the Centre Labor Party and active in the work of the Jewish Agency.
30. In 1948, the Arab population of Lod was 1,100 and the Jewish segment was 150. By 1974, Arabs were 3,700 and the Jews 30,200. *Source*: *Statistical Abstract of Israel*, 1975.

CHAPTER 3

Emigration from India: 'When We Came to the Land of Milk and Honey...'

This chapter begins the story of emigration. I seek to recapture the narrative of how Indian Jewish communities began to consider emigration from India as a serious option. What were the ties that held them back and what were the attractions that spurred them on? What did they imagine Israel to be and what were the sources of that imaginary—family stories or emissaries from overseas sent to encourage world Jewry to emigrate to Israel and enhance the demographic strength of the new Jewish nation? These are important questions in themselves. But they constitute only one half of the story. The other half is about arrival and about the beginnings of acculturation. Hence this chapter is also about what sixty-five year old Naomi described as 'When we came to the Land of Milk and Honey...'. Theoretically, however, Jewish emigration from India needs to be understood at multiple levels. Personal stories need to be placed within socio-historical frames to understand the broader implications which illuminate the nuances of emigration and immigration. Hence, I begin this chapter by first examining a broader national and international canvas against which individual men and women in India began to focus on the Jewish Homeland as an attractive destination.

HISTORY AND REGIONAL POLITICS

Jewish emigration from India was closely inter-linked with historical and political developments in India in the late 1940s. Similarly, developments in the Middle-East influenced the 'pull' for immigration to Israel. I wish to suggest that Indian-Jewish immigration may be theorized as *distinct* and *context-specific* for a variety of reasons. To begin with, Jewish emigration from India must be distinguished from the East European or North African example. We know from previous anthropological and historical research discussed in Chapter 2, that Indian Jews were scattered across different linguistic regions where they had led their lives as settled communities for hundreds of years whether in Maharashtra, Gujarat, Calcutta, Bombay or in various parts of Kerala. Unlike persecuted Jewish communities living in ghettos in East Europe, Indian Jews lived amongst their religious 'Others'. They did not need to huddle closer to Jewish communities living elsewhere in India. For example, Cochini Jews did not wander closer to their brethren in Bombay or Gujarat. The Baghdadis in Calcutta maintained links with extended networks of Baghdadis in China or elsewhere, but even among the Baghdadis many families were three generations old in India. Jews did not move around within India as communities. They moved as other Indians—who undertake *internal* migration which may be employment-driven or linked to marriage. In short, it must be noted that the 'push factors' for Indian Jews to emigrate were not necessarily those that applied to Jewish communities in Eastern Europe, Northern Africa or West Asia. It is true that, in their prayers, Indian Jews reiterated the desire to be in Jerusalem 'next year' as their brethren elsewhere, but the material realities generating the incentives to leave their settled lives in India were *not* related to being *Jewish-in-India*. Secondly, Jewish emigration out of India needs to be contextualized—historically and politically. To better understand the complexity underlying the push to emigrate, we need to historicize and place Indian Jewish migration within the context of the political and historical developments of the late 1940s and early 1950s. This was a time-span within which salient political developments took place, affecting the future/s of both India and Israel.

After the formation of Israel in 1948, Jews were invited from all over the world to collectively claim the 'Homeland'. This created compelling 'pull factors' for Jews all over the world. Along another axis, this coincided with important changes in the country of origin—India. In 1947, when India was freed from colonial rule and partitioned by the British into India and Pakistan, the end of colonial rule meant that some Westernized elites, previously supportive of the British administration felt uncertain and anxious about forging new alliances within a self-ruled India. Communities which had been perceived sympathetic to British rule or had benefited from colonial patronage by being favoured for employment and benefits were understandably anxious about switching loyalties. This was the case with the Anglo-Indian communities especially living in Bombay and Calcutta, and also a large section of the Baghdadi Jewish community, a trading community spread across Asia with kinship networks connecting families in Calcutta to others in Hong Kong, Rangoon and Shanghai.[1] In general, the Partition of India had serious implications for millions who lived in the region. Hindus and Muslims were displaced on both sides of the border. As Pakistan was declared an Islamic Republic, millions of Muslims left India and chose Pakistan and millions of Hindus fled Pakistan, seeking shelter and work in India. Many Indian Jews, mostly Bene Israelis had settled in Karachi, doing businesses and holding government jobs. During 1944–6, the years immediately preceding India's Independence, when violent Hindu-Muslim riots broke out, many Jewish families fled Karachi seeking their friends and relatives in Maharashtra and Gujarat. Diana Benjamin now in her eighties, narrated how she and her family were among the last shiploads who left Karachi around Partition and sailed for Bomaby. When Karachi was finally declared a part of Pakistan, the Jews had the choice to opt for India or Pakistan. Some of the interviewees narrated how initially, they did opt for Pakistan in 1947 in order to hold on to their jobs, hoping to somehow skirt the Hindu-Muslim antagonism, of which they were no part. However, as a minority in an Islamic Republic, Jews had to re-think their options in Pakistan. Simon, one of the respondents for this research who was from Karachi, narrated that in 1948–9 many Jews employed in Karachi were asked to resign their jobs in favour of Muslims. The violence and civil unrest in Karachi also made them insecure, and they were forced to leave Pakistan. For most, the obvious first step seemed to be India which guaranteed constitutional equality to all religions. Moreover, India apart from being culturally and linguistically a 'comfort zone', was also a home to thousands of other Jews. However, among the 'Karachi Jews', as they are sometimes referred to within the community, not all had family networks in Bombay or Gujarat. In 1947, millions of Indians were displaced refugees newly arrived from Pakistan. Millions were uprooted, unemployed and penniless. Finding housing and jobs was difficult in newly independent India, and in this situation many of the Karachi Jews emigrated to Israel, within months of coming to India.

I met several individuals in Israel whose families had moved after 1947 in ships and steamers out of Karachi into India and onto Israel, either as a family or in segments. Jimmy (*b.* 1945) was born in Karachi, where his father worked as an engineer. 'We had no problems there', narrated Jimmy. But when the political situation deteriorated they moved to Bombay. In 1962, his parents decided to move to Israel with their four children. Naomi, now a retiree in Lod, was a teenager studying at English Grammar School, Karachi in 1946. When Hindu-Muslim riots broke out and killings increased, Naomi's mother decided to move with her daughters and nieces to Bombay. There, they lived with relatives and later managed a small apartment in Bandra, then a middle-class suburb of Bombay mostly consisting of Christians and Anglo-Indians. Emotionally, the family settled in easily. Naomi recalled how '... We used to travel in buses and trains from Bandra to Churchgate even at 6 a.m., when I would leave for hockey practice. . . . Our friends were from all communities.' But times were tough in Bombay. As Naomi finished schooling her older brother, Myer 'felt unsatisfied with his job and decided to move to Israel. In 1949, he was the first one from our family to move to Israel.' In 1954, her sister and brother-in-law also made *aliya* to Israel. Naomi moved with their mother only in 1966.

In the discussion below, I examine the actual processes of emigration—the motivations, decisions, and the circumstances of the individual or family when the choice was made, and what followed thereafter. We may note that, within the national Zionist discourses projected aggressively by the initiatives of the Jewish Agency, for Jews to migrate to Israel or to make *aliya*, was about 'returning home' to the Holy Land. Indeed, when I posed the question of motivation up-front in the interviews, that was the answer I got. When asked *why* they migrated from India, most individuals attributed it to their Zionism. Many of the older retirees said *kyonki, ye hamaara desh hai* (because this is *our* country). However, the detailed interviews revealed sub-texts and meanings, conflicting motivations and incentives which revealed complex layers beneath this simple 'love-for-the-homeland' motif. For this research, there seemed a need to tease out other supplementary considerations that had encouraged families to dismantle settled homes and take off for a 'homeland', thousands of miles away. To unravel some of these complex strands, I collated a wide range of details about the lives and circumstances of the individuals especially around the time of migration. What were the socio-economic circumstances? What was the size/status of the family at the time of emigration? In terms of career and economic enhancement, what sort of future did they visualize for themselves in India? What aspirations did the parents of growing children have about the financial future or the marriages of their sons and daughters? Although 'love-for-the-homeland' was the reason respondents frequently cited in the interviews, they were forthcoming in sharing specific family configurations that clinched the decision to make *aliya* to Israel. They were candid in describing how many joint families lived in cramped suburban housing in Bombay and how they had concerns about homeownership in the future. Some lower income families were anxious about the future of their children and *all* parents were concerned about the marriages of their children, lest their sons and daughters marry outside the Jewish fold. Thus, the data gathered for this study revealed that the choice of *when* individuals chose to migrate, whether they migrated *en famille*, or with a Youth Aliya group, or as an older couple with several children or a young couple with one child, and so forth, was determined by a multiplicity of factors that underlay individual decisions to emigrate.[2]

An interesting commonality emerged during the interviews:

most Indian Jews were very enthusiastic when asked about their early days in Israel. Men and women, regardless of class and educational levels, went into great details (in English, Hindi or Marathi or a mix of all three languages), vividly describing the experiences of that early period in Israel (before 1970). Perhaps my own location as a visitor to Israel, who was experiencing a modern, technologically advanced nation in 2007–8, enthused them to go to great lengths to recapture the 'Israel-that-was'— the problems of an emerging new nation in the 1950s and 1960s, the lack of infrastructure, severe consumer shortages and their own sense of 'shock' when they compared small Israeli towns in the 1960s, with the metropolis of Calcutta or Bombay that they had left behind. Hence, for this project which sought to capture Indian Jewish migration experiences for the first time, it became crucial to incorporate these early experiences so as to understand how Indian Jews had negotiated the early days, months and years, living in transit camps, or subsequently in the remote townships where they were settled. These narrations serve another important scholarly purpose: they capture the Israeli setting of the 1950s and 1960s from the eyes of those who were recipients of the many Israeli schemes of land settlement and immigration absorption, which were put in place for their benefit. Sociological research on Israeli society has offered comprehensive analyses of issues relating to immigrant absorption in the early decades. Numerous sociologists have analysed problems of population distribution and ethnicity after the 'ingathering of exiles'.[3] The experiences of Indian Jewish immigrants add a fresh perspective to this body of scholarship in revealing certain specificities of how displacement led to the need for 're-socialization', which in turn, generated considerable economic and emotional traumas.

Thus, the discussion below negotiates two related sets of questions that accompany migration in general, and more specifically this unique example of migration of Indian Jews to Israel. The first set of questions relates to the *process*, which includes the *motivations* and the actual *Journey*. . . . Who were these individuals and families? What did they hear/know about the Jewish Homeland that influenced their decision to emigrate? What were their sources of information? How were the actual journeys arranged and executed, given the fact that in the 1950s and 1960s the world was hardly transnational as it is today, and foreign travel was a luxury which few could afford. The second set of questions follows from this. It presents the juxtaposition between what potential immigrants heard or imagined about Israel and what they actually encountered. I wish to underscore that questions relating to *what they saw* and *what they experienced* are of particular importance when we consider the early years of Israeli nation-building and immigrant absorption which have been the subject of much sociological research in Israel. As immigrant influxes radically altered the demography of the country and the Israeli state responded to the pressures, infrastructure, employment, housing and availability of food and consumer goods all improved significantly by the end of the 1960s. We may note therefore that, immigrants who came to Israel after 1970 did not encounter the same problems or experience the same struggles. This chapter primarily draws upon the experiences of those who came before 1970—although two women immigrants included in this chapter came in 1970–1.

Through this analysis I seek to provide parallel contexts which, in fact, corroborate many of the hypotheses about immigrant acculturation in existing literature on Jewish immigration. However, some experiences unique to Indian Jews also emerge and merit comment. For instance, the sense of marginalization due to what they termed as 'colour-bias' came as a shock to many Indian immigrants. They explained that they had emigrated out of an ethos of being *different* but not *discriminated* against in India, although they were a miniscule religious minority. To migrate on the basis of a shared Jewish identity and then feel relegated to the fringes of social acceptability was distressing—and many recalled that distress with emotion. Upon doing some research, I realized that these were not just personal stories, but that Indian Jewry of the Bene Israeli community had in fact, endured serious rejection by many rabbinates who questioned their Jewish identity. Although today, this issue has now been buried, its scars lie deep in collective memory and a few comments are in order. In fact, in the early 1950s there emerged a controversy regarding the 'purity' of the Bene Israeli Jews who were the largest group of Indian Jews, with higher levels of education than other groups. Although Bene Israelis practised endogamy and most of the Jewish observances with individual variations, they had adjusted well to their linguistic and social environments doing well professionally and commanding respect in Indian society as individuals and as a community. However, soon after groups of Bene Israelis made *aliya* to Israel, a controversy about their Jewish-ness arose. Many interviewees explained that the cultural symbols that Bene Israeli families had imbibed over the centuries made them appear 'too Indian' and 'not Jewish enough'. This was ironic because the Bene Israelis with their spicy *kosher* food and distinct Jewish rituals had perhaps blended Indian-ness and Jewish-ness to near perfection. In Israeli society, however, they had to provide 'proofs' of their devoutness. Their choice to embrace the Jewish Homeland was not enough. In the late 1950s there existed a directive issued by the Chief Rabbinate which made it mandatory for a Bene Israeli man or woman who wished to be married by a Rabbi to produce documents which would certify his/her Jewish ancestry 'as far back as possible'. Rabbi Nissim's directive infuriated the community and protests and strikes were staged. Bene Israelis from Dimona, Beersheva, Yarukham and other immigrant towns mobilized in hundreds and picketed outside the Jewish Agency office in Jerusalem and on the streets of Tel Aviv. The controversy lasted a few years and got wide media coverage reaching parliamentary debates in the Israeli Knesset and a plea from Indian Jews to the Prime Minister of India, before the Bene Israelis were finally accepted as 'equal' to other Jews.[4] Many Bene Israelis I interviewed referred to this controversy and the enduring scar it left upon them as individuals, and as a community.

Finally, apart from examining thematic issues, this chapter also has another important aim. I wish to highlight the descriptive elements and seek to capture some of the vivid details that marked immigration: how individuals or families finalized their decisions to emigrate from India, the bureaucratic approvals they needed to qualify as future citizens of Israel, the nature of their journeys, and finally, their first reactions to Israel—considering that most had never travelled overseas before. The discussion below examines these and related questions.

THE CALL TO MIGRATE: CIRCUMSTANCES, ZIONISM AND THE JEWISH AGENCY

As millions of Indians were confronting post-Independence displacement, Israel's 'call' to the Jewry worldwide reached Indian Jews through various channels. Although the educated Jews living in metropolitan cities like Bombay and Calcutta had access to foreign news broadcasts and print media through which they knew about the anti-Semitic persecutions in Europe in the mid-1940s, most Indian Jews with vernacular education had little awareness of the holocaust. It was too far away geographically and too remote from their own well-acculturated worlds in which they worked, studied and lived alongside millions of non-Jews, while saying their Jewish prayers and observing *kashruth* dietary laws and *shabbat* according to individual preference. Jerusalem figured in their prayers of course, but for most families, the motivation to emigrate had to be created. The land of Israel as a 'home', as a 'new country' and the 'Land of Milk and Honey' with new opportunities had to be packaged and brought to the thousands of Indian Jews who were scattered in different cities. This was a large and difficult project—and this is where the Jewish Agency and organizations like ORT Schools came in. Families had to be reached out to through synagogues, schools and community gatherings. The Jewish Agency's networks were carefully organized and emerged as effective and powerful. It is important to understand the genesis of the Agency in the Israeli context.

The Jewish Agency was set up as a public body to support the 'establishment of the national home and the interests of the Jewish population' in accordance with Article 4 of the Mandate for Palestine. It was enlarged in 1929, and till 1948 wielded power as almost a shadow government. In pre-state Israel, the Jewish Agency for Palestine administered the land settlement programme, co-ordinated the efforts of the other organizations like the Jewish National Fund which controlled the land, and the Foundation Fund which raised the capital. With its mandate to build up the Jewish community in Israel, it also oversaw Departments of Immigration, Absorption, Land Settlement, Youth and Pioneering,

Education and Culture and those concerned with its administration and financial affairs. It also maintained a Political Department, which was much like a foreign ministry. *Haganah*, the underground defence force, was also under its authority. Although, after 1948, some of these branches became departments and ministries of the Israeli government, the Agency retained primary responsibilities for immigration and several other areas. It therefore retained 'quasi-governmental' functions in many fields—both for the outreach to bring new immigrants, and also as an arm of the bureaucracy in directing the development of Jewish settlements and agricultural villages.[5] For most Jews outside of Israel then, the Jewish Agency became the conduit that began forging connections between them and Israel through aggressive outreach programmes. In India, representatives of the Jewish Agency were active. Visiting Zionists conducted evening programmes seeking Indian Jewish communities especially young boys and girls who could be future citizens of Israel. One cannot minimize the role of the Jewish Agency outreach in this regard. The print media or even the radio did not have the impact which the Agency achieved through its network and initiatives. The interviewees for this study invariably mentioned that either they, or a family member or a friend, had met an Agency representative to discuss the prospect of emigration to Israel. Interestingly, when asked about the Agency's powers or mandate, most respondents were rather vague!

The activities of the ORT schools also played an important role in drawing together Jewish youth. The ORT India Schools operated in India in affiliation to the parent network of World ORT Union, a Jewish organization which ran vocational and technological schools in many countries to impart technical education and training knowledge to Jewish youth free of charge. Personnel from World ORT network travelled around and trained local youth to become trainers and local leaders. Indian Jewish children used to be chosen for these programmes which also included familiarization trips to Israel. For instance, in 1957 when Pnina Naogaonkar (*b*. 1939), finished her high school education from the Elly Kadoorie School, Bombay, she was chosen among a group of five other boys and girls for such a trip to Israel. Upon her return she joined undergraduate studies at Bombay University but also became active in Jewish community affairs. Running classes to teach Hebrew and Jewish subjects in the evenings and on Sundays, Pnina travelled to Jewish communities in neighbouring suburbs of Chembur and Thane. In time, she began delivering religious talks in synagogues. Through the ORT School they used to organize camps for Jewish youth not only in the Bombay region but also as far as Cochin. This was all Jewish Agency sponsored work. Through the ORT School, Pnina met her future husband who was a Tunisian Jew posted in India. Both served as ORT School instructors for over two decades, emigrating to Israel only in 1986. Pnina's example illustrates that the Jewish networks had to operate along a number of channels. They had to rely on local human resource and do capacity-building locally in order to be effective in sending out the Zionist message to scattered Jewish families. Indeed, many of the interviewees for this study had attended after-school activities or weekend picnics sponsored by ORT. Clearly this was an effective strategy for forging community bonding because it brought Jewish boys and girls *away* from their usual circle of schoolmates and friends (who would have been Hindu, Muslim or Christian) and brought them together on the basis of their shared Jewish identity. As they learnt about Israel and heard visiting *kibbutzim* sing Israeli songs, images of the 'Land of Milk and Honey' became interwoven with youthful aspirations for a future in Israel.[6]

In general, however, the Indian Jewish response to the Zionist outreach varied across class and region. Individual circumstances and age were important factors. In lower income families, *aliya* to Israel offered an escape from the anxieties of educating and settling six or seven children. Even the prospect of owning a home could be a huge draw in such cases. But for others the excitement of boarding an aeroplane and going to a new country was not enough attraction to give up the tracks of higher education they were on. If all young people were not enthusiastic, then the older generation had more complex dilemmas still. Many felt unsure about giving up steady jobs and uprooting social networks but felt the need to ensure a Jewish future for their children. Some moved reluctantly with their children, others followed the children who left in Youth Aliya groups. Still others resisted and simply lived on in India. . . . But the examples below suggest that *aliya* was also about self-perception as a religious Jew or simply the ambivalences in being 'Jewish-and-Indian'. The Baghdadi Jewish community of India, for instance, is an illustration of this ambivalent identity. As discussed in Chapter 2, the Baghdadis, a Westernized community particularly in Calcutta, thrived economically and socially during British colonial rule. While the elite families sent their children to study in Europe or in England, even the less well-off had adopted a Judeo-British identity and spoke English at home. As a religious minority they were concerned about getting assimilated, and maintained a strong and separate religious and cultural identity. India's Independence created a point of crisis for many Baghdadis, and as prospect of living in an India ruled by Indians appeared unattractive, emigrating as British subjects to the UK or seeking migration to Canada or the United States became the preferred option of many upper-class educated Baghdadis.[7] Many extended families of Calcutta Baghdadis began to spread across Israel, Britain, United States and Canada. Some who made *aliya* to Israel as children with their ageing parents, also moved on after completing their education to open businesses in North America. For instance, Emma, Sammy and Yakov were born in Calcutta and moved to Israel in 1950 with their parents. From this family of eight siblings who grew up or initially worked in Israel, only two sisters and a brother remain in Israel. The others built their lives in California, England and Canada and only visit the Jewish Homeland periodically.

However, this sense of ambivalent identities was not shared by all Indian Jews. If the Baghdadis were alienated from local Indian society, then the Jews of western India mostly Bene Israelis were comfortably settled in Gujarat and Maharashtra, where they all spoke the vernacular with ease. In fact, the earliest Indian Jews to make *aliya* to Israel were not necessarily the best educated or professionally well-placed. Given that Jews did not face obstacles in professional or social advancement, many were working in the Indian armed forces, or in government jobs. The Indian film industry had its share of Jewish men and women and there were professionals who were medical doctors, academics, architects or businessmen. Rachel, one of my interviewees living in Hadera, spoke of her father Reuben Simon Reuben (1912–91) an architect, civil and structural engineer and real estate valuer in Bombay who retired eventually as a chief engineer working for Government of India. Her maternal grandfather was Hon. J.J. Solomon, a high court judge. Avner who lives in Ashdod, and his sister Sarah who works at the Technion at Haifa, spoke of their father, who was a senior Brigadier in the Indian army in the 1970s and 1980s, who chose to stay on in India even after his children migrated. Reuben (*b.* 1949) came from a family which has founded successful private schools in Ahmedabad. His siblings and parents never migrated to Israel. All the interviews for this project confirmed that in India they constantly interacted socially and professionally with non-Jewish people as friends, neighbours and colleagues. Those who had been schoolchildren in the 1960s, confirmed that they had plenty of non-Jewish playmates with whom they shared their social and cultural lives. In the 1950s and 1960s, which were the decades for the bulk of Indian Jewish emigration, upper middle-class urban Jewish families were not easily attracted to consider uprooting themselves from their homes, jobs and social networks in Bombay, Delhi, Ahmedabad or Poona, disrupting their children's education and relocating themselves in a new country, to negotiate a new and difficult language, new system of education and begin a career all over again.

For the same reasons, however, migration was strongly appealing to those who were either avid Zionists, deeply religious Jews or socio-economically on the margins of mainstream society. For the deeply religious Indian Jews migration meant being able to observe all the Jewish rituals in a demographic environment where being Jewish was the *norm*. For the religious it was wonderful to imagine a society organized such that eating *kosher* food, observing Jewish rituals and prayers did not need juggling as it would need in India where all communities observed their religious rites in a pluralistic environment. For Zionists, making *aliya* was to transform the dream of a Jewish Homeland into a reality. But for many others, practical life-choices were a pressing reality. Unsteady employment, low educational levels or just the economic struggles in lower income families, which compelled large extended families to live in two cramped rooms, made the prospect of a new life and a new house very attractive. For instance, Shlomit Talker and her husband made *aliya* in 1964 from a suburb of Bombay where he was involved in the liquor trade. These were days of state prohibition banning the sale of liquor in Maharashtra state in which Bombay was the main business centre. This made liquor-trading a lucrative but dangerous business. Shlomit recalled how her husband expressed a hope for the future of his children when he chose to enlist with the Jewish Agency to make *aliya*. Israel offered not only a homeland for this young Jewish couple but also the possibility for a 'turn-around' in their lives, although they were neither starved nor unemployed in India. Ironically, Shlomit recalled immense economic hardships, including unemployment upon coming to Israel. She bore and raised her children in very challenging circumstances in a small 'development town' in the desert area of the Negev, where she lives even today.

However, these stories of distress were not the norm and the early immigration experiences were too varied to fit into a neat template. From among the Jewish community settled in Kerala—around Cochin and elsewhere, the earliest *organized* immigration group left Kerala in 1949. This 'pilot' group of nineteen people comprised adults and children. These families sold their belongings and some community property in Kerala to pay the Jewish Agency for their expenses. They arrived in Bombay in December 1949 awaiting the Jewish Agency's arrangements to fly them to Israel.[8] Older members of Cochini Jews in Israel, who came to Israel more than 45 years ago, had a wealth of information to offer about the earliest 'post-state' immigrants from India to Israel. For instance, 76 year old Eliyahu, now living in southern Israel, who was then a young lad in Cochin, knew some members of the first group. He explained that, 'the group had to wait for two weeks in Bombay for a flight to be arranged for them. . . . Finally, when they took off, two hours after take off, their flight from Bombay developed a petrol leakage and the plane returned to Bombay. . . .

It took off after two weeks of repair. Thus, those who had left in December 1949 arrived in Israel only in January 1950!' From Cochini elders from the Rosh Pina area in northern Israel, as well as from those living in the Negev, there emerged references to a Jewish officer by the name of Meir, who was serving in the British Air Force in Bangalore some time in the late 1940s. Meir clearly took a keen interest in the community of the Cochini Jews and according to Eliyahu my Cochini respondent, 'Meir knew about developments in Palestine at the time. . . . He brought messages to the boys of the Cochini Jewish community, that a Jewish state was being established. He had addresses and references of people in Palestine, of Jews who would help other Jews to settle in a new proposed Homeland. . . .' Eliyahu described how the older men were wary of this influence and thought Meir's plans of encouraging the youth of the village to be 'crazy', since most of them 'had never even ventured outside the region of Kerala!' However, many young Cochini Jews did become enthusiastic as Meir wrote to many organizations in Palestine explaining about the Cochini Jews and their desire to make *aliya*. Eliyahu knew Meir personally in the early 1950s and recalled Meir's advice while he was awaiting the Jewish Agency clearance to make *aliya*. Eliyahu was enrolled for an undergraduate degree in Maharaja's College, Ernakulam but Meir advised him to switch to some technical training 'I proceeded to learn wireless communication and then acquired training in radio technology . . . to prepare myself for Israel'. In 1955, when Eliyahu was in his twenties, he made *aliya*, along with his sister and his 56 year old father. His younger sister Rivka had gone a year previously as part of an Agency sponsored Youth Aliya group.

Indeed, for many Jewish families in India, whether Bene Israeli, Cochini or Baghdadi, it was young teenaged children who introduced enthusiasm to emigrate to the Jewish Homeland, while the older generation were harder to convince. Elias Ashtemkar recalled how Jewish Agency representatives organized group outings, which were seen as 'fun'. They also heard and learnt Israeli songs from visiting Israeli *kibbutzim*. Thus, many a youthful heart was won! Many a Jewish young boy or girl fired by the

Jewish Agency's 'invitations' to make *aliya* returned home to his/her parents and expressed a determination to go to 'The Land of Milk and Honey'. Elias came from Bombay in 1971 in a Youth Aliya group sponsored by the Jewish Agency. He was thirteen and a half and his father was not keen to send him. When he was insistent on going to Israel the father did not wish him to be isolated, so he sent Elias with his two other children—younger brother Daniel aged 12 and their sister aged 16. The children already had some members of the extended family in Israel. Jacob Miller (*b*. 1934) from Bombay came in 1952, when he and his brother were in their late teens. In this large family of modest means, Jacob's older brother was attracted by the stories of Israel from the Jewish Agency representatives and decided to leave his modestly paid job and try his fortunes in Israel. Their father, then in his mid-fifties, was against emigration. Jacob recalled how his father had voiced his opposition using a metaphor in their mother-tongue Marathi: *Kai ko Navi Viti, Navi Dandu?*[9]

Sometimes, reluctant parents came along. In some cases, they followed but in some unfortunate cases, they got stuck because the Jewish Agency's preference for younger (read: socially more productive) members prevented parents from joining their children for several years. Daniel (*b*. 1956) and his brother Moshe (*b*. 1954) came as children (when they were ten and twelve respectively). They came in a Youth Aliya group in the mid-1960s. Their mother was able to come only twelve years later. The Jewish Agency office refused to sponsor her, and the family in India were too poor to pay for her fare. Finally, her brother from Beersheva offered to pay her fare. Only then was she reunited with her sons. She died in Israel within two years of her arrival. The case of Solomon's father Hanukh Chincholkar who worked as a bus-conductor in Parel, suburban Bombay, before he came to Israel in 1963, is an interesting example of how age and economic factors played a key role in the process of emigration. As the new Jewish nation was being built, not all new immigrants would be as valuable. The young ones were wooed more avidly and Solomon's father was already 50 years old. Although Hanukh applied two years earlier than his cousin Ofer (who was ten years younger), he was not accepted for *aliya*. 'For us the economic reasons for migration were important'. Solomon explained that Hanukh hoped that in the new nation, his five children would be able to make better lives and improve their living standards. Hanukh was eventually granted clearance papers to make *aliya* on one condition: he had to give two of his five children to become part of a permanent *kibbutz* community somewhere in northern Israel. It was a hard decision but he finally agreed and Haim (aged 20) and Sepora (aged 18) were separated from their family upon arrival at the airport in Israel. Haim and Sepora were sent to a *kibbutz* near Haifa in the north and the rest of the family with the smaller children was sent 120 km away to Ashdod in southern Israel. The politics of age is an important and perhaps understudied issue in the process by which citizens were valued more or less in the new nation of Israel. For many their advancing years were a painful reality—of feeling less valued as citizens of the Jewish Homeland.

Gender and Marriage

Although families in India rarely allowed young daughters to travel about unescorted, many single women migrated to Israel through the Jewish Agency. Jewish parents encouraged their children to migrate because they were anxious about inter-faith marriages in the family. Given the pluralistic society in India and its constitutional provisions, inter-faith marriages could take place easily as registered civil marriages in court—without either party having to change their religion. Given the small numbers of Jewish people in India, parents believed that migration to Israel would ensure that their sons and daughters would marry other Jews. This seemed to be a widely held view among all Indian Jewish communities regardless of the socio-economic background of the family. For instance, Esther Bamnulker (*b*. 1941), who was one of six children of a millworker in Bombay, came to Israel in 1966 by herself. Although her uncles and aunts from Ahmedabad had made *aliya* previously and were living in Beersheva, her parents did not come.

Muzel and Triffine, daughters raised in a Baghdadi family, were 20 and 19 respectively when they emigrated from their home in

Calcutta in 1965. Their parents encouraged them to come to Israel on a tourist visa, live with their aunt in Tel Aviv and 'try out living in Israel'. Rosy (b. 1952), a Bene Israeli from Delhi, whose father was a senior officer working for the Government of India, emigrated in 1971 as soon as she completed her B.Sc. in Chemistry from University of Delhi and her younger sister Lizzy (b. 1956) did the same three years later. Both joined *kibbutz* communities for some years in their early phase in Israel and later married and raised families in Israel. Their parents chose not to migrate.[10]

Indeed, many parents were so concerned about mixed marriages, that they were glad to dismantle their own settled lives and migrate, as their children reached their twenties, for fear that their sons and daughters would not find partners within the shrinking Jewish community in India and end up marrying outside 'the fold'. Ruth (b. 1956) grew up in an upper middle class, educated family, graduating from Bombay University in 1978. When her only sister, who was married, decided to emigrate with her husband, Ruth's parents suddenly decided to emigrate too. Ruth narrated, 'I would have liked to continue my studies in India and get a degree in Law but that was not to be. My married sister made her *aliya* to Israel and my parents decided to follow suit. We made our *aliya* to Israel in August 1978 and six months later I was married to Reuben.' Just as Ruth was on an educational track which she did not wish to disrupt by emigrating, there were other young Indian Jews who were reluctant to jettison their academic careers. Zviya (b. 1947) who grew up in Cochin and was doing a Master's degree in Chemistry when her parents decided to make *aliya* narrated this:

My family immigrated to Israel in 1970 because of two reasons. First my youngest sister was ill and needed surgery for which it was suggested by the specialists that treatment was more difficult in India and that we could try in Israel . . . (sadly she passed away on the surgical table in Israel). Secondly, my parents wanted their children to continue to have a Jewish way of life by marrying Jews. . . . Since Jewish life in Kerala was getting very limited due to a shrinking community, migration seemed to be attractive. I was sorry to leave India, I wanted to finish my studies and get a Ph.D. (doctoral degree) in Chemistry, but my family had already left India and I had to follow them.

THE JOURNEY

Decisions to migrate were individual and varied, but once they were made there was a process to be gone through, which involved getting documents from the synagogues, which would certify Jewish-ness and certificates from schools or hospitals which would certify the date of birth. The clearance procedures were uneven and arbitrary. For the skilled or professionally qualified individuals or young single men and women, procedures were quicker. The older parents commonly had to wait longer—unless they were travelling with three or four grown-up children who could become productive citizens upon arrival. Following clearances, Jewish Agency made arrangements for individuals and families to board special flights which would ferry Jews from India to Israel. The 1950s-60s were not a time when foreign travel was easy or affordable for the upper middle-classes, least of all in developing countries. Thus, for a vast majority of new immigrants to Israel, this was to be their first trip overseas, and many described the excitement they felt as children at the prospect of a journey by plane. The flights to ferry the earliest Indian Jews around 1950 had an arbitrariness that could be quite chaotic.

Emma (b. 1930), one of my oldest respondents from a Baghdadi family, narrated how their entire family of eight siblings prepared for the journey and arrived in Bombay in May 1950 after selling all their belongings in Calcutta. In Bombay, they had to wait a few days till the next planeload was planned. On the appointed day when the family lined up to board the aircraft, after her two brothers and father had boarded, it was announced that the flight was 'full' and so the three sisters (aged nineteen, seventeen and four) and their mother were left behind. They were accommodated in a flight only six months later.[11] The most common pattern of the journey was a route via Tehran or Cyprus where sometimes the flight halted for a few hours, and sometimes for a couple of days. Yoshua (b. 1934) came from Bombay with his parents and siblings in the early 1950s. 'The plane in which we travelled was a cargo plane. It was a huge plane carrying mostly young Indian Jewish boys and girls about the age of twelve to fifteen years. . . .

There was space only for four or five families.' The flight from Bombay went via Bahrain, stopping there for two hours, then on to Cyprus stopping there for ten hours. Finally, 'El Al picked up the plane load of passengers from Cyprus and flew us to Israel.'

Disembarking and the arrival at the Lod Airport (later christened as Ben Gurion Airport), became for immigrants the turning point in their lives. After the new immigrants were registered came the big moment of allocations. From each planeload from specific locations, community clusters were allocated locations and packed off in buses to towns and villages across Israel on the basis of some broad logic used by the authorities which did not involve any *choice* by the immigrants. The broad logic seemed to be shaped by the skills or education of the immigrant that could be used productively in the emerging economy. The following chapter on 'Work and Professions' discusses how some immigrants were placed in cities, while others could get stuck in development towns for several years with no scope for upward mobility. But many respondents described a stage prior to that—the arrivals. Arrival experiences raised several questions: how did the administrative authorities treat arriving immigrants? How were immigrant families and communities 'selected' and 'slotted'? What was the element of choice for the immigrants to choose where they were sent to live? As respondents vividly described their arrivals, several issues emerged. It was clear that planeloads of arriving immigrants could lead to haphazard handling in the 1950s. Eliyahu Yakov (*b.* 1935) described how when one of the earliest planeloads of the Cochinis arrived in 1951 and lined up for registration, Eliyahu's father was followed by others who had last names like Pallivathukal which were difficult for the registering clerk to pronounce or spell. In the rush to 'clear' the entire group, he entered all members of this group of 35 people as 'Eliyahu'! Such episodes reflected how individual distinctions were homogenized and 'erased', and new immigrants became just numerical figures with little attention to specificities. A randomness emerged in these procedures. Families unknowingly found themselves in places that were completely unsuited to their skills and situation or involved intense hardships with small children, or places that were 'just depressing'. A vast majority of Indians who immigrated from bustling cities like Calcutta and Bombay in the 1960s were shocked at how 'underdeveloped' Israel appeared and the early months and years raised many questions about the nature of the 'homecomings' they had imagined.

THE 'HOMECOMING': NEW IMMIGRANT PRESSURES AND THE 'COLOUR-BIAS'

Below are instances which present varied experiences of 'homecoming' for Indian immigrants. The examples are drawn from arrivals in the 1950s to the early 1970s. The individual examples reflect diversity of experience and also of responses to the challenges. While their Zionism influenced some individuals to minimize their hardships, others were more blunt in describing their past traumas. The examples here speak of economic hardships, curtailed opportunities, discrimination on the basis of ethnicity, colour and Indian-ness, and also tensions emerging in interethnic neighbourhoods of immigrant communities. We may note that the experiences of discrimination are prominent in the profiles from the early 1950s, as well as the experiences of two women who arrived in 1970–1. Time it would seem did not make a big difference.

The individuals who played down the hardships of the early days were few. The experiences overwhelmingly express a deep sense of disruption that families experienced—not simply in confronting geographical or climatic differences but social displacement in coming from busy cities in India to remote Israeli development towns and villages. Worse still was the psychological and emotional trauma in being marginalized and mocked for what was perceived as their origins from a 'poor', 'undeveloped' country. Given that Indians have a range of brown skin tones, the ones with darker-brown skin tones commonly confronted what they called a 'colour-bias' which translated itself from being an aesthetic standard to becoming an index of ability and intellectual (in-)competence. Indian Jews who had lived among Hindus and Muslims without feeling on the defensive about their Jewish-ness, were unprepared and clearly upset at encountering racism and being marginalized for their Indian-ness—in the homeland which was meant to end all discrimination. Elias's father Solomon was a small-time trader in fish and watches in Parur, Kerala. Solomon was among the first group of Cochinis who came to Israel in 1949–50, and Elias claimed that the *aliya* story of his was unique. Although they were contacted by the Jewish Agency representatives, unlike most other immigrants whose travel expenses were paid by the Jewish Agency, these Cochinis paid their own expenses to come by selling property that the Jewish community owned collectively. This group of seventeen Jews from Kerala heralded further *aliya* from the region and by 1954, 85 per cent of community had made *aliya*. Elias claimed that 800 Jews came from Kerala between 1950 and 1954. Initially, from 1950–5 they lived in *ma'baarot* near Kfar Hasidim (near Haifa). Elias narrated that the community was provided with schooling for the children and medical facilities. 'They were ideological people and inspired by the spirit of Zionism. . . . They liked it. . . . My father always enjoyed himself, did not mind the circumstances he lived in. He never went back to India'.

However, narrations which celebrated adversity were rare.

Moses (*b*. 1934) came from Bombay with his parents and two brothers in 1952.

When we got off the aircraft at Lod, they took us to the gate specially marked for immigrants and we were assigned to go to Shar Aliya, near Haifa. This was a stop-gap arrangement where we were put up for fifteen days. During this time people from nearby *kibbutzim* came to invite us to join them. They wanted young people to work on the land and the *kibbutz* economy. We had a problem. My elder brother was mentally challenged and my mother refused to go to a *kibbutz* where he would be separated from the parents. After two weeks at Shar Aliya, one day a big truck came and four of our Indian families were taken to Kiryat Shmona (previously called Kfar Halsa). At Kiryat Shmona the families were housed in barracks. There was nothing else for miles . . . just barracks of new immigrants. . . . There was no toilet, no refrigeration but there was water.

Moses shook his head and said, '*Khana* (food) was a big problem'. He recalled that bread would arrive in a van from the bread factory which was distributed to families who had been dropped off in these remote neighbourhoods with no access and no mobility to go anywhere.

The bread factory was in Tiberias and the van would distribute bread to all the neighbouring *moshavs* and temporary shelters. But Kiryat Shmona was a long way off and the children had to wait till 11 a.m. or even later for their breakfast. . . . That is when the van would finally arrive at Kiryat Shmona. Subsequently, coupons were given for food and the families had to reach the government grocery store called *tserkhaniya* (store for all you need). A stock of coupons used to be given to last a month. During these days there was no rice and meat was not given to us more than once a month. There was no chicken. Sometimes a strange rice-like grain used to be available, which the Indians called 'Ben Gurion rice' (because it was nothing like the rice we got in India!). Once a week we could get fillet in the shops against special coupons. . . . Whenever, mother could get vegetables she would cook Indian-style *bhaji*. . . . Life was rough. My older brother who was a trained homeopath had no job . . . I told him that, after his level of study, I didn't want him to do a low level job. So he went to acquire education and training in Haifa, and I started doing small level jobs for the family's survival.

Rivka (*b*. 1955) came from Parur in Kerala after finishing high school. An excerpt from a profile she wrote and submitted for this project is worth quoting:

. . . As our flight from Tehran to Israel did not come on schedule, our relatives were not at the airport . . . they had waited there a day before. Some other relatives heard that we had been taken to a place called Kedma which was in south (near Beersheva). But we were actually taken to a place called Kadima which was in the north, near Netanya! . . . We wanted to live in Ramla, where my uncle and aunt were already settled but the immigration clerk at the airport said there were no apartments ready in Ramla—which was a lie, because it was the immigration authority's policy to scatter the newcomers all over Israel. He also said that 'many Indians lived in Kadima . . . so you will have a community'. We arrived in Kadima in a lorry—yes, a lorry, not a minivan or a minibus—and we met the Indian family—the one and only Indian family from Bombay! . . . In 1970, Kadima was a small settlement, with families from Morocco, Iraq and Yemen. Nobody spoke English except the Indians. Their culture was entirely different from ours, there was a lot of shouting . . . while we Indians spoke gently and remained calm. . . . The children in our neighbourhood called us 'Negro' as they couldn't tell us apart from Africans. . . . It was a struggle for survival. . .'.

Oren and Hana (husband and wife), retirees living in Ashdod, had come from Bombay to Israel with their families in the mid-1960s, when they were twelve and nine respectively. They grew up in Israel and went to school in immigrant towns. Oren recalled

the early days were hard . . . in the mid-60s when I was a young boy, one large pita bread had to be shared by seven of us in the family. My mother was in her forties when we came here and had never worked outside the house. But she was not an educated woman, so when we needed an extra income, she had to take to manual labour job for which she had to leave the house at 5 a.m. In those days, around 1966, my siblings and I frequently lived on a diet of bread and jam.

Hana came as a twelve-year old in 1964. Her family was in the Haifa region in one of the immigrant neighbourhoods where she went to school. She narrated that as Indians they were perceived locally as 'poor people'. 'They didn't like India. . . .' We would be mocked as 'Hodi Gali-Gala' (Hodi means 'from India') . . . 'because we spoke a language nobody else understood.'

Senora (*b.* 1954) and Avner Bamnulkar (*b.* 1952), now retirees in Ashkelon, came with their respective families from Bombay in the mid-1960s, when they were school-going children. Attending Israeli schools with other immigrant children, they remembered that as Indians they were mocked for many things—most often for their dark skin colour. Senora said 'they would laugh about my black skin . . . and call me *kushi*' (which is the insulting term equivalent to 'nigger'). Neighbours of other ethnicities living in apartment buildings 'hated the smell of Indian spices and complained about our Indian cooking'.

CHALLENGING THE SYSTEM: EXCEPTIONS AND RESISTANCE

Although a vast majority of Indian Jews had either confronted or sensed discrimination, there were exceptions. Thus, this last section presents examples of exceptions—of immigrant resistance and also of favourable exceptions made for some by the Absorption authorities. Some individuals resisted the procedural methods which gave total control to the Immigrant Absorption authorities by refusing to board the buses which would drop them off in remote locations to live out their struggles for many subsequent years. On the other hand, the Absorption authorities made exceptions for those whose educational qualifications were needed in the emerging nation.

Administratively, several factors were important in 'selecting' new immigrants. Age was important, so was gender. Young men and women had better prospects since they were free of childcare responsibilities and could be sent to a *kibbutz* or an *ulpan*. Similarly, those who came with education and qualifications were singled out, especially in the 1950s and 1960s, when the emerging nation needed all the technical manpower it could get. The randomness in some of the examples above was not experienced by all. For instance, Shlomo and Sylvie arrived in Israel in 1961 with their little three-year old daughter. They travelled in a planeload with other families from Bombay, whom they did not know. Shlomo was a certified marine engineer working in a shipping company in Bombay. His papers had been cleared by the Jewish Agency and he arrived with a job offer in hand from the Israeli Zim Shipping Company. Sylvie narrated that upon disembarkation only two families, Shlomo's and that of another marine engineer, were segregated from the others. 'We were told that someone from the Jewish Agency was coming to interview us from Jerusalem.' Shlomo was carrying his certification papers and the letter confirming his appointment.... Someone came late at night, checked the papers, and told the families that there would be a car next day to take them to Haifa.... 'There was no contact between us and the large group of Indian immigrants who were housed elsewhere on the airport premises. We were taken straight to Haifa.... I was told later that the others were taken to Yarukham and Kiryat Shmona.'[12]

Interviews revealed that although Immigrant Absorption authorities were all-powerful in sealing the fates of new immigrants, there were examples of resistance and documenting them enables us to evolve a more layered picture of the immigration experience. Mozel (*b.* 1955) came to Israel from Bombay with her parents and siblings in the early 1960s. When Mozel's father landed in Israel with his four children, he was asked to go to Dimona or Ashdod where other Indians were being settled. Mozel's father, however, insisted that he had relatives in Haifa and would only go there. This was not an easy process and Mozel recalled camping at the airport—sleeping on sheets on the floor and with erratic food supplies—for four days before the family were given permission to move to the Haifa region.

Noah Gadker (*b.* 1954) came with his parents in 1967 when he was thirteen. Upon arrival bus loads of new immigrants from India were being sent to the Negev. Noah's parents had heard of the hardships and resisted going south. Noah claimed that the allocating authorities assumed that all Indians came from a 'hot' climate and were, therefore, fit to go to the desert! 'But, both Bombay and Kerala were on the coast and had long monsoon months of cool breeze!', he chuckled. Noah described how when they refused to board the buses for the Negev, they were ignored and days passed. . . . 'We wanted to be sent to the North . . . *Hum jaisey hartaal pe the* (we were on a sort of a strike), so we were housed in empty hangars at the airport because we were resisting the allocations. . . . Some with very small children decided to leave and go wherever they were sent . . . finally, after a week we were sent to Kiryat Yam, an area in the North where new buildings were ready for immigrants arriving.' After 40 years, Noah still lives in Kiryat Yam and works on a low-paying job with the Israeli Postal Services in Haifa. His wife offers to care for small children who need a foster home through the welfare system.[13]

CONCLUSION

What emerges from this analysis is a complex picture. Undoubtedly, making *aliya* was a complicated affair. The underlying imperatives that created the zeal to emigrate differed from one individual to another—depending on who they were, how old, where they lived, and what they did before they emigrated. It is evident that the choices made by individuals and families were poised on different axes: religious, emotional, Zionist or just practical. More crucially, the experiences reveal how after choosing to migrate, many immigrants had little choice or control over where they lived, which in turn, influenced what they did. This confirms that after the large unwieldy bureaucratic system took over, individual families were practically powerless to change their lives. Research also revealed that the immigrant experience was not homogeneous. First, it was time-specific. Those who came in the 1950s or 1960s lived with challenges that confronted Israel at that time—coping with a swelling immigrant population coming in from diverse cultures and climates, speaking neither Hebrew nor each others' languages. Those who came in 1970 (or later) experienced a different ethos. Second, individual immigrants from India experienced immigration processes differently depending upon their age, personal circumstances, especially their education and skills. Although, a fortunate few were able to by-pass the typical immigrant traumas, acculturation was never free of challenges.

It is important to recognize that instances of discrimination were encountered by many, most commonly emanating from issues of colour. A vast number of respondents remembered derogatory remarks about their 'dark' skin-colour and about their country of origin as a 'backward' country, conjuring images of the starving millions. For children of school-going age, this had been a common experience. In the adult world, these images were translated as indicating lower ability and competence levels among those who came from India. Although the few who could flaunt a professional degree or British-accented English, had fewer brushes with such prejudice, Indian Jews whether they came from Kerala, western India or Calcutta were not accustomed to being singled out for such censure or stereotyping. Although they remembered class distinctions between affluent Indian Jews and others who lived very modestly, none of the respondents described a life of starvation in India. They did not come from the lowest strata in Indian society. Thus, to encounter prejudice in Israel, where they came expecting total affirmation for their Jewish-ness, was heart-breaking. This perhaps explains why even 40 years later individuals vividly remembered the derogatory remarks and the discomfiture of those moments they had experienced.

In the next chapter, I explore some of the long-term implications of the politics of spatial location. How did location determine the degree of *choice* new immigrants had over the work they did? How did the work they did enhance or mar their chances of upward mobility and status attainment in the immigrant society? Was professional success and achievement determined by age? Time of immigration? Or mainly upon skills and education that Indian Jews brought *from* India? And finally, how do all these questions facilitate a better understanding of our themes in this book—the role of ethnicity and location in the process of acculturation and the formation of community identity?

NOTES

1. Silliman, p. 30.
2. This chapter draws from examples which suggest broad trends only. There could actually be many individual reasons to migrate. For instance, one man from a well-established family of doctors chose to emigrate claiming that he wished to excel in his profession without the social encumbrances of belonging to an eminent family of physicians. Another woman chose to emigrate because she wanted to marry a close relative of hers which was frowned upon in her Jewish Indian family. After the man secured Rabbinical permission from Israel, they married and preferred to live away from their immediate family in India. Such examples of highly personalized choices have not been included here because in this chapter I wish the discussion to be sociologically relevant.
3. Weingrod, 1965; 1966; 1985; Curtis and Chertoff, 1973; Matras, 1973; Deshen and Shokeid, 1974; Smooha, 1978.
4. See the following articles in the *Jerusalem Post*: 'Registration of Bene Israel Couples Expected This Week' (4 July 1962); 'Bene Israel Reject Proposals: Mass Rally Called Here for Wednesday' (3 August 1964); '2,000 Bene Israel March' (6 August 1964); 'Cabinet Discusses Bene Israel' (10 August 1964).

5. Weingrod, *Reluctant Pioneers*, p. 24.
6. I am grateful to Mr and Mrs Joseph Guedj of Karmiel, Israel for providing useful information about the work of ORT schools. Guedj served as a Director of two ORT schools in India.
7. Silliman, pp. 15–18.
8. This was corroborated by Dekel whose parents came in this first group and were settled in northern Israel. Dekel was born in 1950 in Israel and is now an active community leader in the Rosh Pina area in northern Israel.
9. The metaphor is taken from a street game that children in India often play using two sticks of wood. The implication of this basically was 'why start all over again . . . with a new set of sticks . . . we have everything here'.
10. Only after the loss of their father did their mother migrate in 2005.
11. During that gap they stayed with distant relatives and one of the daughters found herself a groom in Bombay and married and stayed back.
12. I met a few other individuals who had been marine engineers, technicians in the shipping industry or pilots who had worked in the Indian Air Force or commercial airlines who were approached in India and offered jobs with excellent salaries and benefits. Such cases were very few in number.
13. Kiryat Yam is part of the outlying 'Krayot' immigrant towns about 125 km from Tel Aviv. This is where I interviewed Noah and his wife in March 2007. His parents, now in their nineties, live in a nearby two-room apartment. Noah has not been able to provide higher education for any of his three Israeli-born sons.

CHAPTER 4

Accountants as Watchmen and Clerks Digging Roads: Negotiating Work and Professions

At Eilat, the southernmost tip of Israel (bordering Egypt and Jordan) I met Dr. Reuven Yoseph, an eminent ornithologist and founder-Director of Israel's International Birding Research Center (which studies the five million migratory birds that pass through Israel annually). At Haifa in the north, I met Prof. Lael Benson Best, Chief of the Department of Thoracic Surgery at Israel's prestigious Rambam Hospital. Both were born in India. In the desert region of the Negev I met seventy-six year old Eliyahu whose innovations in agriculture (mainly growing high quality roses for export in greenhouses) won him the Prime Minister's award for floriculture in Israel (1964) and, the *Pravasi Bharatiya* Award (2006)—an honour bestowed by the President of India on distinguished Overseas Indians.[1]

In this chapter I take migration experiences forward to examine how issues of work and professions shaped the lives of Indian Jews in Israel. While I cite individual experiences such as the above to point out specificities, an important concern of this chapter is to present broad trends that emerged through the extensive fieldwork conducted for this study. Migration had a huge impact on the work and professions that Indian Jews could access in Israel. Just as in the preceding chapter I discussed how housing and location became key issues in the lives of the early migrants, this chapter presents a variety of individual migration stories of men and women to demonstrate the challenges that Indian Jewish immigrants faced in the world of work and professions. In the first part of the chapter, I present a discussion. I examine the question of access and the allocation of jobs by the state agencies responsible for immigrant absorption. I draw attention to the linkages between work allocation and family income levels and how all of this was related to social class and status attainment. I also raise the issue of chronology and how the time of migration mattered in the lives of new immigrants. Gender and the educational levels of individual migrants were also important variables which are discussed. Finally, I also challenge some existing stereotypes of Indians in the workplace by presenting a wide variety of experiences. The discussion of these and related questions is followed by several individual profiles of men and women collected during the fieldwork. These personal stories of first generation Indian Jewish migrants across gender, age and class illustrate the questions I present in the discussion below.

Broadly speaking, Indian Jews in Israel occupy a wide range of professions with consequent variation in economic situation and huge differences in class and levels of status attainment. There are professionals holding white collar managerial positions, entrepreneurs with independent businesses and the less well-paid lower-level office workers, both clerical and secretarial. At the lower-end are those who were in a wide range of skilled and unskilled work in factories or in agriculture from the mid-1950s or 1960s. This last category is where many of the first generation immigrants found themselves, although many were educated, none had done manual work, and nor had they any taste for it. Over time, some individuals acquired skills through state-sponsored training opportunities and moved into office jobs as clerks, accountants, assistants and middle-level managers. Many Indians (mostly Bene Israelis and Baghdadis) joined the travel business through the Israeli national carrier El-Al where Indians still have a large presence. Many are part of the service industry in Eilat, working at hotels and holiday resorts at levels ranging from managers to cooks and cleaners. To a large extent this is due to the fact that many Indian Jews, who had studied in Calcutta or the Bombay region, brought with them English language skills that were better than many new immigrants who came from non-Anglophone countries.

If we look at community-based distinctions then, compared to the Bene Israelis, Cochini Jews were a smaller, less dispersed and a more closely-knit community in India. Since they migrated to Israel in large organized groups of families, they were settled in clusters. As discussed previously in Chapter 3, although only some Jews from Kerala had worked in agriculture in India and many had been small merchants, in Israel they were settled primarily in *moshavs* and began as agriculturists—growing grains, fruit or rearing poultry. Their hard work led to some exceptional innovations in floriculture and by the 1970s, Cochini *moshavs* in the Negev came to be associated with highly successful yields of export-quality roses and other flowers fetching high prices in the European markets. Even today, *moshavs* Mesilat Zion and Taoz near Jerusalem and *moshav* Nevatim in the Negev and Kfar Yuval (in the north) are perceived as 'Cochini' strongholds. Although Cochinis in large numbers were settled in the agricultural villages, Bene Israelis rarely worked in agriculture. Among the Baghdadis I did not meet any who had worked in agriculture as a new immigrant (although some had done manual work while still in the *ma'abarot* transitional camps in the early weeks and months after landing in Israel). In general, many Bene Israelis had fairly high levels of education.[2]

It is from the lower-level white-collar jobs that a certain stereotype of the Indian community emerged. The many Indians who worked at lower and middle-level jobs in Israeli government offices, private companies and municipal offices came to seen as 'good workers', 'gentle' and 'polite'. In a society which encourages its youth to be 'brave' and 'fearless' soldiers and where the military service is perceived as a citizen's contribution to sustaining a strong nation, combat roles in the military are considered the most prestigious. In such a milieu, being 'gentle' and 'passive' are not likely to rank high as 'virtues', and may well suggest a low competitive spirit and lack of 'drive'. Many Indian Jews interviewees explained how this stereotype, in fact, does colour community perceptions even today. From the early days after migration, individuals described how they found it frustrating to negotiate this stereotype because for them being 'pushy' in social and professional behaviour was culturally a form of 'crudeness'. Although I discuss the issue of 'Indian-*ness*' and 'Israeli-*ness*' more elaborately in the last chapter, it is relevant to quote a few examples here to show how this intersected with issues of identity in the sphere of work. For instance, Yakov, one of the interviewees, who came to Israel when he was in his late-teens, and who now owns a successful travel business in central Israel offered an explanation worthy of record. Yakov explained that 'Indians did not aggressively make demands for benefits even from the State . . . we are a little timid . . . when there is a conflict or a confrontation we say *koi baat nahin* (never mind), and move on'. Daniel, now a retiree, who came as a teenager and member of a Youth Aliya programme in 1971, believes he still retains 'Indian-*ness*' in his attitude. Daniel said, 'when Indians work with colleagues, they don't strategize to push out their colleague and move up to take his place'. Instead the more typical attitude is to say, *main tere baaju main baitha hun* (I am content to sit beside you). He explained that Indians widely preferred non-confrontational workplace relations and accepted parallel (or even subordinate) positions, rather than generate antagonistic competitive relationships. This they believe, is culturally misconstrued as 'lack of ambition', which in turn, fuels derogatory stereotypes.

It is these stereotypes that I seek to challenge. For this project I rearched for broader patterns as well as, for *variety*—for Indians who were professionally doing 'different' work rather than what was widely perceived as 'typical'. The research for this chapter revealed that Indian Jews have pursued a wide range of occupations and professions, although high achievers or the very successful may be few. To begin with, it is important to note that early migration experiences revealed that work allocation was a decision largely made by the Immigration Absorption authorities. This allocation could be completely arbitrary and contrary to individual abilities and skills. City-based individuals who came from a bustling metropolitan port-city like Bombay were parked in remote, desert areas to dig roads, although they had held salaried office jobs in India: how a man who had worked as a bank clerk in Karachi till

1961 was made a security guard in Yarukham; how some young educated women of Baghdadi origin with secretarial experience in India were readily offered well-paid jobs in American companies in Tel Aviv while another with similar qualifications from Bombay was repeatedly turned down because she looked 'Indian' (read *dark-skinned*) and was sent by the employment agency to sweep floors in a café. In this analysis, I wish to highlight not only the obstacles that new immigrants faced in finding jobs, but also to underline the complexities that enhanced or marred an individual's chance of securing employment and then climbing up the professional ladder. Secondly, I also wish to argue that *chronology mattered*. The challenges that individuals faced in terms of work were less daunting from the 1970s. This was so, because the immigrants who came after the 1970s encountered Israel as far more developed and technologically advanced than the early immigrants of the 1950s and mid-1960s. Also, Indian immigrants who came later came with higher levels of education *from* India.[3] Those who came in the 1970s or later had apparently identified suitable career opportunities for themselves in Israel. Thirdly, this chapter seeks to highlight the range of occupations that first-generation Indian immigrants were engaged with. If Cochinis are widely perceived as *moshavim* living in the Negev, and Bene Israelis to be in Ashdod or the less prosperous neighbourhoods in Ramla, Lod and Beersheva, then the fact remains that over the decades there are instances of upward mobility and there are some Indian Jews who live in posh villas in Carmel (Haifa), or in expensive seaside neighbourhoods like Herzliya and Netanya. Among such individuals there are medical practitioners at prestigious Israeli hospitals like Hadassah and Rambam, woman professionals who are chartered accountants, freelance marketing consultants, validation experts for pharmaceutical companies; and team leaders within Israeli hi-tech companies. Among the first generation Indian retirees there are those who in the 1970s had served as pilots and flight engineers in El Al (Israel's national airline), commanded ships in Israeli shipping companies like Zim, and those who have worked in Bedek the Israeli Aircraft Industry on managerial posts.

Notwithstanding this, it needs to be stated that such achievers remain the exceptions. The majority of first-generation Indian immigrants were professionally not on 'fast-tracks'. Even the few who live in privileged neighbourhoods took several years to reach there and they would still not be among the wealthiest Israelis! Hence, while acknowledging the success stories, this chapter lays greater emphasis on analysing the professional tracks of those who illustrate broad trends within the community, rather than the exceptional few.

There is little doubt that for the majority of Indian Jews who migrated to Israel, access to work and professions were widely shaped by spatial location. Development towns like Dimona, Kiryat Shmona, Kiryat Ata loomed large in immigrants' narratives as they described their struggles for work and upward mobility. In the 1950s and 1960s there was little work to be had in development towns. We may note that from the late 1950s, the Israeli state offered incentives to industries which would be located in the 'periphery'. Setting up a manufacturing unit in a new immigrant town was supported by major monetary incentives, so that employment opportunities would be generated for new immigrants who had been part of the 'population dispersal' plan of the Israeli state.[4] It was believed that factories in remote regions would assist in the wider strategic plan to settle immigrants in remote locations and reduce the attraction (or desperation!) for internal migration. However, in many cases, this was less than successful (as one of the profiles below reveals). Industrial units in the peripheral regions were too few.[5] Indeed, many units used the incentives given in remote northern areas but in a few years the factories closed down declaring losses. Thus, struggling families were stranded and only those who were young and single could re-locate in search of job security.

The search for job security had long-term consequences. It meant that even the children of the generation settled in the development towns grew up with severe economic pressure. After some basic school education, followed by the mandatory military service meant that such children were already in their early twenties. At this age, families who did not have a secure economic future could neither sponsor nor supplement their children's higher education. The sooner the children of new immigrants could become economically independent, the more secure they felt. It was no surprise then, that in Indian Jewish families in development towns, the children who grew up in the 1980s or early 1990s, have followed 'vocational tracks', as opposed to university education. Only the rare few managed university education, moving up professionally and socially. They are the ones who also moved spatially: *out of* development towns and into cities in central Israel although hardly any to Tel Aviv.

For most immigrants, age emerged as an important variable. Flexibility and adaptation was related to age but in complex ways. For instance, immigrant traumas were probably the worst for those who came in their late forties or older—especially men, because as primary breadwinners their need to find work was critical for family survival. Yet, as potential employees they ranked low. If they had no special technical qualifications, their experience with office-work was of no use in an emerging economy. Although they had knowledge of some English and at least one Indian language, they did not know Hebrew. Approaching fifty, they were least able to make a 'turn around' in their lives. Mastering a new and difficult language and beginning a new career was too daunting. This research also revealed that we cannot simplistically assume that all children in families adapted easily just because they were the 'next' generation. In fact, this too was age-specific. The examples below strongly suggest that when large families migrated, older children (in their late-teens) suffered long-term consequences of displacement, while younger children, that is those below ten or twelve, fared better in 're-socializing' in their new homeland. For eighteen or nineteen-year olds in newly arrived immigrant families, continuing higher education or joining universities was not an opportunity they could afford. Those teenagers who were from modest backgrounds where educational levels were low to begin with, dropped out of schools, because the high school work in Hebrew was too challenging and teachers rarely paid them the individual attention they needed to catch up with it. Besides, an extra contribution to the family income was so welcome that for such young men and women their education and professional skill-enhancement halted at that point. Although some pursued skill-enhancement programmes in secretarial or office jobs offered in their workplaces, hardly any returned to universities to acquire higher degrees. Either way, large numbers of young men and women became what I would term 'circumstantial drop-outs' as they embraced income-generation roles. Age was also an important factor for those who came as children in Youth Aliya groups. Scattered in boarding schools or among *kibbutz* communities, some benefited from the early induction into immigrant society, but most children recalled their family separations as times of deep sadness and emotional isolation.

The analysis in this chapter specially turns the spotlight on gender. A gendered lens broadly underlies this entire chapter on work-related issues. Being mindful of gender issues is important for several reasons. At the most obvious level, it is important because many Indian Jewish women had never done wage-earning work outside their homes in India (and may never have done so!). As struggling new immigrants in Israel, however, they felt compelled to enter the workforce to stretch family incomes—even those who had little education and no special skills that they could market in the workplace. Gender dimensions are equally important in the case of families where men were traditionally presumed to be in bread-winning roles because those were the pre-migration family structures. In some of the profiles below, gender, class and 'colour' intersected to give some women advantage over others. Although in terms of colour all Indians are brown, those who spoke English with a 'British' accent and 'did not look Indian' (i.e. were less dark) fared better when they applied for office or secretarial jobs.[6]

The sections below illustrate the complex range of circumstances which Indians confronted as 'new immigrants' in search for work and livelihood which eventually had long-term consequences on economic or social mobility and in more subtle ways, on reinforcing ethnic stereotypes and community self-image.

MIDDLE-AGED PARENTS, YOUNG-ADULT CHILDREN, AND DEVELOPMENT TOWNS

Among the families whose emigration from India was sponsored by the Jewish Agency in the 1950s and 1960s, many were large units with five or more children, with parents in their late forties or older. Typically, the father was a salaried person with a steady modestly paid job who was able to send children to school. Few wives were working women. In general, Bene Israeli women were better eduated than Cochini or Baghdadi women but broadly speaking, they were usually secretaries or school teachers.[7] As new immigrants, such families underwent a virtual churning in their life-patterns in the new homeland. Although most Indians speak two languages (either two Indian languages or English and a vernacular), the new immigrants who were middle-aged men and women had limited potential to master a new foreign language. From being blue-collar salaried workers or in clerical positions, without a knowledge of Hebrew, they were virtually 'unemployable' in the new economy unless they could demonstrate specific technical or mechanical skills. Hundreds were handed shovels to do manual work on the many building and digging projects that were characteristic of early Israel. If the men were too old to learn new careers, the women who were accustomed to being housewives felt compelled to seek paid work to supplement the meagre wages that their husbands were paid. Given that women from such modest backgrounds had low levels of education, they got stuck in small odd jobs in manufacturing units, food processing plants or textile mills, a few of which emerged in new development towns. Needless to say, these odd-jobs meant exploitative conditions: doing 'piece-work' jobs, no coverage by labour laws, without pension benefits or minimum wage stipulations. However, the impact of this configuration was most critical in shaping the lives of the *children* of such immigrant families. If the older children in immigrant families had completed matriculation in India, joining the workforce was easier because many had a good working knowledge of English from their education in India. If the families had been upper middle-class in India, their children had often been to missionary schools and had acquired good English skills. This rendered them attractive employees in Israel—as soon as they could learn some Hebrew through an *ulpan* in Israel. The really young children managed well because they were thrown in early into the Israeli school system along with thousands of other immigrant children of different ethnicities. They swiftly picked up Hebrew and became interpreters for their parents! The brunt of the emotional dislocation was borne by the teen-aged children, who were pulled out of schools in India, away from friends and playmates, only to arrive in transit camps in Israel and wait for weeks and months before they could join another school. What followed could be more traumatic—being plunged into a system where the curriculum and language of instruction were all foreign. Cultural adjustment posed another set of issues—coping with widely held stereotypes of being 'dark-skinned' Jews from a 'poor' country.

For instance, Diana (*b.* 1950) now a retiree living in Ashdod, came from Bombay with her family in the early 1960s, when she was in her mid-teens. Her father who had been a bus-conductor in Bombay was nearing fifty and had only basic school education. After several weeks of waiting at a transit camp near Haifa, he got a poorly paid job at the Haifa Oil Refinery. He struggled on, took some training and tried to improve his prospects. But the children felt the economic pressure to supplement family income, and as Hana finished high school she took courses in book-keeping and through her father's connection at the Oil Refinery, she was able to get a job as a book-keeper at the Haifa Oil Refinery. Her brothers meanwhile, grew up and joined the military, which could become a career option after the mandatory period of two or three years had been served. During the fieldwork for this research, I met dozens of people like Hana who came to Israel when they were in their teens. Despite the diversity of circumstances in which they were living in their retired lives in 2006–8, there was one marked similarity. What they shared in common was that they had *all* been plunged into the workforce at an early age.

Plate 1: David Negrekar, holds the Indian flag, leading dancers in his troupe (dressed in *saris* to match the Indian tricolour) as they perform to *Vande Matram,* a patriotic invocation to Mother India. Negrekar is the founder of the dance troupe *Namaste Israel* (Ashdod).

Plate 2: The *Nirit* Group: First-generation Cochini women dressed in traditional Kerala dresses present Jewish songs in Malyalam and Hebrew. Indian Ambassador's Residence (15 August 2008).

Plate 3: Lilly Diana Benjamin (*b.*1928) poses with her three children Ruth (left), Rosalind (right) and Ben Sion (back). The siblings migrated to Israel individually during the 1970s. Lilly's late husband Joshua M. Benjamin was the Chief Architect, Government of India and she made *aliya* (2006), only after her husband's death. (26 January 2008.)

Plate 4: Eliyahu Bezalel (left) and Galia Hakko (right) are Cochinis who live in different parts of Israel. They pose at the reception on 15 August 2008. Indian Ambassador's Residence, Tel Aviv.

Plate 5: Hundreds of Indian-Israelis converge socially at Indian Embassy receptions. Uriella Solomon (left) had commuted from northern Israel over 100 km away, to attend the reception on 15 August 2008.

Plate 6: Aviva Israel (b.1982), a second-generation Indian-Israeli student participated in the Government of India sponsored 'Know-India' programme (2005), for youth selected from Indian diaspora communities worldwide. Aviva speaks of her 'Know-India' experience at Indian Embassy reception on 26 January 2006.

Plate 7: Mai-Boli programme (May 2008): Bene Israeli men and women present literary readings at this annual programme which celebrates Marathi—widely spoken among first-generation Bene-Israelis. The programme coincides with Maharashtra Day (May 1).

Plate 8: Noah Massil (b.1946 in Raigad, Maharashtra), an active Bene Israeli community leader, editor, *Mai Boli* journal in Marathi. Massil is a long-standing president of the Central Organization of Indian Jews in Israel (COIJI). Notice the *Mai Boli* stage banner in Marathi.

Plate 9: Annie Rohekar (left) and Elizabeth David (right), senior members of the Indian Women's Organization, Lod pose with author. IWO, Lod is the oldest and most active of Indian women's networks (see chapter 6).

Plate 10: Shayela Israel (centre) from Gan Yavne, poses with Bene Israeli singer Itzik (left) and his wife Nurit (right) from Beersheva. Shayela works at the Embassy of India, Tel Aviv. Photo courtesy: David Israel, July 2008.

Plate 11: Second-generation inter-ethnic marriage: Ben Ami Eliyahu, a Cochini, and his Russian-born bride Natasha Losoub hold up the *ketuba* marriage document. Ben Ami is the Israeli-born son of Eliyahu Bezalel (*b*.1930) who made *aliya* from Kerala in 1955. They live in Moshav Sha'haar (Negev).

Plate 12: Dan Shishoren and his wife, a young Bene Israeli couple perform and choreograph Bollywood-based dance sequences for Indian cultural programmes. Kiryat Ata, December 2007. Photo courtesy: Dan Shishoren.

Plate 13: Abrahmee Mazgaonkar, among the senior-most Indians settled in Kiryat Ata being honoured with a plaque at the Indian community programme, Kiryat Ata, December 2007. Photo courtesy: Dan Shishoren. (See Chapter 6.)

Plate 14: Rebecca Yehezkiel, a Bene Israeli artist poses with her grandson Shai at his Bar-Mitzvah in 2008. Rebecca's painting is the cover image of this book.

PROFILE 1

Baghdadi family (Aliya from Calcutta: 1950)

Rachel, Esther, Rami, Jackie, Jimmy and Betty were six of the nine children of their parents who decided to migrate to Israel in 1950. Rachel was nineteen, Esther eighteen and the youngest Betty was only four. When they packed up their home in Calcutta, two of the older sons in their twenties, decided to migrate to Britain in search of better prospects. Their parents Ellis and Sarah were both Calcutta-born Baghdadis, who were moderately educated but both spoke fluent English, which was the language in which the family communicated. The father's job in a cigarette company and his small side-business as an optician brought in enough money to educate the children and afford some hired help for domestic work. Esther explained how representatives of the Jewish Agency had convinced their family that 'better prospects' awaited them in Israel. Esther's father arrived in Israel at the age of fifty with no knowledge of Hebrew. His search for jobs was in vain. His work experience as an optician did not count because he had no certification papers. So he was given to do manual labour. 'They gave him stones to break . . . to make pebbles by crushing stones manually for a building under construction in Haifa.' The family lived in *ma'baarot* for almost a year and their standard of living plummeted. The older daughter Rachel who had done secretarial training in India, joined the workforce and the second girl hastily chose to marry a man who worked as a chef on a ship and several years her senior. Esther explained that their sister had made a conscious decision to accept this man's proposal, who was a holocaust survivor who had lost his entire family. She saw her marriage as a pragmatic decision to ease the family's economic struggles. From the ship where she would be with her husband, at least she would be able to bring quantities of food to supplement the state-allocated meagre rations given to the family. Esther, grew up doing much of the domestic work because 'my mother had never needed to sweep and clean in India, she could always afford help'. Over time, the children became the main earning members and the family moved first to

Lod and then with some 'pushing with the authorities' eventually, to more stable housing in Kiryat Ono. From this family of many children, the older daughters worked in secretarial jobs for several years in Tel Aviv—their English learnt from their mother was a huge asset. Betty, the youngest child from this large family who came at four, grew up in Israel, going to school with hordes of immigrant children, learning Hebrew as well as, the rough and tumble of being jostled about. She settled well into the Israeli school system, speaking Hebrew like a native while speaking English to her parents! After completing her compulsory military service in 1970, she was sent to Paris on a government assignment which was part of the Israeli Embassy to France (on a 'purchase mission' she preferred not to discuss). To her Hebrew acquired from school, she added her fluent English, social skills and her exposure to English literature and Western music acquired from her mother. . . . Subsequently, she was chosen to be part of the Israeli delegation to the United Nations in New York for a period of two years. At the end of it, in 1973, she was offered a continued assignment in the Foreign Ministry in Jerusalem but by then chose to marry and start a family. She subsequently married an eminent Israeli nuclear physicist from a well-known *Ashkenazi* Jerusalem-based family. They spent several years in the United States and have now settled in their villa in a seaside neighbourhood outside Tel Aviv.

The other siblings from this Calcutta-based Baghdadi family had longer years of struggle but through their jobs, businesses and marriages are now eventually well-settled. All except one, married Jews of *Ashkenazi* origin. They are scattered across Israel, the UK and the US.

PROFILE 2

Bene Israeli family (Aliya *from Bombay: 1952*)

Jacob Yehezkiel (*b.* 1934) finished his matriculate in Bombay and was the son of a building engineer living a comfortable middle-class existence in Shivaji Park, Bombay, where the family had Hindu, Muslim and Christian friends. 'We lived in good conditions...'. The elder brother Yoshua was inspired to make *aliya* although their father was resistant to 'uproot their settled life'. The father's sudden death, however, clinched the family's decision and Miriam (*b*. 1901) the widowed mother arrived in Israel in 1952 with her four sons, one of whom had a congenital disability. After the immigrant camp they were assigned to Kiryat Shmona and housed in *ma'baarot* consisting of barracks. As his two brothers left to find work in Haifa alongside thousands of other new immigrants, Jacob could not leave Kiryat Shmona with the responsibility of his mother and disabled brother. 'We suffered a lot here... we had no support... for many months in 1952 when unemployment was high in the Israeli economy I used to find work only for two weeks in a month.' Jacob described that in those days of hardship, even after having been in the region for six months, he had not even seen the city of Haifa! 'We had no money to go anywhere.' Around this time, an Israeli businessman opened a diamond polishing factory in Kiryat Shmona where Jacob secured a job at a pitiful sum of 5 lirot a day, which was barely enough to buy basic food. He explained: 'if you were a bachelor you were paid only two and a half lirot a day'. Since he was supporting his mother, he was paid 5 lirot. In 1956, 'I started learning to polish diamonds'. After six months he was trained to polish all varieties of diamond facets. Subsequently, he began instructing newcomers. However, the owner of the diamond factory was based in Central Israel in Ramat Gan, traditionally the centre of the diamond trade in Israel. As Jacob explained, it was clearly not attractive for this manufacturer to shift his business to a remote development town in northern Israel. Thus, in two to three years the Kiryat Shmona manufacturing unit for diamond polishing was shut down and Jacob became jobless. There was no choice but to chase employment security and Jacob moved to Netanya, closer to central Israel, living in a rented room and continually anxious about his family responsibilities in Kiryat Shmona.

In 1960, finally, Jacob moved to Tel Aviv. He felt that the only way out of extreme poverty was to move to central Israel where wages were significantly higher. He found employment at one of the diamond polishing factories where 'I was the only Indian working there'. Jacob's mother died in 1961. By then he was able to afford enrolling his brother into an institution and plan to marry and have a family himself. When interviewed at their home in Petah Tikwa in 2007, he and his wife were living modestly as retirees. None of their children have received higher education. Their daughters are matriculates, one works in a secretarial job. Their son is a plumber.

PROFILE 3

Bene Israeli family (Aliya from Bombay: 1961)

Sarah's father was a modestly placed employee in the Indian Railways in Bombay in the mid-1950s. Sarah (*b.* 1941) was one of his six children. When Sarah's eldest brother Ezkiel got married he could not afford to live separately and applied for immigration to Israel. After Ezkiel settled in Israel, the entire family decided to move in 1961. In this group the son was aged twenty-three and Sarah and her sister were nineteen and seventeen. The family was initially assigned to a *kibbutz* where the young children worked and studied as per *kibbutz* regimen of morning lessons and afternoon hands-on work. Although the family chose to leave the *kibbutz* in six months to move to a non-communal way of life, the children continued to be the earning members. Sarah got married in 1962 to another Bene Israeli (originally also from Bombay). They were sent to Beersheva, from where she worked in factories and weaving mills for several years, doing simple tasks like making bundles of threads. Furthering their qualifications or upgrading their skills was not an option for any of these children. Sarah and her husband are retirees living in Kiryat Gat, another development town in the Negev. Their children are not educated beyond matriculation and are stuck in jobs with little prospects for social mobility. For instance, one son works as a basketball coach at a school, a daughter is a kindergarten teacher and another is a helper at a hospital.

PROFILE 4

Karachi-born Bene Israeli woman (Aliya from Bombay: 1966)

Naomi Joseph is a retiree living in Holon. She was born in Karachi and came to Israel in 1966, as a young woman of twenty. Although her brother, uncles and aunts had made *aliya* previously and were there to receive her, her parents remained in Bombay. She had basic schooling—knew Hindi and Marathi and a little English.[8] She described how her brothers had advised her against joining a *kibbutz* and she had begun life looking for odd jobs. She landed herself a job at a paper mill in Hadera, working as a waitress in the canteen. Naomi did a Diploma in waitressing. 'My English helped me. . . . I also worked extra hours in the evening as a waitress at a Wedding Hall nearby where I used to get 10 to 12 lirot per hour and additional tips. . . . In a few years, my accumulated savings were much higher than my two younger brothers, because they were working on salaried jobs'. Naomi claimed that she saved money to pay for the expenses when her brothers got married. '*Badi bahan mummy ke barabar. . . . Ye India ki reet. . . Israel main aisa nahi hota*' (an elder sister is like a mother. . . . That's how it is in India . . . not so in Israel). Naomi played the maternal role supplementing expenses to settle her younger brothers because she was able to earn more, although her brothers had more stable careers. Naomi married a modestly paid electrician, but after their divorce she raised her daughter Anat, as a single mother. Anat a diligent student, worked her way up, completing high school compulsory army service to continue her higher education. Having worked to pay her way through university and getting a law degree, Anat is now an attorney. She is a confident and accomplished woman, perfectly bi-lingual in Hebrew and English.

In her interview Naomi rationalized her waitressing work as well-paid and clarified that she only 'served' and was not a 'dishwasher'. I wondered if this was related to the fact, that in India, men and not women, do waitressing jobs—except for a more recent trend in some luxury hotels. Waitressing would be seen as 'unbecoming' for girls from 'respectable' families. Subconsciously, Naomi probably still carried some of those cultural values and perhaps in speaking to me felt the need to clarify how her professional work had been not only a lucrative option but also locally perceived as 'respectable'.

PROFILE 5

Immigrant Children and Upward Mobility

Jimmy Garpkar's (*b*. 1945) life is another example of the long-term impact of displacement in a teenager's education. But Jimmy's later life presents an unusual example of how two immigrant children growing up in development towns acquired some degree of upward mobility as a couple through an unexpected trajectory. Jimmy was born in Karachi where he did his early schooling. He arrived in Israel in 1962. Like many other Jews who left Pakistan, Jimmy's family arrived first in India and stayed in Poona for several months before they moved to Israel in 1962.[9] Jimmy narrates, 'It was the parents' decision to come to Israel . . . and we faced many problems upon arrival. . . . In Karachi we had begun studies in Urdu and English, in India we could use both languages and also knew Marathi, but in Israel we were stuck. My father who had worked as an engineer had a problem finding work and our standard of living went down completely. My father had a college degree but no Hebrew. . . . We were sent directly to Beer-sheva. . . . The first work my father was offered was to be a watchman. He had to do that for over a year so as to generate a family income.' Jimmy grew up in the development town scenario as the family moved from Beersheva to Dimona. For several years, he served in medium level accountant's position in Dead Sea Chemical Works near Dimona. Jimmy's wife Elizabeth (*b*. 1946), who grew up in a lower-income family in Bombay, was sent to Israel with her younger sister as part of a Youth Aliya group in 1964. The family was united once their mother and five other siblings arrived in 1966. They were sent to Dimona. Elizabeth's adolescence was marred by bitter memories of helping her mother, an uneducated woman, to cook and fry Indian snacks and popular delicacies at home which they would sell within the surrounding community to support their large family. Elizabeth and her sisters forfeited the possibilities to study and raised younger siblings with these culinary sales. When Elizabeth married Jimmy, she continued making small supplies of Indian food items and snacks for income-generation. Over the years, her 'kitchen-craft' became a business for which she employed workers, began supplying packed Indian snacks to Indian shops. She has been joined by her son and by Jimmy after he retired. The men look after marketing and distribution to Indian stores in Israel. Elizabeth personally supervises production and manages the finances. Elizabeth and Jimmy now have a thriving unit producing Indian snacks, sweets and ground Indian spices which are retailed under their own brand name in Israel.[10] They own a retail shop in *Merkaz Dimona* (the city Centre at Dimona) and also offer private catering services. Elizabeth employs nine full-time workers who cook, prepare, fry and pack the snacks, savouries and sweets.[11]

In January 2005, when I first met this couple they were marketing a wide range of Indian savouries and delicacies at the annual Indian community weekend cultural get-together in Eilat where there were about 2,000 Indian Jews. Elizabeth and Jimmy have a son and a daughter, both of whom have degrees from Ben Gurion University in Beersheva. This couple is an example of how immigrant struggles were successfully transformed to gain some degree of social mobility by innovative entrepreneurial choices. We may note, however, that even this economic betterment has not enabled them to move out to a prosperous Israeli city like Tel Aviv. They are comfortably off but are far from being part of Israeli elites—socially or economically.

YOUTH ALIYA

When large lower-income families filed their papers to the Jewish Agency for *aliya*, the representatives engaged with many parents personally so as to persuade them to send their teen-aged children first as part of Youth Aliya—a scheme whereby groups of boys and girls aged between twelve and seventeen were flown into Israel and sent off to boarding schools or a *kibbutz* where they would do a combined work-study programme. Indian parents, regardless of class and religious faith, were protective about their children and preferred them to have a family member in charge of their child. Gender was important and girls in particular had to be chaperoned. Family reluctance to send their children separately softened over the years, as young sons in Jewish families were excited about going to the 'Land of Milk and Honey' from what they heard through ORT instructors, visiting *kibbutzim* or other sources. As word spread, more families became willing to send children in Youth Aliya, but it was typically the lower income families with six or seven children who were willing to send off one or two, hoping for better prospects for them. More importantly, those children did not recall that separation without bitterness. The final outcome of course, depended hugely on the sort of institution that the Jewish Agency assigned to the young immigrant as the two profiles below illustrate:

Karachi-born Yakov Eliyahu (*b*. 1935) came to Israel in 1950 with his sister. He was aged fifteen and his sister sixteen. They came as part of a Youth Aliya group sponsored by the Jewish Agency. They were settled at *kibbutz* Mayaan Tzvi (near Zikhron Yakov in northern Israel), where Yakov worked the *kibbutz* regimen and studied half the day (mostly Hebrew language, Torah study and Mathematics). He joined the *kibbutz's* garage and began to learn mechanical work. In 1953, when he joined for military service, he was assigned to the Israeli Navy where he began to train as an electrician. Attending evening classes, he completed his Matriculation and after completing his mandatory service, he stayed on with the Navy. He upgraded his skills, and in 1959, when the Israeli Navy bought a submarine from Britain, he was sent as part of a large contingent of Naval personnel. In a team of 55 people, he recalled being the only Indian Jew. In 1967, he was sponsored by the Israeli Navy to study at the prestigious Technion (Israeli Institute of Technology). At the Technion he qualified as a Practical Engineer.[12] Although the 1967 War disrupted his study and he was enlisted into active service, when the war was over, he resumed his study. As a sailor in the Israeli Navy, Yakov was an eligible young man and married Orna, a woman of Iraqi origin. Yakov and Orna clearly planned their family finances carefully because they bought a house in Haifa for which they were able to pay through joint earnings and savings. Yakov retired from Navy in 1982 as an engineer drawing a salary of about 500 lirot—which would provide a comfortable upper middle-class lifestyle.

Equipped with professional qualifications, Yakov did not experience the financial hardship that many others in his generation did. It is important to note, however, that since he came as a young lad and his parents migrated later, he was not forced to earn a living as soon as he came. Yakov also showed determination to keep upgrading his education. His children are highly educated—two of his daughters are lawyers, one works at a hi-tech company and another is a qualified nurse. He spoke proudly of his children's achievements.

Shlomo came in 1966 at the age of twelve, with his brother Eliyahu aged thirteen and a half. Shlomo and Eliyahu were sent to Kiryat Tivon Boarding School. 'I used to cry missing home and my parents. . . . I cried all the way on the plane.' The two brothers looked after each other. They got a monthly allowance of 5 lirot, apart from clothes and food. 'I used to save even from this bit of money and we used to buy small plants and grow them in a little patch of green in the school. Then we would sell the flowers or the plants in the weekly market on Saturday or a holiday.' They learnt from an early age to scrape and generate an income to build savings. Shlomo's early life in Israel was spent at the boarding school where the group of young boys and girls from Iran, Morocco, Argentina, Brazil, Romania and India was brought together. Shlomo recalled that there were 36 Bene Israeli children, thirty boys and six girls. There were no *Ashkenazis* at the school. In subsequent years, Shlomo worked in the upholstery business as a worker taking client jobs to fix and sew upholstery on furniture. In 2007 he said, 'I still work'. Architects sometimes call him when they have a project to do. He said that there were very few Indians in his trade. All through the years, Shlomo's struggle was to save money—which would be enough to send to his parents to buy them a ticket to Israel. He claimed that the sponsoring office showed indifference in helping his parents to make *aliya* 'because they were old and unproductive members of society'. Shlomo and his uncles raised the money to pay for his mother who eventually came in 1973. His father managed to come only in 1979.

Both died soon after. Shlomo recounted his story with bitterness.

Shlomo's children did not study beyond high school. His daughters are in lower level jobs in factories and his son is a bus driver. Shlomo's life is an example which illustrates how thousands of new Indian Jewish immigrants struggled with adds and eked out opportunities for themselves and even then were not able to acquire the means to put their children through the excellent professional and technical higher education which Israel could boast of.

SKILLED AND UNSKILLED WORKERS

I met a number of first-generation families who came as young couples with one or two small children. Among the younger immigrant families if the men had been skilled workers in India—mechanics, electricians and so forth—they found work easily and their young families with small children settled in without too much distress. It is important to note that such skills were in great demand in an emerging nation, as Israel was expanding infrastructure and facilities to cope with thousands of immigrants who had poured in, especially till the end of the 1960s, possibly later too. In contrast, in India even in the 1970s, such skills were ranked fairly low in the job market and lower-level technical work was poorly paid.[13] Thus, many such families from a crowded metropolis like Bombay, would have lived in cramped one- or two-room suburban housing. Upon making *aliya*, however, such technical workers were readily absorbed on relatively good salaries. The additional support of being given a house with three or four small rooms with some basic furniture was an immediate boost to their level of comfort.

Diana and Shmuel Talkar came in 1964 with their three small children. Diana had elementary education and Shmuel was a factory worker in a textile mill in Bombay. 'As soon as we arrived we were taken to Dimona directly from the airport. There were two textile mills: Kitan and Sibi. My husband was an experienced mill worker, so he was given a job in Kitan, where he received a salary of 250 lirot per month. At that time the lirot was equivalent to the Indian rupee and in India he received a salary of only Rs. 150 a month. This made him very happy with the conditions.' Shmuel Talkar's experience as a weaver in Edward Mills in Bombay proved to be useful given that Dimona's main industrial production was in textiles. With Shmuel's salary in Israel and the supplementary support through state housing, basic furniture and household effects provided by the government agencies, this family settled in and Diana had three more children in Israel. Shmuel and his wife raised their children in Dimona. It's only the next generation who were able to find middle-level office jobs in central Israel.

Shaul Collet (Kolatkar) came from Bombay to Lod in 1953. In Bombay, Shaul was a aeroplane mechanic working with the Indian national carrier—Air India. His wife had a clerical job at the Jewish Agency office in Bombay. The Jewish Agency representative offered Shaul a job in Israel with a free visit to check out his options with El Al and IAI (Israel Aircraft Industry). He left for Israel in 1953 and a year later returned to take his wife and child to Israel. In the early 1950s trained technicians and mechanics were welcomed by Israeli companies. In India at the time, such technicians were modestly paid, and would have taken years to save enough to buy their own homes. To be offered housing, children's schooling and sometimes higher salaries than they were drawing in India was very attractive. Over time, Shaul was asked to approach other young Jewish Indian technicians in India with job offers in Israel. Thus, through networks, cousins and Jewish friends working for Air India he emigrated. For such individuals *not knowing Hebrew was no obstacle.* They raised families in reasonably comfortable environs. However, their economic well-being did not necessarily translate into social mobility. Even 35 years later, numerous such families live in Ramla and Lod, which have high concentration of Indians but are not prosperous cities.[14]

YOUNG WOMEN, SECRETARIAL WORK AND THE 'COLOUR-BIAS'

A number of women who acquired a good high-school education in India prior to migration in the 1960s and 1970s, found it easy to get secretarial jobs in Israel. Most such women had done a

Matriculate or a Senior Cambridge Certificate (ten or eleven years of schooling respectively). All students who had passed high school in Bombay or Calcutta brought at least a good working knowledge of English with them, but the schools which offered the Cambridge Certificate taught a high standard of English. Although in the 1960s, Hindu and Muslim middle and upper middle-class families in India were commonly not in favour of their daughters joining the workforce, except as medical doctors or teachers, Christian, Anglo-Indian and Jewish families (the Baghdadi Jews, as well as the Bene Israelis) seemed much more comfortable about their daughters working in offices and doing secretarial jobs. Among middle-class Jewish families who favoured the idea of their daughters joining the workforce, secretarial courses and montessori training were the favourites. This opened up income-generation possibilities to work as school teachers or secretaries in offices. Some women worked even after they got married although many did not. But when young married women with secretarial experience arrived as new immigrants from India, they were able to secure jobs easily. For instance, Abigail Talkar (b. 1945), now a retiree living in Lod was a wife and mother when she emigrated with her husband and children from Bombay in 1970. She was a matriculate and had done additional training as a kindergarten teacher, and a stenotypist. Her secretarial experience and English typing skills secured her a job easily: 'I was lucky to get a job as a secretary to the Chief Aeronautical Engineer at Ben Gurion Airport. After one year, I got a better job as a typist at the Head Office of Bank Leumi.'

Ruby Israel (b. 1950) also a retiree living in Lod was a matriculate from Bombay. Her first job after she came in 1966, was a clerical one with the Telrad Telephone Company, where she worked for many years subsequently.

Through the interviews, however, some subtle differences emerged: almost all the Baghdadi young women had received a more anglicized education and socialization. This was less common among the Bene Israeli women who came from Bombay or Gujarat.[15] Some Bene Israeli women were married and their securing jobs in Israel brought in the much-needed supplementary income into the immigrant family budget. The Baghdadi women also commonly had more exposure to a Westernized social life, exuded more self-confidence and spoke a more 'British' English. Although hardly any of the Baghdadi women from Calcutta had a university education, they secured well-paid secretarial jobs easily with reputed Tel Aviv based companies. Their life-histories revealed that many furthered their careers as the years went by, and kept moving up economically and socially. 'Moving up' socially also meant making friends and finding husbands among more established Israeli families, as opposed to struggling in 'immigrants towns' away from the best job opportunities.[16] In the example below, social mobility emerges as a complex issue, available to some more easily based on age, gender or Westernization, yet elusive for others.

Anat Sopher (*b.* 1952) came to Israel in 1971. She belonged to a middle-class Jewish family and had a Baghdadi father and a Cochini mother—an unusual combination. In 1971, when Anat and her sister came to Israel, they were young women just out of high school and 'ready to "spring" and make a new life'. Anat explained that in the 1970s, fluent English was a useful skill in the Israeli job market, because 'most immigrants who were persuaded to come from non-Western countries did not have English to offer. Indian Jews from post-colonial India had this huge advantage compared to those who came fromYemen, Morocco and so on. . . .' Anat landed herself a job easily mainly because of her English language skills as she said. I may add, however, that Anat's energetic personality and cheerful persona undoubtedly added to her assets! Subsequently, Anat changed jobs, married, divorced and raised and educated her children mostly on her own. For the last several years, she has held a well-paid job at one of the embassies in Tel Aviv. Two of her three children have degrees from college and her son is serving his mandatory military service.

In 1964, Rivka Sassoon (*b.* 1945) and her sister Triffine came to Israel from Calcutta. They had studied at Loretto House, a prestigious Christian missionary high school for girls in Calcutta, and spoke good English. After completing a secretarial course, Rivka had worked in Calcutta for a few months prior to her departure. In Israel, soon after their *ulpan*, the sisters managed to secure jobs and carved out a stable existence for themselves, living in a rented apartment in Tel Aviv. In 1965, when the Hilton Hotel opened in Tel Aviv, Triffine got a job at the hotel. Once again, good English was an asset. Similarly, Rivka worked for many years at various embassies.[17] Through these two sisters I met Rebecca, also a Baghdadi from Calcutta who came in her twenties. She had finished her Senior Cambridge School Certificate in 1958, was trained as a secretary and had worked in the well-known firm Jenson & Nicholson in Calcutta. Her skills and her English also ensured her job security. Over time, these women became part of the social circles in and around Tel Aviv. All three are married to *Ashkenazi* men and now live in various parts of central Israel. These women explained how in the 1960s and 1970s, Indians with good English language skills were widely hired by companies and banks and even more so, in the hospitality trade. Jobs at the airport or with the airlines welcomed smart Westernized women from India because they were considered hard working, persevering and 'quiet' workers. In the 1960s, for Indian immigrants, office skills and English was a viable combination for the job market. However, if good communication skills was an asset, a Westernized projection was all-important—as the profile of Mina Penkar below illustrates.

The experience of Mina Penkar (*b*. 1932) who came from Bombay in 1966 bears special attention. Mina's[18] experience shows that many eager Indian immigrants who may have been confident of their job-oriented skills arrived in the Jewish Homeland to confront bitter disappointments. When Mina left Bombay in 1966, she resigned from her job in the Jewish Agency there. She had held that job for several years and had been appreciated for her work and her excellent English language skills. By then, she had met many visiting Israelis and her siblings were already in Israel.[19] In 1961, the Agency had given her a free ticket to Israel. In short, she was not unfamiliar with Israel yet this is what she narrated in her clear well-articulated English:

Upon arrival I had a terrible experience . . . they gave me such a rough time . . . I had worked for the Jewish Agency but the people I had worked for were in Jerusalem. They offered me a job in Jerusalem but since I was solely responsible for my elderly mother, I needed to be near extended family living in Tel Aviv and Lod, so I could get support. . . . I was miserable and used to cry everyday because I found no job. . . . The lady at the employment exchange was rude. . . . She was like a Nazi. She would say, 'No Hebrew, No job'. On one occasion, she got me a job. When I went to the address, I found it to be a café where I had to clean the floors. . . . It was miserable. . . . I will not forget that time. . . . Finally, I managed to get to an *ulpan* in Haifa. . . . I enjoyed the Hebrew learning for five months, but my Hebrew was not good enough for me to work only in that language. . . . I tried for many jobs. . . . When I would speak on the phone in English would call me for an interview. But at the interview they would see that despite my excellent English I was not a 'white' person but an Indian, and I would be told that there was no job! My friends were also unable to help . . . at the time colour prejudice was much more than now. . . . I applied to the American Embassy and also to many other places. . . . On one such occasion, at the TWA office I just walked in and enquired. Upon being interviewed there I was hired as a telex operator for 350 lirot a month . . . a fabulous salary at the time.

These early experiences of struggling in the job market in Israel reveal how the variables on which acquiring a good job depended could be many. Apart from the obvious ones like education, age and gender securing a position was also about finding the right 'break' or a 'connection'.

MEN AND WOMEN PROFESSIONALS: ROLE OF HIGHER EDUCATION

Indian Jews from upper middle classes in India came with higher levels of education. Like other Hindu or Muslim upper middle-class parents in India, Jewish parents also laid considerable stress on their children's education. Many of the interviewees for this research mentioned studying at Elly Kadoorie School, Bombay and Jewish Girls/Boys' School in Calcutta. Of the Karachi-based Jews many had fathers employed with the British Railways. This provided the children with ready access to special English-medium schools run by the Railways for the children of their employees. Two men and a woman I interviewed, who were successful professionals in hi-tech industries in Israel, came from the small Jewish community in Delhi and had graduated from institutions like St. Columba's School, Convent of Jesus and Mary and St. Stephen's College, University of Delhi in the early 1970s. All of these missionary institutions offered premier education. Those who had finished a college degree or a professional degree in India, found entry into the Israeli job market easily. It is important to note that, from such highly qualified Indian Jews, all did not make *aliya* to Israel. Many preferred to migrate to the United Kingdom and United States. The ones who came to Israel fared very well. Two senior medical specialists, and three professional sailors who commanded ships for Zim and other well-known Israeli shipping companies described how they had been approached and offered jobs by Jewish Agency representatives in India before they landed in Israel. One of them had been flown in for an interview previously and all arrangements were in place when they arrived. Needless to say, such professionals were settled in Tel Aviv, Haifa or elsewhere in Central Israel. Not knowing Hebrew was immaterial for the highly qualified medical doctors or commanders of ships. Their technical degrees were an important resource. Many such professionals were carefully identified by the Absorption authorities. They were allotted better neighbourhoods and their immersion as new immigrants was cushioned socially, economically and logistically.

PROFESSIONALS IN SHIPPING, FLYING AND MEDICINE

Rabin (*b.* 1934) made *aliya* in 1961. He was a certified Master Marine living in Bombay and worked for the prestigious Great Eastern Shipping Company in India (1953–61). His certification as a Master Mariner, qualified him to command a ship. In 1961, before he left Bombay the Jewish Agency had completed the necessary paperwork and Rabin had a job in the Israeli Zim Lines Shipping waiting for him in Haifa. Rabin explained, 'there was a great demand for this profession in Israel at the time. Unlike lawyers or teachers my profession had no language barriers, because all our manuals on the ship were in English'. Rabin's knowledge of English was a great asset because at the time the shipping companies in Israel employed many non-Jewish personnel due to a shortage of Jewish-Israeli trained professionals in shipping. Rabin later moved to El Yam—another marine company and in 1963 got command of his first cargo ship. After 1970, for several years he worked for the Ashkelon Pipeline Company as a harbour pilot. In 2000, Rabin retired after a fulfilling professional career. He and his family have settled in Haifa and live in an upper-class neighbourhood which is predominantly *Ashkenazi*. Both their children are highly educated. His daughter (born in India) teaches at an Israeli university.

Similarly, Rabin's brother Izak (*b.* 1927), when he arrived in 1970 had a smooth induction into the Israeli job market. Izak had been a Wing Commander in the Indian Air Force. After seeking early retirement from the Air Force, he had joined the national carrier Air India. When he migrated to Israel he had no problem on the professional front. He was recruited by the Israel's national carrier El Al as a pilot and flew Israeli aircraft for many years. Another cousin from the same family who was a medical doctor secured a job easily when he and his wife migrated in 1966. Their sister was married to a medical doctor. When they migrated in 1966, Dr Apticar got a job at the Holy Family Hospital in Nazareth where he worked for several years and chose to retire and settle down in Nazareth.

Rubin Binyamin came to Israel in 1964, when he was nearing thirty. He came from an upper middle-class Bene Israeli family from Poona and many of his cousins and uncles were highly educated and well-placed in government jobs in India. Rubin resigned his job with Goodyear Tyres (an American Company) in Bombay. His Director arranged for Rubin to get a job with a tyre factory in Israel. Thus, upon completing six months at an *ulpan* in Beersheva, Rubin got a managerial level job with Samson Tyres in Petah Tikwa. He narrated that soon after joining, in one of his assessment reports about the factory he pointed out the flaws in the production process (based on his experience in Goodyear Tyre factory in India). 'They thought it was shocking that an Indian should criticize their factory. . . . They did not realize that our best companies in India were functioning very efficiently.' As a result of this friction with the management, Rubin quit the job and decided to switch gears professionally. To his Indian degree of B.Sc. (Bachelor of Science) he added courses to become a marine engineer. He qualified as a marine engineer from Haifa in 1968. Upon a friend's advice, when he applied to international airlines, both British Airways and TWA offered him jobs. Subsequently, for over thirty years he worked for TWA in their ground office at the airport, where he was part of a team that briefs the crew about the operational plans prior to take-off. 'For this I did not need Hebrew—but my good knowledge of English mattered', said Rubin. In our conversation, Rubin confessed that 'my Hebrew is still not as good as my English! With his own Israeli-born children he spoke English, but 'my grandchildren correct my Hebrew' he said. Rubin lives in an elite neighbourhood just off Tel Aviv and his children are highly educated.

Jacob, a Bene Israeli made *aliya* in 1979. He was a medical doctor working at a government hospital in India and belonged to a well-established family as his father was also a highly reputed medical doctor. When he decided to emigrate he was flown in for an interview at one of the premier medical institutions in Israel. When he migrated with his wife, his assignment at one of Israel's biggest hospitals had been secured. When he completed his residency requirement in his medical specialization, he claimed that his salary and benefits in Israel were 'fantastic' compared to what he was getting in India. He grew to become a widely respected professional for his specialization in Israel and has been recognized and awarded several honours by the Israeli government. This children are highly educated.

CORPORATE AND PRIVATE BUSINESSES

There were also those who came from well-paid jobs in the corporate sector in India. Typically, these corporates were in Bombay or Calcutta but there could be exceptions like Danny Sopher, a Baghdadi who had been Senior Manager in National Tobacco Company in Calcutta and Shillong. Similarly, there were other interviewees who had worked for Johnson & Johnson (Bombay), Goodyear and Dunlop (Calcutta). All these companies typically recruited candidates who were smartly turned-out and spoke English well. The corporates would have provided salaries and benefits that would ensure lifestyles of great comfort, with domestic help and a company car, etc. For such individuals, upon coming to Israel, although jobs were not an issue, their Indian degrees and professional certifications (like Chartered Accountants) were often disregarded. The jobs they were offered in Israel hugely compromised the standards of living that were accustomed to, and many were bitter that were pressured to 're-qualify' themselves in Israeli universities to clear the obstacles in their professional development. For instance, when Solomon Morris a Bene Israeli came from Calcutta with his family in the mid-1960s, he was in his early thirties and had left behind a job as a Financial Controller with the Dunlop Rubber Co. (India) Ltd., where he was a senior officer. They lived in a privileged neighbourhood and had a bustling social life with the corporate elites of Calcutta. In 2007, when I interviewed him about his entry into the professional world in Israel, he said,

When seeking a job I was amazed at the lack of recognition of professional accountants. In fact, the first job that I secured was as an Assistant to the Chief Accountant of Israel Aircraft Industries Ltd. (Bedek), Lod, who himself was a Chartered Accountant from South Africa ! There were many emigrants from India working at this plant. . . . While working there, I qualified as an Israel Certified Public Accountant in 1966. . . . After that I was offered a job as the Controller of the new plant that Bedek was setting up in Beersheva.

By the end of 1966, he switched jobs and joined Motorola Israel Ltd., which was a young company at the time. He kept moving jobs and furthered his career, later joining Mennen Medical Ltd. (a company in medical electronics specializing in real time reporting of patient medical data) as Financial Controller. He worked with Mennen for 17 years thereafter. Post-retirement he still does consultancy and investment activities.

The career trajectory of Ronny is another interesting example.

Ronny's father was a licensed liquor distributor in Bombay at a time when the state prohibition on the sale of liquor made such business lucrative. Thus, Ronny's family had socio-economic stability. As a high school student he was fluent in English, Hindi and Marathi. Before emigrating, his father also asked him to do an electrician's course, which stood him in good stead in Israel. In Israel, Ronny began working in the tours & travel industry, initially with the Avis Car Rental Company. In time, he became the station manager for Avis at the Ben Gurion Airport. Noticing his enterprise, one of his superiors encouraged him to start his own company and assisted him with the financial investment. This is an important recollection for Ronny who argues that he did not encounter racism. His first benefactor and business associate was an *Ashkenazi*. Ronny's company was started in 1980–1 and the various businesses have since grown in these last thirty years. From the 'rent-a-car' business, he now has a travel & tour business. He owns an agency for cable networks which beam in Indian TV channels in Hindi and Gujarati into homes across Israel. This is a thriving business. He plans to add Zee Marathi and Sahara channels soon.[20]

When Issac (*b.* 1955) came to Israel in 1977, he had completed degree education in Calcutta. He had a Bachelor's degree in Commerce from St. Xavier's College, Calcutta and had worked briefly as a foreign exchange and money market broker. Upon coming to Israel he was sent to a *kibbutz* which he left after eighteen months to join Tel Aviv University to take a degree in Social Studies. He worked in Israel with Budget Car Rentals, and international airlines like Pan Am and Swissair for over fifteen years after which he became an entrepreneur. Today he owns a successful freight handling company.

WOMEN PROFESSIONALS

Nurit Talker (*b.* 1966) came as a qualified chartered accountant in 1993. In India, she had completed her BA degree from Bombay University, and subsequently had become a certified chartered accountant, working with KPMG (a multinational firm of chartered accountants). She was one of their chief auditors (1992–3) drawing a good salary. Despite this, in Israel 'I had to prove to them that my degree was equal to the British qualifications which were recognized in Israel' she said. Today Nurit is a proud and successful woman professional. As a professional who has surmounted some of the challenges, Nurit analyses perceptions about Indians and the difficulties of workplace stereotyping. 'The problems with the Indians who came in the 1960s was that they took what they got. . . . Even those who knew English got only clerical jobs.' She believes that although some went into businesses, they stayed with the same small businesses importing Indian items, spices and small items. 'The allotment of location where Indians were housed was an important determinant of their future economic success. . . . Those early years of insecurity and settling-in shaped the way the next generation was raised. . . .' Nurit believed that 'as individuals, not enough Indians have tried to push and break boundaries'.

CONCLUSION

For immigrant families from the lower socio-economic strata and low levels of education, life in Israel was extremely tough and many have struggled on for years in 'development towns' which never became the developed industrial towns that they were visualized to be. University-level education even in the Israeli-born children in such groups is rare, and the spiral of being (and remaining!) under-privileged has been difficult to break. Most children of such families followed just a vocational track and are plumbers, electricians, mechanics, clerks, or employees of the Israeli government or police at lower-level positions. They have remained not only geographically in 'peripheral regions' but also economically and socially peripheral to the spin-offs of Israel's technological and economic growth since the 1980s. On the other hand, those men and women who *brought* skills from India whether they were English communication skills or technical training, fared much better. After the initial displacement and hardships, they settled down and have raised children who have middle-level managerial positions, good jobs in the Israeli military, or have emigrated to the US or Canada to further their prospects.

In terms of chronology, those who came in the 1970s found career opportunities more easily. Some key reasons for this may be: first, typically, the latter day immigrants from India were better-educated than their earlier cousins had been. Like all urban middle-class Indians, who grew up after the mid-1960s, they were beneficiaries of widely available and relatively inexpensive college-level education in India. Armed with better qualifications, they were more confident and put up a tough resistance when their qualifications were not recognized in Israel. Most importantly, they also came with a confidence that coming to Israel was not an irreversible decision. If professionally or economically, Israel proved to be too daunting, they could either return to Bombay, where they had strong ties with friends and social networks or they could move on to the UK, USA or Canada. Dozens of individuals I interviewed in Israel, spoke of cousins and siblings who had moved to the US and Canada or siblings and cousins who chose never to emigrate from Bombay because they were 'doing well' economically and socially. So we know that many *did* exercise these options. These 'recent' better-educated immigrants were predominantly Bene Israelis, usually Bombay-based, because the Cochinis and Baghdadis who wished to emigrate from India had already done so before 1970, and the remaining numbers are small.

There are also other reasons for latter day immigrants faring better. Most obviously, they were coming to a fast-growing Israel, even if 'the periphery' sadly lagged behind. Those who migrated later, came with a far better understanding of what the Jewish Homeland was all about. They were well-primed by the stories from relatives and kinsmen in Israel and had a much better sense of how to 'get ahead' after making *aliya*. They were careful to resist authorities and avoided settling in development towns in remote areas, and displayed a clear sense of the economic geography of Israel. Their higher educational levels and job experience from India put them on a stable footing to negotiate with employees and authorities alike. Cultural hesitations to push ahead or the need to maintain a modest posture were put aside. Individuals better understood the need to jostle ahead.

As Helen, one of my respondents said, 'After years of working at the Technion's academic office I learnt that I had to fight for my case and had to *ask* for a raise . . . and that's how I got it. . . !'

NOTES

1. Since the examples above cite the professional achievements of certain individuals, their original names have been retained.
2. A study of the Indian Jewish community at Lod done in the early 1970s showed that the average number of years of schooling that a first gene-ration Bene Israeli had was 9.5, which was the same as the Israeli national average in 1973–4. The average number of years among African and Asian countries was 6.6 years. Shalva Weil, 'Bene Israel Indian Jews in Lod, Israel: A Study in the Persistence of Ethnicity and Ethnic Identity', Ph.D. thesis available at Haifa University, vol. 1, p. 127.
3. I mean those who made a carefully planned decision to make their future lives in Israel—I do not mean older relatives or parents of those who were already settled in Israel.
4. Erika Spiegel, *New Towns in Israel*, Stuttgart: Karl Kramer Verlag, 1966.
5. In Dimona residents spoke of Dead Sea Chemical Works (50 km away) and two textile factories ('Kitan' and 'Sebi') and in Yarukham they spoke of a glass bottle factory as the main employers for all the immigrant communities in that area.
6. The women who fared better were less willing to admit to the 'colour-bias'. The ones who had felt marginalized were more candid in voicing it.
7. This was the case among both Bene Israelis and Baghdadis although among the latter community and the Cochinis there were also merchants who traded in small businesses.
8. For the interview, we conversed in colloquial Hindi because she was more comfortable speaking Hindi.
9. Migration to Israel from Pakistan was not possible directly because Jewish Agency offices did not exist in Pakistan and Jews usually contacted the Bombay office to arrange papers for *aliya*.
10. They make authentic Indian delicacies like *besan ladoos, pede, namkeen*, and the Maharashtrian *puran poli*.

11. Two of the women employees were Indian and two were Russian immigrants who had learnt to make the Indian snacks!
12. This is a notch lower than a full-fledged engineer because this requires a shorter course of two and a half years, instead of four years.
13. From the 1970s, Indian engineering colleges were producing hundreds of graduates each year. For those with low skills living in a thickly populated metropolis like Bombay, there were challenges and very tough competition for jobs, low salaries and expensive housing and so forth.
14. Although the children tend to move out of those towns, among the first-generation, only a few have moved from their original homes to smarter newer areas in Rehovot, Rishon le Zion or Shoham.
15. The Baghdadis were English-speaking. The Bene Israeli were often fluent with one or two Indian languages as well, whereas, most Baghdadis spoke a broken street-version of Hindi which they were accustomed to using with their domestic help in India.
16. In 2006–7, I met many women of Baghdadi origin who had come to Israel from Calcutta in the 1960s as young women, beginning their life as secretaries. Many of them had married well-educated *Ashkenazi* men and were now living in expensive neighbourhoods around Tel Aviv.
17. Later she married an *Ashkenazi* of Polish origin and raised a family in comfortable socio-economic conditions.
18. Mina, a retiree living in Lod, was one of my most articulate respondents—fluently speaking English and Hindi—both languages which she learnt at Indian schools almost forty years ago.
19. She and her mother were well-settled in India and moved only because the family in Bombay had diminished and as the mother aged, the dwindling support system posed a concern.
20. His clients in the travel business are foreign tourists and also the Indian Embassy, which patronizes his car-rental agency for its constant stream of delegates from India.

CHAPTER 5

Raising Jewish Families in Israel: Gender, Religious Practice and Life Cycle Rituals

Migration and the concomitant displacement have been two important underlying strands of this book. But what were the gendered implications of displacement on women, home and family? An important part of the research was to reach out to Indian Jewish women of the first-generation particularly those who came before the mid-1970s. I wished to capture their experiences as *olim* or new immigrants who flowed into the Jewish Homeland along with thousands of other immigrants from North Africa and West Asia. Although immigrants also came from Europe and America, *olim* of *Mizrahi* non-European origin were frequently settled alongside each other although many interviewees mentioned that in some *moshavs* and development towns, small groups of immigrants from east-European countries like Rumania, Bulgaria or Hungary were also settled with them. This could accentuate a sense of cultural displacement and isolation for women who coped with the immigrant struggles as wives and mothers. But did women have *gendered* immigration experiences as they settled into the Jewish Homeland? This research revealed that they did. The questions that needed to be asked were:

- What did immigration do to gender roles in the family? How did women experience responsibilities of motherhood and parenting in the Jewish Homeland?
- How did women's work in the immigrant society re-shape their lives?

Taking these questions further meant examining the layers of acculturation and asking:

- What are the trends in family organization and lifestyle among Indian Jewish families today that show assimilative tendencies? And what are the ways in which families cling to what is 'Indian' —family values, codes of behaviour, modes of address in the family, responsibility towards elderly parents, etc.
- What about religious experssion? How is 'Jewishness' experienced and what are the Jewish practices in families? In the community?
- Has this been transformed since their move from the pluralistic society in India to the Jewish but multi-ethnic society in Israel?
- What are some 'Indian-Jewish' practices and rituals still prevalent in the life cycle rituals of Indian Jews in Israel?

Bearing these questions in mind, in this chapter I turn from issues of work and profession to issues of family, home, and personal choices in religious practice. The distinction between discussing professional issues in the previous chapter and 'personal' issues in this one is organizational, and not an ideological one. I recognize that the 'personal' can hardly be fenced off from the 'public', i.e. social, professional or community issues. In fact, the discussion in the previous chapter has established that for a majority of new immigrant families their personal or home lives were overwhelmingly affected by the social structures in which they found themselves and the jobs that were allotted to do. Thus, this chapter examines important issues which remain yet unexplored in this book: issues of gender, marriage, family life, life cycle rituals and religiosity. On one hand, this chapter examines how migration re-shaped women's lives in relation to conjugality, marriage and motherhood. On the other hand, this discussion analyses how the religious identities of Indian Jews as a community were *re-framed* so to speak, from being a distinct religious minority in India to being distinct by ethnicity as *Indian* Jews in Israel. The schematic divisions below flow from these two trajectories of discussion.

The first part of this chapter is on gender and family life. This section highlights the specific ways in which women experienced migration—the churning in women's lives as they crossed over from the cultural and social ethos in which they were born and raised in India to become part of the vast sea of new immigrants that poured in from other cultures into Israel. We know from Chapter 3 that for hundreds of lower- or middle-income Jewish families, the villages of Kerala, the suburbs of Bombay and even those displaced from Karachi, the migration package arranged by the Jewish Agency offered the stability of owning an independent home by couples, who could not have afforded to buy real estate in their pre-migration financial status. While this was an important draw, there were other drawbacks that emerged as nuclear families of young couples separated from extended family networks and migrated to the Jewish Homeland. While young married women gained more autonomy from older women in the family, especially domineering mothers-in-law, their independence came at a price. For instance, motherhood for a young immigrant woman brought new challenges. Although women who were interviewed did not complain about the availability of medical facilities for childbirth in Israel, women commonly recalled the trauma of returning home with newly born infants to cope with housework and childcare while their husbands were away for long hours digging roads or performing other hard manual work. Nurit in Kiryat Yam spoke of returning home with her three- or four-day old babies to resume housework. Ruby of Yarukham spoke of giving birth to triplets—none of whom survived after a few days. Such phases of the immigrant experience were a harsh reality for these women. Lost was the extended family support and long weeks of pampering that women could expect in most middle and even lower middle-class families in India where sisters, mothers of sisters-in-law took turns to spend time routinely in helping with infant care and post-childbirth settling in. For many of these women, their extended families were either still in India or scattered in other *ma'abarot* or development towns, struggling with their own livelihood issues.

This examination becomes an entry point to consider the following: what were the gendered imperatives in the new immigrant society in which women had to be 'Israeli' wives and raise 'Israeli' children? How was family life re-structured and how have Indian-Jewish families evolved in the Israeli context? This includes a whole range of issues related to family and home in the broadest sense which would include parental expectations of children's behaviour, inter-generational family ties, the role of first-generation women as grandmothers, how families observe holidays and festivals at synagogues and at home, the languages they speak to each other, what they cook and eat at home, and how ethnicity is articulated consciously or otherwise in all these choices and observances.

What naturally follows from this is a discussion of life cycle rituals and religious observances among the Indian Jewish community. This forms the second part of this chapter. It is important to state however, that this chapter does not aim to offer an analysis of religion or Judaism *per se*. What is pertinent to a sociological study of the Indian Jewish community is the ways in which religion finds expression in the religious practices at home, in the synagogue or in the observances of life cycle rituals. Thus, for instance, it is important to emphasize that many Indian communities across Israel pray in their own Indian synagogues (as do some other ethnic communities). Although the prayers in Indian synagogues follow a broadly *Sephardic* tradition, there are some specific observances like the *malida* ceremony which make the worship in Bene Israeli families distinct. Similarly, there are Indian touches that make Indian Jewish weddings ethnically distinct—both in what people wear, do and eat at the weddings. Thus, in this section I deal with religiosity and 'Jewishness' in a broad sociological sense showing how ethnicity and religion blend in the traditions that Indian Jews observe. It must be stated at the very outset, that the levels of strictness in following Jewish customs and rituals varies enormously within the Indian Jewish community—with some being deeply religious in what they wear and do and strict in following the *shabbat* and *kashruth* dietary restrictions, while others are much like other secular Israelis in observing Jewish holidays in a traditional fashion but not following ritualistic injunctions. The discussion about religiosity and Jewish-ness among Jewish communities in different societies has attracted many anthropologists. Indian Jewish communities have been studied for their rituals and observances that they preserved or modified as they lived in India among non-Jewish communities.[1] Within Israeli sociology also there has been an interest in examining aspects of the religiosity of the different immigrant communities who came from non-European Jewish traditions in North Africa or West Asia.[2] However, there is little scholarship on Indian-Jewishness in Israeli society although there are some distinct facets that bear analysis. This discussion draws upon my own observations during wedding and pre-wedding ceremonies, circumcisions, synagogue services and other national Jewish holidays in Israel.

GENDER

Altered Gender Roles and Decline in Family Networks

Migration created an upheaval in women's lives although the degree to which this could be exciting or traumatizing depended upon age, education and social class. Disruption was experienced differently by a twelve-year old girl who came in a Youth Aliya group, a young educated single woman who came from Calcutta or Bombay in her twenties, or by a woman from a lower income family who came as a young wife and mother. It was a whole different experience, from all of the above, for a woman who was herself in her late forties and came along with her grown-up children, all of whom were uprooting themselves emotionally, socially and psychologically. For the young girls of Youth Aliya (who tended to be from large but modestly-placed Bene Israeli or Cochini families), the trauma of separation from parents and siblings was a major shock. But most were sent with a sibling or a cousin and after the initial months of homesickness or once the parents made *aliya* and were re-united with the children, these girls settled in as new immigrants floating alongside many others like themselves. We should remember though that being able to 'float along' did not mean that they found avenues for upward mobility, which was in fact severely limited for those who were growing up in remote development towns like Dimona in the south or Kiryat Shmona in the north. If the women were from upper middle-class families from Bombay or Calcutta and were inspired by their Zionism to make *aliya* or encouraged by parents who hope that in the Jewish Homeland they would soon find eligible Jewish men to marry, such women usually found themselves in and around Tel Aviv, Jerusalem or Haifa. Following their *ulpan* Hebrew study, jobs were easy enough to get. For them, the upheaval resulting from migration had a different character. For them the new society offered both exciting freedom from protective parental supervision as well as, immense responsibilities to take their own decisions. Not many such young women were used to jostling about alone in public transportation in India, nor were they used to fending for themselves without domestic help at home. For them migration meant freedom as well as responsibility—whether it was in matters of finance or their marriages—issues which were invariably parental responsibilities in India whether the parents were Hindu, Muslim or Jewish.

Then there were those women who came from the lower middle classes but were used to a highly urbanized metropolis like Bombay. Many such women found themselves in small development towns, with husbands or fathers stuck in poorly paid manual jobs which compelled them to join the labour force although they had neither education nor any special skills. Culturally, such women came from an ethos in India where neither they nor their mothers and sisters had ever worked outside the home. Women could take it for granted that women relatives from the extended family were around to support them through their pregnancies, childbirth and subsequent childcare problems. Supportive family networks or strong neighbourly ties among women were the norm rather than the exception. Emigration severely disrupted all this. They arrived into situations where the best they could take for granted was housing—and many not even that because they found themselves in the *ma'abarot* or immigrant camps. The uncertain work situation for the men forced them to take on paid work which more often than not was manual work like fruit and vegetable-picking as farm labour, cleaning jobs in commercial or government buildings or lowly paid factory labour.

The clothes they traditionally wore, the food they were used to cooking for their families and the division of labour in the house as they understood it, suddenly became unsuitable for the transformed life in the development towns or the *moshavs* in which women found themselves. They could neither jump in with their *saris* into the vans that transported them to factories or farms, nor did they return home after the manual work with enough energy to cook their traditional curries for their families.

Given the outreach of the Jewish Agency and its preference for young singles and couples, and also the fact that many of the older generation were hesitant to uproot their settled lives in India, it was common for the Indian *olim* in the 1960s to be young families with small children but without a grandparent generation nearby to offer a family support system. Given this configuration, women, who came as young wives or mothers of toddlers, and were sent to development towns, experienced a huge churning in their lives. For many, it shook the foundations of what they knew and had experienced in their gender roles in India. It catapulted them into scenarios where their inherited wisdom about their roles as wives, mothers and daughters was put to a severe test and their previous support networks snapped as they found themselves jostling among other women immigrants from Morocco, Iraq, Yemen, Bulgaria or Romania who were their neighbours in the immigrant towns. How women coped with the collapse of previous support systems, how they experienced the pressure of being belittled for not knowing the language and the prevalent mores of the new society and their being 're-socialized' within the new bureaucratic culture of immigrant authorities, these are the questions this chapter highlights.

For the older women, the disruption was the most painful—alas, for this section my respondents were the fewest since most of those women are no longer alive and many are too unwell to handle interviews. About them, the information comes from their daughters who recall their mothers as women who were 'always a little lost', 'never really adjusted . . . and remained unhappy. . . .' Shirley's mother Segula was a Baghdadi Jew born in Calcutta. She spoke fluent English and was educated up to high school.

But when she was 45 years old, her husband decided that they would move to Israel. When Segula came to Israel in 1950, along with her seven children aged between twenty and three, her life took a turn that she could barely comprehend. With life beginning in the tin-roofed *ma'abarot* immigrant shelters near Haifa, followed by cramped housing in Lod, Segula never really got used to either the physically tough conditions, the Hebrew or the struggle of staying afloat in the immigrant rush. She made few friends, relied on her grown-up daughters to assist with Hebrew and housekeeping in Israel. She died at the age of fifty-six, 'a graceful but an old and tired woman' as Shirley described her to be. Osnat described how when their father who was a businessman in Bombay decided that the family would make *aliya* in 1970, she herself was just out of high school and her mother who had borne and raised three children in Bombay, was accustomed to a comfortable life at home with some basic domestic help. More importantly, she had a social life centering around her own women friends and Bombay was 'home' in every way. She migrated reluctantly, found Hebrew too difficult and the 'culture' of Israel 'too rough'. She kept returning to Bombay annually to visit her friends and many relatives who had decided not to migrate to Israel. In the early 1980s she became terminally ill and could no longer travel back and forth. Referring to her death, Osnat said, 'Had she not left Bombay and felt so uprooted and unhappy, I am sure we would have had Mummy around for longer.' In Kiryat Yam I interviewed Hanna whose husband works on a low-level job in the Israeli postal service and whose family history (since *aliya* in 1965) presents a rather typical immigrant family struggle in a development town. She referred to her mother- and father-in-law living in the adjacent building. They were neither able to better their circumstances and move out to a better, less depressed neighbourhood, nor did they blend into a Hebrew-centric culture. Today, both are in their nineties and ailing. Their children help out but no one has the resources to hire care-givers as thousands of better-off families in contemporary Israel do to look after their family elders.

My oldest respondent for this research was born in 1924 and

three other women born in 1927. The above remarks were important as a tribute to those for whom my research in 2007–8 was already 'late'. This realization deepens my commitment to capture the narratives and voices of those women who were the 'next-in-line' to bear the brunt of the immigrant experiences, and are now grandmothers and retirees in their sixties and seventies, as well, as those who came as younger children in families and are now in their late fifties. The profiles of women presented below seek to capture some of the flavour of the early immigrant experiences.

WOMEN IN DEVELOPMENT TOWNS, *MOSHAVS* AND CITIES: SOME PROFILES

Ruth Bhastikar came to Dimona in 1970 with her husband and infant son. When I interviewed her in February 2008, she was still living in Dimona, a widowed retiree, and her family size seemed a bit unusual. She spoke of having only two children, sons born in 1970 and 1975, the first in India and the second in Israel. When I asked for her story, she narrated:

I was a trained nurse and had worked for ten years at K.M. Hospital, Bombay before I and my husband emigrated with our infant son (*b.* 1970). When we were sent to Dimona, I recall that although we were given a newly built apartment, I was shocked at the level of underdevelopment. . . . After Dadar, Parel and suburban Bombay, Dimona was rural!. . . Dimona had no jobs. . . . My husband who had always done clerical work was given common manual work in the glass bottle manufacturing factory in Yarukham. His salary of about 200–300 lirot was barely enough. I didn't work for the first seven years after coming to Israel, during which I conceived triplets. The childbirth was difficult and none of the babies could be saved. . . . Maybe with today's available technologies, my babies would have been saved. . . . But I also felt that we weren't treated so well and the facilities in Dimona were really basic. . . . Later, I lost another child but the next one survived. . . . After I lost my triplets, I began to work as a nurse. I worked in *Kupat Holim* (the national health care system) and served as a nurse in Beersheva, Dimona and Yarukham. My salary used to be almost double that of my husband! I worked for twenty years in Israel.

Ruth's husband died of a heart attack several years ago. With a great deal of equanimity, she said, '*Mere husband ne mere liye ye do anmol rattan chhode hain*' (My husband has left behind these two priceless jewels for me!). Despite the tragic developments, Ruth's having only two children to provide for meant that they got better opportunities, and she and her husband were able to send their sons away to a boarding school in Jerusalem. One of her sons lives with his family in Dimona, although he works in one of resort hotels over 50 km away. He works as a room-service helper and the hotel transport ferries him to work. Her younger son works at the *Kamaag* (the Nuclear Installation) in the Dimona region on a medium-level, non-professional job. Ruth still volunteers as a nurse. Twice a week she visits families where there are elderly or cancer patients and she writes reports about them for the health care system which supports their care. She is actively engaged in raising small funds for cancer patients in her neighbourhood. When I asked about divorces among the community and in her own generation, she said, '*Yahaan Israel mein, divorce to fashion jaisa ban gaya hai*' (Here in Israel, divorce is like a fashion!). One of her sons had married a Moroccan woman but they were divorced. She had never considered re-marriage for herself.

Yerusha Eliyahu (*b*. 1936) was the most articulate of the group, spoke fluent English and I learned that she had moved with her husband and five children from Karachi to Bombay. They came from Karachi via Bombay to Israel in 1968.[3]

We moved in with our five children into the tiny apartment given to us. Living in cramped housing, we decided to send two of our children to a boarding school.[4] 'I could not afford to see them every week so they used to come once a month. They would take a bus to Beersheva and from there to Dimona. . . . That toughened them and made them independent.' . . . My husband was very resentful and kept battling with the authorities and we finally changed to a better house in Dimona itself after eight years. . . . In general, we who came from India were shocked at the rudeness here. . . . We thought of Israel as our homeland but many of us were guided by a euphoria that could not be sustained when we actually came to live here. . . .

Bathsheva ('Bati' to her friends) came as a child in a Youth Aliya group from Cochin in 1954, and studied at a religious school in northern Israel till her parents came in 1958. In 1958, her marriage was arranged by her family to a young Cochini Jew (eleven years her senior) who had migrated in 1955 and was living at a *moshav* in the Negev. They were married at the synagogue on the *moshav* and Bati recalled that a day after their wedding she wore a sun-hat at 5 a.m. and joined her husband on the farm that they would both till and sow for many subsequent years. Bati's husband subsequently became a successful and reputed agriculturist in innovating and producing high-quality roses for export to European markets in the 1970s. Alongside giving birth to her four children Bati became something of a specialist herself experimenting with plants in her own independently managed greenhouse.[5]

When I asked Bati about her life in the *moshav* and the conditions forty years ago when she had been giving birth to her children, she responded in a matter of fact by telling me that the nearby medical centre for the region had been adequate. Her mother had come from Jerusalem to help her with her first baby. Subsequently, she had been able to manage with the help of her husband. Over time, Bati acculturated smoothly. She spoke Malyalam with her husband and Hebrew with her children. A strong, determined woman she tended to the farms and looked after her children in the years that her husband served in Israeli wars and later as a reservist in the military. In her sixties, she not only continues with her farm work, but also looks after her two grandchildren on weekdays till their parents return home from work. Bati is a spirited woman who enjoys Israeli folk-dancing, has taken lessons and drives 20 km on weekend evenings by herself to dance with a group of about fifty people who gather from neighbouring *moshavs* in a community hall.

These examples from women in remote towns and *moshavs* recreate the early scenario during which immigrant women were 'broken-in' to a new ethos of work and family responsibilities. In fact, it is important to underscore that post-migration life had its challenges even when the young women were educated and *not* in remote towns. For example, Jeanette was married to a medical doctor in India and came to Haifa within two years of her marriage. She narrated:

My husband's work in the hospital was not easy at all. He had to work thirty-six hour shifts and he used to come home only every alternate night. . . . I had a lot of difficulty coping with the loneliness and was homesick for years because my husband kept studying to further his qualifications. . . . Recognition for Indian qualifications was not easy to get here. . . . Salary-wise, even in the 1970s, young doctors got terrible salaries in Israel. . . But I had learnt from my mother how to manage with little, and money was never really an issue. . . . Although I had lived a sheltered life in India, I started working in secretarial jobs. . . . Once the children were born, I had them to give me company after a long day's work. . . . I was homesick for years.

Conjugality, Sexuality and Gender Roles

It must be emphasized that women immigrants who started life in Israel in development towns and *moshavs* experienced immigration struggles in specific ways and their experiences had little in common with the women who were able to secure a foot for themselves within cities in Central Israel.[6] In discussing marriage and conjugality, I must emphasize that this research revealed a variety of patterns. While a large majority of first-generation Indians married other Indian Jews, I also came across dozens of men and women in their fifties and sixties who were married to non-Indian Jewish Israelis from other ethnic groups—very often of *Ashkenazi* origin. Other interviewees also told me about siblings who had married non-Indian Jews in Israel. In this section, on marriage, sexuality and family, I begin by making brief comments on conjugality and marriage practices as they existed in India *prior to* migration. I believe such cross-references are crucial to understand the sociological mutations in personal lives and family structures in the post-migration context.

From existing studies on Cochini, Bene Israeli and Baghdadi Jewish communities in India we know that there were some broad similarities in marriage patterns among Jewish communities in India despite other important cultural and linguistic differences.[7] Below, I underline some of the similarities. In general, marriage among Jews in India was seen as normative. Men were to be the bread-winners and women home-makers, mothers and amicable additions to larger family networks. Wives were invariably younger. In fact, many women narrated that their mothers had been married in their late teens and that the fathers were eight to fourteen years older than their mothers. This seemed common regardless of their being Baghdadi, Bene Israeli or Cochini. Daughters were carefully chaperoned among Jewish families as they were among other Indian families. Given that girls were married at a young age and lived protected lives before that, their chances of meeting eligible men on their own were few and dating (in the Western sense) was unacceptable for daughters from 'respectable' families. However, family weddings and other extended family get-togethers were cited by many women as occasions when young men and women met each other or parents spotted eligible marriage partners for their children after which families negotiated and clinched the marriages. So, for instance, Jean and Solomon, both Bene Israelis saw each other at a family wedding, fell in love and the families were gradually persuaded to perform the wedding. Judy and Daniel who were married at the synagogue in Nagpada in Bombay in the late 1950s were first cousins related through their mothers. They had grown up seeing each other and nurturing the desire to marry as the years went by. But the final decision was taken by the parents. Even if the brides and bride-grooms had seen each other, many had exchanged only a few words at a formal encounter before they were wed. For the woman marriage meant leaving her parental home and going to live with her husband's extended family which would include his parents, younger siblings or older married brothers with their wives and children. Newly married young women got the privacy of living with their husbands as a nuclear family unit mostly if the husband's job took him to a city away from his parental home base. Divorces were rare and frowned upon although families tacitly believed that women maintained social silences about domestic conflict and cases of marital abuse. While Jewish communities lived in India, widow remarriages were rare—especially among the Bene Israelis. This may have been the influence of the surrounding (predominantly Hindu) culture because in Islam and Judaism widowhood is not stigmatized.[8]

Migration disrupted all these traditional living arrangements and tossed girls and women into the immigrant flow. At one level, this also liberated them from obsessive chaperoning, sexual policing and oppressive joint families, it also pulled away from them the protective networks that their mothers had always taken for granted. Although Indian parents were protective about their daughters and reluctant to send them alone, hundreds of teen-aged Jewish girls came in Youth Aliya groups, sometimes with a sibling or cousin in the same group. Such girls were rarely from urban upper middle-class families from Bombay, Calcutta or Ahmedabad. Instead they tended to be from large Bene Israeli, Cochini or Baghdadi families of five to eight children where sending away a son and daughter to Israel seemed a wise parental decision for the future prospects of the child. By the mid-1960s enough families had migrated to Israel for parents to feel confident and send their grown-up unmarried daughters under the family umbrella of uncles and aunts who had migrated in previous years. Shoshana and her sister came in their late teens with a Jewish Agency sponsored group, and their parents (with their seven other children) came a few years later, after which all were sent to Beersheva. Rina came from Mattancherry in Kerala in 1956 when she and her distant cousin Rivka (aged eleven and thirteen respectively) were sent by the family with a Youth group of Cochini Jews. Rina had lost her mother when she was a child and her father made *aliya* six years later with the rest of his children when they were sent to a *moshav* in northern Israel near the Lebanese border.

Young Indian girls like Rivka, Shoshana and Rina who grew up in Israeli development towns, attending schools for new *olim* did not acquire the education or the social skills for upward mobility. Economic pressures pushed them hastily into semi-skilled jobs, sometimes before the end of high school. This had important consequences for their marriages. Being outside the well-paid labour market and stuck in far-flung *moshavs* or development towns meant that they had little access to eligible young men in well-placed professional jobs. They met their prospective husbands in their own socio-economic circles or their marriages were 'arranged' by parents or uncles and aunts who suggested grooms from the community, although there was more flexibility in letting the young people meet a few times before weddings were fixed, than there may have been in India in the 1960s or 1970s. However, it must be emphasized that this *too* was class-specific. Young women from urban upper middle-class families who came from India came with a reasonably good education, and the English-medium schools they attended had given them literary exposure as well as some personality grooming. In India, such girls would have been chaperoned and dating men would meet with severe parental disapproval. However, when such girls were sent to Israel by themselves, they were broadly under the care of aunts and uncles who had made *aliya* previously. Even when their parents did arrive they were much 'freer' about permitting dating and most such girls found themselves in *ulpans* with other English-speaking *olim* from America, South Africa or Australia, among whom they also met their future husbands. For instance, Mazaal, Rachel, Naomi and Fleurette all of whom came in the 1960s from Baghdadi families in Calcutta, were sent by their parents either alone or as two sisters, starting life in central Israel. The *ulpans* they attended were for English-speaking immigrants (from America, South Africa, Australia and so forth). They were also located in good neighbourhoods like Netanya or Ra'naana—not far from Tel Aviv. These *ulpans* became their entry points into a much higher social strata, and set the tone for their future social circles in Israeli society. A young girl growing up in Kiryat Shmona, Dimona or Kfar Yuval was unlikely to find such social breaks.

Gender Roles and Housework

In general, marriages among first-generation Indian Jews largely replicated the patterns that had existed in India prior to migration. Between couples who had been married in India, the gender equations did not change dramatically or suddenly from what they had been. Among those who got married after migration, over time, the division of labour in the home revealed significant mutations in the new cultural climate. Upon migration, as women's traditional family support systems collapsed and they struggled with new economic pressures to join the labour force, most women recalled that initially, the division of labour in the family was resistant to change. Women who were interviewed with their husbands, smiled as they looked at their (now retired) husbands, recalling those early years of subtle negotiation in gender relations, when husbands were compelled to share the chores in a nuclear family because, as Esther said, 'there was no one else to help me'. Although many women said that things had changed over the years, an interesting exception was reported by *all* the women interviewed. Those who were married to Indian men reported that even when the husbands helped with housework, cooking was rarely a chore they helped with, and men smilingly confessed 'cooking, I cannot do!'

Retiree Women, Widowhood and Inter-ethnic Marriages

Through the interviews and focus group meetings with Indian Jewish women's organizations, I talked to dozens of women retirees who were widowed and living alone. Some had lost their husbands twenty years ago, others more recently. None of these women had remarried, although the ones I met were varied in their educational levels and were dispersed across Israel, living in Lod, Ramla, Ashdod, Dimona, Haifa or Jerusalem. The oldest among them were in their early eighties. But in spite of their age they were fit enough to live in independant households and manage on their own (although there were instances of a woman who had brought in an older sister to move in with her, and another one who had moved to her daughter's house). When I asked them about the option to remarry, most replied that though, 'it is okay in Israeli society', they had personally not been interested in remarriage. At focus group meetings in Dimona, first-generation Indian Jewish women who were now leading low-key but settled lives seemed reasonably contented. As grandmothers who could now devote more time to the hobbies and interests they could not pursue earlier or as women who do volunteer work within the community, they didn't seem to measure their lives by whether or not they could have lived in a more developed or centralized cities. Some of them it seemed had also internalized their 'peripheral' location and accepted it and in many ways the present seemed calm as compared to their turbulent past of struggle and hardships.

Divorces in this generation were rare and I came across no instance of polygamy. The reasons for a low divorce rate also stemmed from cultural internalizations of gender and conjugality. Among the older generation, more than a few made oblique references to marital disharmony, but they were couched in a delicate language, describing their husbands as 'difficult' or 'short-tempered'. Indirect references suggested that among the early immigrants in the 1950s, and early 1960s, especially among the lower income groups, alcoholism among the menfolk had upset the family life of many. However, the women were quick to point out that the men had been very unhappy with their economic and work situation in those days and their anger and alcoholism had been a kind of vent for their powerlessness and frustration at poor access to opportunities in Israel. None of the women admitted to having experienced domestic violence in their marriage although a few said they 'had heard of a few cases'. Apart from the interviews, more than 40 women contributed to this research data by way of writing profiles about their immigration experiences. From all these, only two women spoke of divorce and about raising children on their own, although both prided themselves on having taught their children to 'respect their fathers'. There were, however, a few divorcees among the comparatively younger women, who were in their fifties at the time of this research. Most such divorces were from inter-ethnic marriages where the husbands were of *Ashkenazi* origin.

This, however, merits explanation of another aspect of gender and conjugality: inter-ethnic marriages. I encountered a widespread perception about Indians in Israeli society that 'they don't inter-marry with non-Indians'. I found this to be a context-specific issue and not an absolute truism. Among the Indians born in the 1930s and 1940s, those who came to Israel rarely married non-

Indians, for many reasons. First, in development towns there were enough Indian families for suitable marriage partners and displacement from a shared linguistic environment brought Indians together—whether Malyalam-speaking Cochinis or Marathi-speaking Bene Israelis. But beyond language and food, many Indians felt that cultural gaps between themselves and other Jewish communities settled there were too wide to bridge. Many interviewees from Dimona, Kiryat Shmona, Kiryat Ata, Yarukham, even Ashdod and Petah Tikwa, openly said that they had encountered aggression and hostility routinely from their neighbours who may have been Moroccan, Iraqi or Turkish. Indian immigrant youth growing up in such environments were also slow to fall in love with girls and boys from other ethnic communities by whom their families felt belittled. However, generalizations are problematic because among Indian youth who grew up on *moshavs* or in cities, many met and married across ethnic lines. So in fact, Indians did begin to marry outside the Indian Jewish Communities by the 1970s, but because the couples did not necessarily return to live in areas of Indian-Jewish concentration, they were less visible and integrated into the Israeli multi-ethnic society.

In fact, there is a class of Indian immigrants among whom inter-ethnic marriages were quite common but remain unnoticed because they do not constitute a stereotype. There were the young, educated Indian men and women who came from the bigger cities and from upper middle-class families with considerable exposure to English and the international world before they migrated. When they arrived in Israel they were sent to *ulpans* for English-speakers. Their induction into Israeli society took place at a much higher level. For instance, among the more 'anglicized' women or those who came with an English education from India, many did marry *Ashkenazi* Jewish men. A noticeably large number of Baghdadi-Indian women are married to men originally from Poland, or other European countries or to *Ashkenazi* men who came from the early Jewish families in Israel. Thus Rosie and Diana, Baghdadi women from Calcutta whom I interviewed together, were both married to *Ashkenazi* men. Their closest social circle of friends comprises other women of Baghdadi-Indian origin who were raised in British colonial Calcutta, went to school there and came to Israel in the late 1950s, often without their parents. None of their group of women are married to Indian or Baghdadi Jewish men. Similarly, Betty and Rachel, sisters born of Baghdadi parents who came as young children from Calcutta and grew up in Israel have both married *Ashkenazi* men. Betty's husband is a well-established scientist who has many patents to his name, while Rachel's husband was a child-holocaust survivor from East Europe.

Among the Bene Israelis, inter-ethnic marriages were rare in the generation born in the 1940s. Miri, a young attorney I interviewed told me that her mother Eti who had come from Karachi had met her *Ashkenazi* husband at a factory where they worked. However, this marriage ended in a divorce and Miri, an only child, was raised by Eti. Among those born in the 1950s, inter-marriages became more common among the Bene Israelis. David married Esther, his Algerian sweetheart whom he had met in Dimona. Jimmy married Nili Weinberg whom he had met at the School of Fashion where they studied. Nili's parents were Israeli born but of Russian and Romanian descent, a well-to-do family, which had migrated to Israel in the 1930s.

The research revealed that among those who did have inter-ethnic marriages in Israel, the women were more likely to be the partner of Indian origin. In general, however, inter-ethnic marriages followed an uneven pattern among the Indian Jewish community in Israel.

RELIGIOUS PRACTICE: FAMILY LIFE, LIFE CYCLE RITUALS AND RELIGIOSITY

Family life among the Indian Jews reflects many of the patterns carried over from pre-migration days. In the early decades in Israel, the community remained well-connected—enough to be able to conduct match-making for those who came as children and grew up in Israel, although such 'arranged' marriages did decline over time. Community contacts were strong among groups who were settled near to each other. For instance, the Ramla and

Lod communities knew each other quite well and they knew many others in Ashdod—all broadly in the same region. In the Haifa region those who lived in the Krayot knew others who were scattered in Kiryat Ata, Kiryat Motskin and Kiryat Bialik. They were less likely to interact with those who were deep south in Dimona. The reason for this seemed clear. Economic struggles prevented most people from travelling around—even in a country as small as Israel and among the first-generation hardly anyone could afford a car. However, generally, the connections among the first-generation have endured well as I discovered during this research because individuals constantly helped me to follow-up and find Indians living in distant *moshavs* and small towns.

On a micro-level, connections between families have remained strong, and weddings and life cycle rituals bring together cousins, uncles and aunts. This is broadly true whether they are Bene Israelis, Cochinis or Baghdadis. However, since the Cochinis and Baghdadis from Calcutta and Bombay are smaller communities, and have had more inter-marriages, this had diluted some of the traditional family patterns. For instance, among the Bene Israelis, family life still retains many 'Indian' cultural patterns. First-generation Bene Israeli parents continued to speak Marathi or Hindi at home, and their Hebrew-speaking children have a much better familiarity with those languages than those who grew up in Cochini families. Another important point is about modes of address in families. In Indian families, regardless of regional, religious or linguistic variations, modes of address reflect family hierarchies showing respect to elders and different titles for uncles and aunts depending on whether they are maternal, paternal, younger or older than one's parents. This was maintained among the first-generation. For example, Moshe from Jerusalem referred to his older sister as 'Shanti ben' (sister Shanti) and his nieces called his wife *maami* (mother's brother's wife). In Israeli society where everyone uses first names, this practice underwent a sea-change. As the first-generation aged, the young women and men their children dated or married called them by their first names—something unheard of in Indian families even today. It would be considered disrespectful and churlish behaviour. When I asked individuals about how they felt about this their replies were like Noah's who smilingly said ,'*Yahan, Israel mein aisa hi chalta hai*'(Here in Israel, this is how it works), or Eliyahu, who said in English, 'This is the way here, my niece calls me "uncle" but my daughter-in-law is Israeli, she calls me "Eliyahu".' The other practice in family arrangements that bears mention is that of elderly parents living with their children. From being the norm in India, this practice has become the exception, although I did meet women who spoke of their husband's parents living with them in the same household in Ramla, Lod and Ashdod. Frequently, a closer questioning revealed that there had been a gap of several years between the arrival of the two generations in Israel, but had decided to live in a shared household due to economic reasons. In general, the elderly in families are moving to facilities for assisted living. The one in Dimona for instance, already has a few of the very senior Indian Jewish immigrants.

Life cycle rituals followed by the Indian Jewish community reflect a strong impact of the contemporary Israeli culture. Burial rites or periods of mourning (*sheva*) vary only slightly within groups or communities, and those differences are more likely to stem from how religiously observant or orthodox the family is, rather than the ethnicity of origin. For happier occasions like weddings and Bar-Mitzvahs the ethnic distinctions are also on the decline, obviously because most celebrations are becoming commercially catered affairs held at halls which are hired for the party to which guests are invited. The economic status of the family determines the nature of the hired premises, the lavishness of the food, décor and the entertainment programme of music or dancing that may accompany the package of festivities for the evening. However, most first-generation immigrants have memories of weddings held in Israel in the early decades which reflected legacies of the pre-migration days. For instance, when Rachel, a Cochini, was married in 1958 to Amir, also a Cochini living on a *moshav* in the Negev, their wedding was solemnized at the small synagogue on the *moshav*. As a bride, she wore a white Indian *sari* as Jewish brides do in Kerala. The older women of the family together cooked Cochini food for the 250 guests attending the wedding dinner. Rachel today lives on the same *moshav* and her two married children had weddings which were performed by the Rabbi at a wedding hall a few miles beyond the *moshav* and the food was catered. The brides wear white 'Western-style' bridal gowns. Rachel, however, added that among their Cochini friends who live in Nevatim, the pre-dominantly Cochini *moshav*, weddings still retain more of an ethnic flavour because the synagogue in Nevatim is a replica of one in Kerala, and the strong presence of the Cochini community facilitates following traditional customs in food and other rituals.

Discussions with several Baghdadi women who came from India revealed that even in pre-migration days Baghdadi Jews living in Calcutta or Bombay had weddings which reflected a high degree of 'Westernization'. Brides wore white bridal gowns and men wore suits. The well-off families hosted the occasions in hotels and Western music performances were an important accompaniment of the feast. Lower income families had festivities on a smaller scale limited to their family only but most weddings were performed by the *rabbi* in a synagogue. Thus, post-migration weddings among the Baghdadis did not undergo major transformations, although in keeping with current trends, wedding ceremonies are also being held at halls rather than at synagogues.

It is among the Bene Israelis that life-cycle rituals, especially weddings, show a distinctness and cultural character which is a blend of Jewish and the 'Indian' presenting a mix of colour, music and ritual in the observances, which I as a non-Jewish Indian found fascinating. In 2007, in Ashdod, I saw a bride being given a handful of rice to throw over her head 'back' into her parental home, symbolizing a daughter's severing of ties with her parental home to begin a journey of embracing her husband's family as her own. This was a familiar ritual I had seen dozens of times at Hindu weddings in India. A few months later, in Lod at the home of Hana and Hannan I saw the video film of their daughter's wedding where a *mehndi* ceremony was held a day before the Jewish wedding. The *mehndi* ceremony is a widely popular pre-wedding festivity in India (among Hindus and Muslims) when the brides palms are decorated with intricate patterns of henna paste.[9] Traditionally, involving singing and dancing by the bride's women friends and female relatives, *mehndi* has become a trendy fun evening usually on the eve of the more formal religious wedding the day after. The video recording of Hana's daughter's *mehndi* ceremony showed me the spectacle of a lively celebration with most people dressed in bright Indian dresses, dancing to the tune of Indian Bollywood film/pop music and the bride being carried in an improvised 'palanquin' quite like a 'princess'.

Watching Hana's daughter's *mehndi* and wedding party on the video in an old apartment in a poorly maintained immigrant building in Lod, was a very interesting moment in this fieldwork. It sharpened my sense of how acculturation and assertions of identity operate in complex ways in diasporic communities. Hana and Hannan had both come to Israel as children, who met and married in Israel. Their Hindi was rusty but functional for this interview. Their children however, barely knew a few words of Hindi. It made me starkly aware that most young people in the video dressed in Indian clothes and dancing to the energetic rhythms of Hindi songs, had never been to India, they were 'Indian-Jewish-Israeli', barely understood a few words of what they were dancing to. Yet, ethnic and cultural assertions were clearly important. Other weddings among the Bene Israeli community which I attended also broadly replicated a wonderful blend of ethnic and religious elements. The wedding ceremony was Jewish, but the celebrations around the wedding, the colours, the music, the food and other expressions of culture surrounding the wedding carried unmistakable markers of ethnicity. At a wedding in Dimona where one parent was Bene Israeli and the other Algerian, the wedding celebrations were preceded by the *mehndi* or 'hina' party which combined North African and Indian elements in the ceremonies, music and food. Experiencing multiple ethnicites is common for all young Jewish Israelis, including those of Indian origin.

The economics of weddings can be extremely daunting. Since weddings and *mehndi* ceremonies in Israel today are almost entirely catered affairs as working women have little time or energy to do in-house preparations, some individuals have floated small-scale enterprises to service community needs. For instance, Moshe and wife Ofra of Dimona offer catering of Indian *samosas*, *vadas* and so on, which can be served as appetizers before the regular dinner party menu is served. Ofer and his wife Esther, who live in Petah Tikwa, have an 'event-management' service and plan and execute the *mehndi* ceremony for families. They bring traditional Indian *saris* and textiles to decorate the location, a 'palanquin' to carry the bride, brightly painted traditional earthernware pots, flowers and other bric-a-brac that re-creates an 'Indian' ambience and transforms a dull hired hall into a colourful 'Indian' scene with blaring Hindi melodies and wedding songs—a heady, irresistible mix for a fun evening! The economics of the wedding has yet another aspect. These weddings are expensive. Several of the parents gave me figures between 65,000 and 80,000 shekels spent at a wedding which would include 200–300 guests. Many first-generation families are unable to spend this kind of money for two or three children from their savings. The general custom therefore, is for guests to give presents in cash (200–400 shekels, given in an envelope by a couple who attend the wedding dinner). This helps the host family to defray the expenses of the wedding dinner. The expenses are shared by the two families. Among Indian-Israelis today, the bride's family no longer has to bear the entire financial burden of the wedding-day celebrations—a practice which is still the norm in India, across class and religion.

Religiosity and 'Jewish-ness'

Nurit Koletkar (*b.* 1950) came from Bombay in 1969 and is a strictly observant Jewish woman. She was pregnant with her first child when she made *aliya*. They were sent to Ashkelon where she bore four sons between 1970 and 1983. For some years now Nurit is strictly observant and prays three times a day.

My husband and my sons all wear the *kippa*. In our early years, we were less strict about observing the *Kosher* diet regulations, because it was hard to make all the lifestyle changes to a strict routine.... From Ashkelon, we used to have to go to Gaza for our shopping.... I had all kinds of friends—religious and non-religious.... Some years ago, my second son Ofer had a very serious road accident in Ashkelon. His recovery from it made him religious. Under his influence, other family members also became religious. We took classes in understanding our religion. Ofer's father-in-law was very religious and used to lead the prayers in a synagogue and through the family's influence we too have become increasingly religious. All my daughters-in-law wear the headscarves. We wear only skirts (not trousers) and even my little grandsons wear *kippas*. My son Ofer does not even have a television because among Orthodox Jews that too is disapproved of, but he does have a computer for his children. My second son's family do have a TV but watch only Channels 1 and 2.

Nurit and her ailing husband now live in a rather poorly maintained old immigrant-housing building in Yehud, not far from Ben Gurion airport. As a retiree Nurit enjoys saving up to go for Indian community cultural shows and loves Indian music and dance. Although she does not watch television on *Shabbat*, in general for her the Zee TV (Indian programme beamed through cable channels from Dubai) are an everyday need for social well-being. In this respect, she is like thousands of Indian Jewish families especially the retirees, who love watching Indian television programmes for a few hours every evening, whether in Hindi or Marathi.

Dani Bamnulkar (*b.* 1958, Karachi) came in 1971 at the age of twelve in a Youth Aliya group along with his brother who was fourteen then and his sister who was fifteen. They grew up in Israeli boarding schools for immigrant children until their parents were able to join them in Israel, after which they lived in immigrant towns in the north. Dani studied only up to high school and has made a modest living in Israel as a worker in fixing furniture. Dani is religious, more strictly so than his family was in India. 'In India the synagogues were very far and it was difficult to keep the *kashruth* laws', he said. When I questioned him about his attitude about God and Providence, he said that he become religious only a few years ago, after an incident when he believed he escaped death by sheer coincidence. He explained:

Twelve years ago I was on my way to my shop in Tel Aviv and was to take a bus to Dizengoff Street at a certain time. My son insisted that I accompany him and drop him to school that day. Consequently, I missed that 9 a.m. bus. A few hours later we heard that there was a bomb blast in that bus which killed several people. I felt that God's hand had prevented my death and given me a new life. Since then, I became a *namaazi*.

Although Dani's and Nurit's case sounds 'episode-triggered', there were many interviewees from the first generation who spoke of having become more observant and stricter about following Jewish dietary and other injunctions in the past fifteen or twenty years. Yaacov, who came from Bombay in 1952, and his wife Nora, who now live modestly as retirees in Petah Tikwa, have also become devoutly Jewish in recent years. He began to wear a *kippa* and she has turned to wearing long-skirts and headscarves. Among some families, one or two siblings are strict about following Jewish injunctions while others are not. Diana from Ramla who always wears a head-scarf which totally covers her head and wears long skirts as other Jewish orthodox women in Israel, explained that two of her sons had become deeply religious and had joined the *yeshivas* (Jewish seminaries), which gave them exemption from the mandatory military service, while her other son was secular and had gladly served in the military. Although the degree of religiosity may vary between families (and within families), some Jewish holidays are almost sacrosanct. For instance, fasting on *Yom Kippur* (the Day of Atonement) is widely prevalent, *Rosh Ha Shana* and *Succot* in the Fall months and *Pesakh* are observed nationwide. The state-declared holidays on all Jewish festivals facilitate these observances more than was possible in pre-migration days.

There are a few Jewish customs unique to the Bene Israelis as a community in Israeli society, which bear documentation. Prominent among those is a practice of 'thanksgiving'—a ritual called *Malida* which was (and is) widely observed by Bene Israeli families in India, in Israel, and elsewhere in diasporic locations. *Malida* is a home ritual observed by family and close relatives to mark a special occasion—it could be just before a wedding, the evening after the circumcision of the male infant, a child joining the army or even getting a promotion or a tenured position at work. A *Minyan* is not required for this ceremony and a *Cantor* may or may not be present to lead the prayers. The prayers are in praise of Prophet Elijah as the precursor of the Messiah, and a very highly revered figure in Bene Israeli legends.[10] The *pizmon-Eliyahu-ha-navi* is first read followed by several different blessings quoted from the Bible, the first of which begins with the Hebrew words *vayiten-lecha*. A large plate or salver is filled with roasted puffed rice-flakes (*pawa*), and a mix of nuts and five varieties of fruits. Fresh coconut, raisins, cardamom and sugar flavour this platter of offering. It is decorated with flowers and is offered to the prophet around which the men and women gather to offer prayers and sing songs in praise of the patron saint for blessings or thanksgiving as the occasion demands. After this, the Bene Israelis eat the bowls of rice-flakes and fruit. This is also known as the *Eliyahu-ha-navi* ceremony. Bene Israelis claim that the practice has existed since antiquity although its origins are not clear.

Another point of distinction is that in Israel, the Bene Israelis are the ones most likely to abstain from eating beef. This has historical and cultural roots in that the majority of their Hindu neighbours in India did not eat beef.[11] Over time, Bene Israeli food preferences were shaped by the surrounding culture and they began to prefer chicken and lamb over beef. Many among the first-generation Bene Israelis in Israel still do not eat beef. Another cultural practice among Bene Israeli Jews which was shaped by the wider Hindu ethos in which they lived for centuries was related to widowhood. Widowhood has long been stigmatized in Hinduism as a result of which widows rarely remarried. Among the Bene Israeli Jews widow-remarriage was rare and even after migration to Israel older women of the first-generation do not remarry. Yet another example is the distinct practice relating to *sheva*—ritual observances surrounding death. Among Bene Israelis white is the colour of mourning, as in India. Even after migration, Bene Israelis wear white, although in Israel, Jews whether *Ashkenazi*, Moroccan, Iraqi or Russian wear black as the colour of mourning. Nora, who has been living in a privileged neighbourhood in Haifa for over forty years has little contact with other Indians. Both her children are married to non-Indian Israelis. But on *Yom Kippur*—the Jewish Day of Atonement—Nora routinely wears a white *sari* all day till she offers evening prayers.

Living for centuries in harmony among Indian Hindus, Bene Israelis were undoubtedly more influenced in their tastes and preferences by the surrounding community and cultural ethos. Some of these preferences have remained unchanged in Israel even decades after migration. Interestingly, Dani in his narration quoted above used the word *Namaazi* to describe himself. *Namaaz* is in fact, an Urdu word used to describe the Muslim prayer and therefore, a *Namazi* would describe a devoutly religious Muslim man. His use of the term revealed to me the ways in which language and colloquial expressions for these Indian-Jewish communities in India were drawn from Hindi and Urdu because neither religion was in a hostile relationship with Judaism in the Indian social context. In fact, in a phone conversation with me in Hindi, Yerusha, a woman from Dimona said, '*Mein Shabbat pe girja jaati hoon*'. I go to *Church* on *Shabbat*). Such snippets of language usage were important to unravel. Most of the individuals who spoke in fluent Hindi with me were Bene Israelis. These free-flowing colloquialisms in language use showed that for hundreds of years, Jews in India who had interacted with local languages and local *non-Jewish* communities were not unduly sensitive about adopting each other's vocabularies. Such cultural flows posed no threat to their Jewish identity.

Given that migration from India was all about migrating *as Jews* to the *Jewish Homeland*, some conclusive comments on levels and patterns of religiosity are in order. First, as I travelled across Israel interviewing Indian Jews from different social strata, what seemed unmistakable was that certain factors shaped the levels of religious adherence. For example, the individuals who had done well professionally and had achieved levels of social privilege, or lived away from Indian clustered-communities or had married Jews of *Ashkenazi* origin, were less likely to be strictly religious. Most families, however, did follow traditions and Jewish religious holiday rituals around *Succot* or *Rosh Ha Shana* (the Jewish New Year) but were flexible about *kashruth* and *shabbat*. Friday was about family coming together and siblings congregating in the parental home for a large (and long!) family meal, but it did not necessarily mean not watching television, or switching off telephones, or not driving over to meet friends over the weekend. Today, in places close to Tel Aviv many shops and restaurants are open on *shabbat* unlike in Ashdod or Dimona and of course, hardly anything is open on *shabbat* in Jerusalem. Indians who live in cities where the communities tend to be secular-dominated rather then religious, are just like other secular Israelis. Rachel living in Haifa on the Carmel said, 'I am not very strict about *kosher*. In India my father was a senior officer in the Indian Armed Forces and often we were the only Jewish family in the city and could hardly follow the strict Jewish rules.... I don't mind having milk and meat together. However, I do not eat pork or sea foods that are forbidden by the Jewish religion. We do not observe *shabbat* or go to synagogue regularly.'

During my research, I did not come across Indian Jews who were ultra-orthodox although at synagogue services I was introduced to religious men who when they greet would not shake hands with women, which is otherwise a customary manner of greeting in contemporary (secular) Israeli society. On the other hand, more generally, I can conclude that on a weekly basis, the Jewish *shabbat* is widely observed among the Indian community, although the degrees of strictness may vary. For instance, if I were to host a dinner on Friday night, most of my interviewees for this research would refuse to come because they would not commute on *shabbat* and traditionally choose to stay home and spend the *shabbat* evening with their children and grandchildren. Also, in a non-*Kosher* kitchen like mine, most of them would prefer to eat only vegetarian food.

CONCLUSION

In the years which immediately followed migration to Israel, there were acute dislocations in families which disrupted living arrangements, gender ideologies and the roles that men and women had been socialized to play in pre-migration days. Changes in food, language and climate disrupted the lives of women and men in the initial years of struggle. However, over time, as the Israeli immigrant society stabilized and different ethnic communities settled down, what emerged through the process of mutation were complex forms of acculturation manifested in altered gender ideologies and family arrangements. Although families became increasingly Hebrew-speaking households in which both men and women were employed, in terms of their home lives, most families reverted to former food habits and some life cycle rituals. After years of having to eat bread or 'pita-bread' with boiled vegetables because there were no Indian ingredients available, many Indian Jewish families reverted to cooking rice, *bhaji* and food with familiar Indian spices. Some life cycle rituals they observed around weddings or periods of bereavement also revealed strong markers of ethnicity and cultural metaphors from the society of origin.

What do these practices and religious observances reveal about self-definitions, identity and 'belonging'? When and how do individuals come together to celebrate a shared culture and ethnicity broadly defined as 'Indian'? What are the ethnicity-based Indian organizations in Israel? How do these networks function and how effective are they in community mobilization? Finally, what do all associational and cultural expressions reveal about the need for community affiliation and identity assertion among the Indian-Israelis?

These questions lead us to the last chapter of this volume.

NOTES

1. Nathan Katz and Ellen S. Goldberg (eds.), *Kashrut, Caste and Kabbalah: The Religious Life of the Jews of Cochin*, New Delhi: Manohar, 2005.
2. Shlomo Deshen, Charles S. Liebman and Moshe Shokeid (eds.), *Israeli Judaism: Studies in Israeli Society*, vol. VII, New Brunswick: Transaction Publishers, 1995.
3. Yerusha's parents were already in Dimona. They came in 1963.
4. The state had set up boarding schools which catered to many of the children who had come either in Youth Groups or where new immigrant parents would send their children from the remote *moshavs* and development towns. Yerusha's children went to a boarding school in Ashkelon where there were children from many other Indian immigrant families.
5. When I visited her, she proudly showed me the hi-yield ginger that she was growing—an expensive item in Israel (usually imported from China).

She had a huge tree of Indian 'curry leaves' and two of 'drumsticks'—which are rare to find in Israel and much sought after by Indians for special flavouring in Indian cooking.

6. Women who began in the development towns came broadly from two kinds of family situations: either young wives and mothers who had emigrated with their husbands as a nuclear family or teenaged (or younger) girls who came along with older parents making *aliya*. This seemed to be the pattern whether the families were Bene Israeli, Cochini or of Baghdadi origin.
7. F. Elias and J.E. Coopers, *The Jews of Calcutta: The Autobiography of a Community*, Calcutta: The Jewish Association of Calcutta, 1974, pp. 47–62.
8. Although, by Indian law, widows are free to remarry, Hindu orthodoxies have long stigmatized widowhood and conservative Hindu families continue to exert overt and subtle pressures on widowed women to lead simple pious lives, give up on worldly pleasures and dreams of remarriage.
9. This ritual also known as 'Hina', is also celebrated by other North African Jewish communities in Israel.
10. The legends have it that on two occasions Prophet Elijah visited them and returned to heaven. The first occasion was immediately after the arrival of the Bene Israelis, the coast of Konkan. On this occasion he revivified the unconscious Bene Israelis who swam to the beach from the sea. The second occasion occurred at a much later period. At this visit it is believed, Prophet Elijah also left behind a footprint at the spot from where he rose to heaven. This spot was in the village of Khandala near Alibag close to Bombay where Bene Israelis go to perform religious rituals (not to be confused with a tourist town by the same name near Pune, also in Maharashtra).
11. In Hinduism, the cow is revered as sacred: a 'mother' figure which provides humankind with milk. Hindus widely abstain from eating beef.

CHAPTER 6

Mediating Assimilation and Separation: Community Networks, National Politics and Indian-Israeli Identity

RACHEL, JERUSALEM

In Jerusalem I met Rachel, a Bene Israeli from Bombay who had come here as a young woman, studied at the Hebrew University, worked for several years as a statistician with the Israeli Bureau of Statistics, married an *Ashkenazi* holocaust survivor from Greece and was now living as a retiree. Although she remembered some Hindi, she said she hardly ever cooked Indian food. Living close to a religious Jewish neighbourhood on the outskirts of Jerusalem, Rachel, herself a 'traditional' Jew, could be classified as 'assimilated' into Israeli society. However, as she showed me family photographs of her four grandchildren, she said she had raised her daughters Orit and Talia on Indian bedtime stories from a Marathi storybook that she had brought from India in 1963. Rachel would read in Marathi and translate the tales for her Hebrew-speaking daughters.

SOPHIE, HERZLIYA

Sophie Cohen, a Baghdadi, left Calcutta in 1950 when she was three and started life in Israel with her parents in a *ma'bara* near Haifa. Life had turned out well for Sophie. In 2007 when I met her, she was a grandmother, with three well-educated children living in the posh seaside city of Herzliya. A light-skinned woman of Baghdadi origin, Sophie had married an *Ashkenazi*. She had no links with India and her siblings are scattered between Israel, England and the United States. On our many meetings, Sophie rattled away stories about journeys in Indian trains, hill stations like Darjeeling, even snippets of Indian songs and some smattering of Hindi. Sophie was raised entirely in Israel but her Calcutta-born Baghdadi mother told her bedtime stories which were dramatizations of an India that she nostalgically recalled as 'home'.... Now herself a grandmother, Sophie still cooks *bhaji* and other Indian dishes for her grandchildren when they visit her on *Shabbat*.

SARAH, HADERA

Sarah came from Cochin as a young woman with a degree in science from a university in Kerala. After struggling with Hebrew and forging ahead through many barriers she managed reasonably well-paid jobs and has worked in a software company on a technical job. Her husband also a Cochini, is a landscaping expert and they own a small villa in Hadera, a modest town north of Tel Aviv. In March 2008, Sarah and her friends invited me to a lunch to celebrate *Onam*—a festival widely celebrated in Kerala although essentially a Hindu festival. When I expressed curiosity at their Jewish *Onam* gathering, Sarah said 'We have been talking nostalgically about *Onam* as we celebrated it with our childhood friends in Kerala, and then four years ago, David and I decided to call in a few friends here and do something for *Onam*. Since then, the numbers are growing and our cousins come to join in.' In Sarah's garden, as we sat beside the traditional floor decorations she had made with coloured rice powder and I ate the coconut-based Cochini curries served to me on banana leaves, not only did I forget that I was in Israel but also that to me (a Hindu from north India), *Onam* meant little when I lived in India! Yet, to my Jewish women friends in Hadera, it became an occasion to bond together with Cochini friends along ethnic lines and reconnect symbolically with an Indian past.

In this last chapter, I move this study beyond the work lives and family structures among Indian Jews to explore identity, culture and citizenship. Here I place previous discussions of the migration experience against a broader canvas, to discuss issues of community identity and group mobilization in diasporic contexts.

While gathering information about the economic and social lives of my respondents and how they conducted themselves in families, I came upon several fascinating details about their lives, such as in the excerpts above which I could classify only very broadly as 'cultural'. For instance, how individuals defined leisure: the movies they watched, the music they heard, the television programmes they watched and even the bedtime stories they told their children. Encountering such narratives during the course of unstructured interviews, I saw the need to go beyond factual information and probe through the layers of what constituted people's cultural lives in the broadest sense so that I could understand issues of identity and self-definition. How did people define themselves as individuals or as part of collectives? For instance, when did ethnicity assert itself and how were citizenship and 'belonging' articulated (as Bene Israeli/Cochini/ 'Indian'/'Israeli'). I sought to uncover the linkages between cultural legacies (from India) and acculturation (in Israel) and I wished to analyse how collective self-understanding functioned in a community.

In the years 2007–8 there was remarkable surge in Indian community activities. Many more cultural events were held than I had witnessed in previous years, where the community came together in different towns and municipalities. There were two important reasons for this. In 2007, India marked the fifteenth year since it established diplomatic relations with Israel, and in 2008 Israel celebrated its 60 years of statehood. The former provided an impetus to Indian Embassy-sponsored activities and the latter inspired many resident communities in Dimona, Be'er Ya'aqov Kiryat Bialik, Kiryat Gat to organize Indian cultural programmes in their respective cities with the support of their municipalities— some of these cities were staging Indian programmes for the first time or at least after a gap of over ten years. This surge of programmes was further boosted by an increased interest in Indian popular culture and Bollywood film music among second and third generation Indian Jewish youth. Many of these young Indian *Sabras* (as Israeli-born Jews are called in Hebrew) have neither

Mediating Assimilation and Separation 187

been to India nor do they know the language of their grandparents. Yet, the audience excitement during the shows was palpable. Popular stars from India attract full houses and Bollywood-based musical shows get a rousing applause. This led me to ask questions about how individuals articulated a cultural sense of 'belonging'. Although such enthusiasm for Hindi films and popular music exists among Indian diasporic communities in the UK, USA, Canada and elsewhere, the case of Israel is different. Migration for Indian Jews to Israel was a sharper snapping of ties with the land of their birth (India) because their change to Israeli citizenship was immediate—just upon arrival. Subsequently, state policy and the social environment sought to erase markers of ethnicity and the languages Jews had spoken in the various cultures they were born in. Indeed, the 'ideal' Israeli was the Hebrew-speaking citizen who had learnt Israeli/Hebrew songs and folk group-dances which are taught widely across schools in Israel. How then did these young third-generation *Sabra* girls and boys of Indian origin swing along (and sing along!) to Hindi Bollywood songs when they would have had to make an effort to relate to the words of the lyrics they did not readily understand? How did communities preserve this musical and linguistic heritage? How did they organize themselves along shared cultural traditions in an ethos which sought to homogenize the *olim chadashim* or the 'new immigrants'? Searching for answers to these questions took me to many Indian cultural programmes in cities and towns across Israel where Indian Jews live and where they have active organizations.

Thus, I began examining group activities, patterns of consumption and other preferences, beyond the cuisine people favoured or the languages they spoke. I collated qualitative information from my observations and the fieldwork interviews when men and women had made incidental remarks on being 'Indian', or being 'Israeli' or when they had referred to 'the Indian community'—sometimes identifying as a part of it, sometimes as *outside* of it. I explore what it means to be 'Israeli' or to be 'Indian'. What do people do as a group to experience or show 'Indian-ness'? What activities do they organize/attend and who is included in these activities by way of other Indians (*non-Jewish*) and Israelis (*non-Indian*)? To uncover these complexities, I researched, Indian associational networks and organizations in different parts of Israel and analysed the importance of the Indian cultural programmes in the lives of the community clusters. However, I also wish to take this discussion of identity a step further by asking the following question: if cultural programmes are manifestations of an ethnic affiliation and a sense of 'belonging' to Indian culture or 'Indian-ness', then how does this intersect with being an Israeli and a patriot of the Jewish Homeland? As a researcher, I was aware that apart from Indian networks and their activities, in the case of Israel where religion and politics are so intertwined in people's everyday lives, the political views of an ethnic community were a significant aspect in understanding identity-formation. Thus, other related questions needed to be asked. First, what was the role of Israeli politics and nationalism and how did individuals define or express Zionism? Secondly, how did Indian Jews who had no history of antagonism with Muslim communities in India re-shape their politics surrounded by what state discourses described as 'enemy states'? Thirdly, where did they place themselves within nationalist narratives of Jewish persecution—which they had never experienced? Finally, what did Indian Jews think of Israeli politics and of Israeli occupation—especially the first-generation Indian Jews who had grown up singing the Indian national anthem and had switched to singing the Israeli one post-migration? In fact, the singing of the national anthem became a useful entry point to pose more serious issues of how individuals and groups define and experience national identity and citizenship and how they choose to display or express it. The over-arching question then was: how did all these specific strands enable us to reflect upon issues of identity—nationalist, Zionist and 'Indian'?

These questions frame my discussions in this final chapter.

A NOTE ON METHODOLOGY

Methodologically, this chapter was more challenging than the previous ones. Early on in the research, I realized that there was no ready source containing statistics or even basic facts about the Indian community scattered across Israel. The Israeli Bureau of

Statistics does not collect ethnicity-based demographic data for cities and towns. The municipalities had no official break-up and the mayors I met at Dimona, Kiryat Bialik, Ramla and Kiryat Gat were reluctant to quote exact figures. The Embassy of India, Tel Aviv which has direct dealings with the Indian segments in various cities and towns across Israel also had 'estimates' about the Indian community presence. The community members living in those locations also offered 'estimates'—sometimes conflicting ones. Although Indians have founded networks in many Israeli cities and towns, the information was not documented. The fact that Indian Jews in Israeli society had not been researched comprehensively, although they hold numerous India programmes and run associations, became an important reason for me to collect and *document* available information about the community.

The various elements which constitute this chapter were shaped over an extended period of time. The information about Indian community organizations spread across Israel and the activities they promote, has been systematically collated for the first time. My documentation and analysis are based on fieldwork and personal observations at over fifty community-related events during 2005–8—ranging from large events held in Eilat, Ashdod and Lod to those held in small community halls in cities like Kiryat Ata, Kiryat Bialik, Kiryat Gat, and Dimona, or in the open-air as in *moshav* Nevatim or simply in gatherings after synagogue prayers.[2]

The discussion below begins with information about Indian communities and their associational activities in different parts of Israel. This is layered with a critique of major organizational efforts and their issues of leadership, funding and so forth. How do these scattered associations function and interact? How do they deal with key issues like gender, finance and leadership? How successful are these initiatives in community mobilization, and why are they not *more* successful and politically visible than they are? The following section discusses 'Cultural Programmes' that are held in dispersed locations. This analysis of cultural programmes as staged and conscious manifestations of ethnic identity becomes an entry point for me to examine the intersection between an ethnic-'Indian' identity and nationalist-'Israeli' identity. The next section then, is on 'Nationalism, Politics and India' in which I analyse how individual articulations about Israeli politics reveal what individuals have internalized as a sense of national 'belonging'. I conclude this chapter by placing these discussions in the broader international context where I examine bi-lateral relations between India and Israel, which have an uneven history since nationhood was achieved by both countries in 1947 and 1948 respectively although Indo-Israeli cooperation has been growing rapidly in recent years.

INDIAN JEWISH ORGANIZATIONS: GENDER, COMMUNITY AND LEADERSHIP

Collecting data about Indian organizations across Israel was challenging. Although community leaders knew of each other (at least among the Bene Israelis) cooperation between networks was uneven and very sporadic. For instance, those in Dimona and Yarukham knew others in Ashdod or Lod, but they had almost no contact with associations in the north as in Kiryat Bialik. Moreover, despite long years of networking and activities, organizations did not have comprehensive records about their founding, and so forth. Individuals willingly offered information about their own limited areas and were appreciative that it would be documented, but the data presented below had to be collected in person, through interviews conducted on location in cities across Israel—from *moshavs* like Kfar Yuval near the Lebanese border in the north, to Nevatim in the Negev desert, and Eilat at the southernmost tip touching borders with Egypt and Jordan.[3]

Broadly speaking, community mobilization of Indian Jews in the decades since their arrival in Israel has witnessed many offshoots. The 1950s and 1960s for most seemed to be overwhelmed with a struggle for survival during which the community usually gathered around synagogues in the neighbourhoods where they lived. Some like Hanna and Hannan, who were teenagers growing up in a *ma'abarot* near Haifa, remembered that Indian families used to flock to watch the Hindi films that were screened by the municipality in a cinema hall on Friday evenings. Those were days of intense physical struggle and little leisure. As the years passed by, many Bene Israelis who had been in white-collar jobs in banks and government offices in India felt the need to organize themselves in Israel. A major impetus was provided by the controversies that emerged regarding the 'purity' of Bene Israelis as Jews. The Bene Israelis were enraged that their harmonious adjustment in the Indian cultural ethos which was reflected in their language and some Jewish rituals, was being used to target their Jewishness as suspect. The protests of the community against discrimination by the rabbinate, is today reminiscent of the situation of recent Russian immigrants.[4] Although these controversies of the 1950s deserve a separate research paper, here I wish to argue that the protests became for the Bene Israelis, a plank on which to organize in common cause as a community across Israel. In 1963, a certain Divekar of Jerusalem was the main initiator of what emerged as the Federation of Indian Jews which became the precursor of the present-day Central Organization of Indian Jews in Israel, discussed below.

I wish to note that at the many community programmes I attended across Israel, the Bene Israelis were at the forefront—as organizers and participants. The only exceptions were at Nevatim which was a Cochini initiative and at Kiryat Bialik where the local Bene Israelis and Baghdadis (from Bombay) collaborated. I examined some of the underlying reasons for this and several possibilities emerged. For one thing, the Jews from Kerala remain close-knit groups *within* their *moshavs*, and have relatives and friends elsewhere in cities but are not in large clusters in cities and towns. They also have a high rate of inter-community marriages, whereby only one partner is of Indian origin which perhaps dilutes the urge for ethnic affiliation. Thus, unlike Bene Israelis, Kerala Jews do not have prominent formal associations which hold cultural programmes and command visibility. The exception to this is the community from *moshav* Nevatim, which I discuss below. The case of the Baghdadis from Bombay and Calcutta is yet a different one. Some Baghdadis are loosely affiliated with the Babylonian Jewry Heritage Center (*Maghen Aboth Le Yehudei* Calcutta) in Or-Yehuda, near Tel Aviv, but in fact, many do not identify with the Jews who migrated from Iraq to Israel after 1948. They prefer to be identified as 'Baghdadis from Calcutta/Bombay' rather than 'Iraqi'. There is a subtle projection of superiority when this identity is assumed as many who came from India believe that their English education and anglicized socialization in India gave them an edge over the Iraqi Jews who came to Israel.[5] The 'Westernized' socialization shaped the cultural identity of the Baghdadis from Calcutta in yet another way. Unlike the Cochinis who bond around Malyalam or the Bene Israelis who bond around Marathi and Hindi, the Baghdadis who had lived in India, had links neither with Arabic nor any of the Indian languages. Speaking English and growing up with Western popular or classical music, they did not have an ethnicity to invoke through a linguistic culture which other Indian Jews did. This also explains why group mobilization around a shared linguistic culture including music and dance is much more successful among the Bene Israelis.

Indeed, the Bene Israelis are the group that engage most prominently in organizational activities in Israel compared to the Cochinis and Baghdadis. Even in areas where the community is small and of modest means, they gather to celebrate festivals or observe Jewish holidays together and have an association of sorts. In general, it was obvious that the synagogue which had served as the nucleus for networking in the early days after migration, continues to be an important conduit to disseminate information among the community, even after well-organized associations have emerged—with officer-bearers, fund-raising and other hallmarks of formal associational activities. What emerged clearly through this research was that cities and towns which have clusters of Indian Jews do have functioning organizations. At the most basic level, they meet and celebrate Jewish holidays together usually at their own Indian synagogues, of which they are very proud, and to which they donate generously.[6] The association raises its own funds and seeks support from the municipality when it seeks to organize a large cultural programme. Such programmes are staged at community halls and are modestly ticketed—between 25 and 50 shekels. The halls may be hired or given free by the mayor's office, which may sometimes also subsidize programme costs by paying the artistes and performers, so that the funds from the sale of tickets become part of the synagogue funds.[7] Theoretically, many of the community organizations have trust funds which are meant to support activities or give student scholarships to children from the community. However, interviews revealed that in their current status most trust funds had no money and activities had to be contributory. Individual members also expressed unhappiness at the handling of trust funds hinting that office-bearers had used them arbitrarily without wider consultations with community. Many Indian associations have their own sports activities—mostly amateur level football and cricket teams.

Broadly speaking, the Central Organization of Indian Jews in Israel (COIJI) functions as an umbrella organization. It was established in 1986. It has 29 branches all over Israel. Individual Indian community associations across Israel either function independently or are loosely affiliated to the COIJI through local resident representatives.[8] The COIJI has its stalwart membership comprising first-generation Indian Jews in the Ramla, Lod, Ashdod and Dimona areas. Programmes held in these locations draw the most committed audiences including those who are scattered in nearby *moshavs* or newer cities like Rehovot, Rishon or Holon which lie on the fringes of central Israel. The annual *Hodu-yada* organized by the COIJI draws Indian Jews from across Israel. Although for such programmes scattered associations collaborate, the relationships between them remain uneven, depending overwhelmingly on personality issues.[9] Although there is a second-generation woman on the committee, it remains a male-dominated organization.

Women have their own organizations, although not in every city where there are Indian community clusters. The oldest one is the Indian Women's Organization, Lod. In 2007, it had 53 active members. Three of its founding members are still around to tell its story and as a tribute to them I wish to identify them by their real names: Sophie Benjamin (*b.* 1924), Becky Isaac (*b.* 1924) and Elizabeth Joseph (*b.* 1928) are proud of this network which they narrated was also founded to spread Indo-Israeli awareness and friendship, even before the Indian Embassy was set up in Israel.

The women of this association wanted to spread awareness about India, since many of them had encountered negative stereotypes about India as they began to settle into the Jewish Homeland. Elizabeth David who has long been an office-bearer in the organization said, 'This was our way of showing our love for Mother India'. Since younger women are working, most regular activities are attended by women who are pensioners. Aside from group activities like yoga classes and Indian music, they have also attended skill-enhancement programmes through which many have now become computer literate. Given that several of these women had done secretarial training in India and many have retired after long years in office jobs in companies like Telerad and Israeli Aircraft Industries, it has not been difficult for them to attain computer skills. The members have a strong commitment to fundraising for their synagogues. The women's organization has other chapters in Beersheva, Ashdod and Ramla. Smaller *mahila mandals* (women's groups) also exist in Dimona and elsewhere in northern Israel where there are clusters of Indian communities but the Lod and Ramla-based women's groups maintain a higher profile. In fact, these groups are important supporting pillars for the *Mai Boli* journal in Marathi brought out by a section of the Bene Israeli community (discussed later). Indeed, in terms of organizing activities for its members the women's organization at Lod is the most visible. I first met a large number of the women from Lod at the Republic Day programme at the Indian Ambassador's residence in January 2006. The women were all around sixty or older and had hired a bus to commute some 50 km from Lod for the 9 a.m. Indian flag-hoisting ceremony. They were dressed in colourful *saris* and many enthusiastically sang along the Indian national anthem that they remembered from their schooldays in India. Subsequently, I met several women and attended their programmes. I attended a special programme that was held on 8 November 2007 at the Synagogue Hall, Eli Cohen Street, in Lod. This was an annual ritual *malida* ceremony which the women's network had organized just before the Jewish New Year to pray for blessings for all in the coming year. There were just a few male invitees that evening. It was totally a women's evening and the *khazan* and rabbi were invited by the women.[10] I was the only non-Jewish attendee and the organizers warmly welcomed me announcing that I was going to document their stories!

Community organizations are registered as non-profit organizations and function independent of each other. At any given time much depends on the enthusiasm of the committee. Below I present an overview of these community efforts being carried on in dispersed locations. This was last updated in September 2008.

INDIAN JEWISH COMMUNITIES:
ACTIVITIES IN DISPERSED LOCATIONS

In the major cities, Jews of Indian origin are scattered like Israelis of other ethnicities. In the Jerusalem area Indian Jews remain dispersed and estimates of numbers were not available. There are two Indian synagogues in Jerusalem—one in Katamon which is of the Cochini origin, and the other in Pisgat Ze'ev which is of Baghdadi origin.[11] There are three Indian restaurants in Jerusalem—two of which are *Kosher*. A prominent member of the Indian community in Jerusalem, Noah Massil, also a long-term President of the COIJI, issues the Marathi brochure-journal called *Mai Boli*. The Israel Museum in Jerusalem has a section dedicated to the Jews from India, with artefacts contributed by the Indian community. A synagogue from Cochin called the 'Pardesi Synagogue' was brought out piece by piece and rebuilt as a replica in the museum. The culture of Tel Aviv and its surrounding neighbourhoods is structured more around social and economic class than around ethnicity. Indian Jews whom I interviewed in areas around Tel Aviv or the privileged Carmel in Haifa or even Jerusalem, were not active participants in community events. Thus, I collected community-related information from cities and *moshavs* where Indian Jews live near each other or choose to socialize with other Indians in a shared bond of ethnicity, language or culture. In the list below, I have included places with an active Indian ethnic presence whether that may be manifest in the local associations, cultural programmes, Indian shops or restaurants. For better clarity, I present the data regionally. (For specific locations see Map of Israel in the Appendices.)

The South

In Beersheva, the Indian organization started in 1978 with six members. The local Indian community then was around 2,000 people. Today, Beersheva has an Indian Jewish community of about 10,000 people. There are five Indian synagogues and a sixth one is in the making. There is one central cultural centre for the Indian community called Tifferet Yehoshua and one for younger members called Shiluv Asarteev, which organizes community events. For three years now, they have held Indian cultural programmes annually at which the Indian Ambassador and members from the Beersheva municipality are guests of honour. Beersheva has three Indian cricket teams and a football team. There are five Indian shops which sell spices, condiments, and Indian music CDs and DVDs of the latest Indian films. There are two Indian restaurants. The women's organization at Beersheva has close links with its counterparts in Ramla and Lod and they attend each other's events.[12] The community is also making efforts to set up a museum of Bene Israel Jewry, but funds and space have yet to be procured from the municipality.

Nevatim,[13] an agricultural village was originally populated entirely with Jews from Kerala, and is still popularly known in Israel as a 'Cochini *moshav*', although inter-ethnic marriages and new residents have diluted this ethnic Cochini domination. In sustaining an ethnic identity, Nevatim is a model. The Cochini Synagogue and Museum are the pride of the *moshav* and the Jews from Kerala proudly show it off. The synagogue is a replica of a synagogue in Cochin. The community raised funds and even procured a Torah from the original synagogue and installed it in Nevatim. The museum was set up in 1996 with community donations and some seed money from the Israeli state. It is clearly a labour of love and ethnic pride and has objects reflecting everyday life food, dress, rituals and material culture of the Jews of Kerala. About half of Nevatim's residents are still agriculturists, while others work in the neighbouring Beersheva and Dimona.

In 2006–7, when I visited Nevatim several times for cultural programmes and interviews, the erstwhile flower-export business had declined in the face of competition from East Africa in the global flower market. To spark off some economic activity, the Israeli government is encouraging ethnic-related tourism urging Cochini families to open guest-houses and offer ethnic food to generate economic activitiy for the community. Nevatim's exploration of alternative economic models and offering domestic tourists 'a Cochini experience' is giving impetus to ethnic pride.[14] Nevatim has a community newsletter distributed electronically within the community. The children are taught Indian dancing and represent the *moshav* in national cultural programmes. A restaurant serving Cochini food caters to tourists. Although Cochinis are scattered elsewhere in Israel, Nevatim has become a symbol of the Cochini community and an ethnic showpiece for the Israeli government. Its synagogue, museum and preservation of an ethnic flavour have attracted visits from top Israeli cabinet ministers, especially those dealing with agriculture and immigrant absorption.

Kiryat Gat has a total population of over 2,000 Indians—mostly Bene Israelis. Although Indian families have long had get-togethers, formally they have had little visibility, mostly due to fund-raising issues, given the low income levels in the region.[15] The Kiryat Gat association, *Amutat Tzedek* which became active around 2005 has a local focus. Its objectives include, 'uniting the Indian community... encouraging integration with other communities... assist financially weak families and new immigrant families in the community... to preserve folklore, tradition and culture of the community (it arranges Indian dance classes)... and to improve the self-image of the community'.[16] The cultural programme I attended in April 2008 to mark Israel's sixtieth anniversary, was the first large-scale cultural music and dance concert that the community had staged in all these decades since migration. Without ample financial support from the muncipality, the community could not have sustained it.[17] There is also a women's organization, which was set up in 1993. Kiryat Gat also has three Indian synagogues and two Indian shops.

Dimona has a concentration of about 5,000 Indian Jews. Among this community, it is easy to get by speaking any of the two Indian languages—Hindi or Marathi. The Indian community in Dimona is active in organizing Indian cultural programmes, but demographically a large number of them are pensioners whose children have moved elsewhere to study or work. Economically, the community is middle to lower income level.[18] For several years, the deputy mayors of Dimona have been of Indian origin although there has never been an Indian mayor.[19] In 2008, the Indian community in Dimona proudly staged a dramatized story-version of the popular Hindi film of the 1960s *Sangam*, a love-story known to many Israelis. The city hired a professional director but the actors were amateurs, predominantly local Indian men and women, who all performed in Hindi, while Hebrew translations were displayed on the screen above. The event was enthusiastically received and featured in an article in the national print and electronic media. The Indian community in Dimona has recently been allotted a modest space by the municipality for a museum.[20]

Eilat, which is a port-city and seaside resort on the southern tip of Israel, employs much of its working population in the tour and travel industry or at the port. In interviews with Eilat community leaders in January 2008, I discovered that Indians who worked widely in hotels in Eilat worked at various levels from cooks and helpers to managers. In my discussions with the community members it emerged that they considered their experience in Eilat to be somewhat different from the way the Indian community had experienced acculturation elsewhere. As Yehuda told me, 'In Eilat, Indians have always been in demand in the travel industry and at the port. . . . They are valued for being respectful, polite and well-behaved. . . . We do not have the same problems of assimilation as others may have told you because in Eilat there are no 'ethnic neighbourhoods' . . . my neighbour can be from any ethnicity and his neighbour may be from a different ethnic group. This helps assimilation'. *Sitar* (named after the melodious Indian string instrument), the Indian Jewish organization of Eilat, exuded a different air in that it appeared more well-knit and cohesive than in other cities. The Indian Jews in Eilat are more isolated because distances prevent them from attending Indian community programmes elsewhere in Israel. There are about 500 people of Indian origin—almost all are Bene Israelis. There is no Indian synagogue and Indian Jews live and worship alongside their neighbours from other ethnicities. This is in sharp contrast to Ramla, Lod, Dimona and Yarukham where the ethnic cluster model is far more pronounced.

The North

Unlike the arid Negev, northern Israel has several fertile stretches where agricultural villages thrive. Around the city of Rosh Pina there are agricultural *moshavs* where many Jews from Kerala were settled. The Indian Jewish community in Rosh Pina consists of about 25 people, mainly Cochini. However, in neighbouring councils a few kilometres away, there are Indian community clusters which give the surrounding *moshavs* the common association of being 'Cochini areas'. Near Rosh Pina is Hatzor, where about 40 Indian families live (approximately 200 heads). Yesod Hama'alah,[21] about 15 km away from Rosh Pina, is a small community of about 1,300 people, of which 230 are Indian Jews. They are mostly agriculturists and have a synagogue of their own. The Indian group has a presence in their City Council. About 45 km away from Rosh Pina is Kfar Yuval, a *moshav* with about a hundred families, *all* of whom are Indians from the Cochin area. This agricultural community has its own synagogue and an Indian restaurant on the *moshav*.

There are no exclusive Indian associations or community activities in these places surroudning Rosh Pina, on account of the smaller numbers and integration through marriage, but members are active and have influence in the wider inter-community context.

North of Haifa are Kiryat Yam, Kiryat Haim, Kiryat Ata, Kiryat Bialik, and Kiryat Motskin which are collectively called the 'Krayot'. The Krayot initially accommodated new immigrants who were to work in agriculture and industry in the Haifa region which with its port, oil refinery, and other industries provided a potential hub. The area has low opportunities for upward mobility and the population of each varies between 40,000 and 50,000. Out-migration from the Krayot is common among its young people in search of better jobs. Of the five Krayot, Indian origin presence is more pronounced in Kiryat Ata and Kiryat Bialik.

Kiryat Bialik presents a very unusual picture of the Baghdadi, Cochini, and Bene Israelis—sharing the same synagogue, which they began to build in the early 1950s with modest means and their own humble contributions while they were still struggling new immigrants. From time to time, they organize Indian cultural events. The Indian community in Kiryat Bialik consists largely of pensioners but some second-generation have done well.[22]

Kiryat Ata has approximately 200 Indian families. There is one Indian synagogue, an Indian shop but no organization. With the growing interest in India, some local community members have taken a private initiative to organize Indian cultural events to which the local mayor and the Indian Ambassador are special guests. In December 2007, I attended an elaborately organized programme of Indian popular music and dance at Kiryat Ata which was planned and executed by a young second-generation Bene Israeli couple who not only perform but also run classes for Indian Jewish boys and girls who wish to learn Bollywood-style dancing.

On the Fringes of Central Israel

The Indian Jewish community in Be'er Ya'aqov consists of approximately 400 heads—mostly Bene Israelis. There is one Indian synagogue which keeps the community connected. It has a hall which can be used for meetings and activities. In the local city council there is a member from the Indian Jewish community.[23]

Ramla and Lod are important cities where Indian Jews, mostly Bene Israelis, built-up an active and connected community in the 1960s and 1970s. Today, the Indians in these cities are overwhelmingly pensioners who have retired either from the Israeli Aircraft Industry or El Al, both of which are located in the vicinity.[24] The parent generation of Indians in Ramla are active participants in community-related activities. They do not have separate Indian associations but in fact, they form the main support base for the COIJI.

Community members claim that there are approximately 3,400 Indian-origin Jews living in Ramla, of whom 20 per cent are pensioners and approximately 8 per cent are soldiers. There are three Indian synagogues, four spice shops, one Indian *mithai* (sweet) shop and two Indian restaurants. They have a basketball, football and cricket team. The cricket team is the best in Israel. Ramla has several Indian dance groups. The community has managed to make this a recognized activity in the Municipality and dance classes are held in the municipal premises. Two prominent groups are *Naach* (dance) for the age-group of 15–19 years and *Bharat Dance* (Indian Dance) for those over nineteen. The Indian women of Lod have an active network which uses the Indian synagogue for their gatherings. The Indian synagogue has a synagogue hall for their meetings—which is not common in other locations.

Lod has approximately a thousand Indian families. It has the largest and the most active women's organization. There is one Indian shop and five Indian synagogues which are centres for community interaction. The Lod community does not have an active local association although its residents are active in COIJI activities and events.

Ashdod has the largest concentration of Indians, estimated by community leaders to be around 15,000. Exact numbers are difficult to ascertain on account of two reasons: inter-marriages and changes in names (from Indian last names to Jewish ones). Indian Jews were settled here from the early 1960s and as a development town Ashdod has fared far better than for instance, Dimona and Yarukham. In Ashdod, Indians have a representative in the City Council, who is affiliated to the religious Shas party. Ashdod has six Indian synagogues. The municipality of Ashdod offers some support for Indian community programmes and activities. There are a few Indian restaurants, and more than eight shops selling an assortment of Indian clothes, spices, Indian groceries and so forth.

Young Indian *sabras* born in Israel, are active in the local football teams and also have their own cricket teams. Ashdod is the home of the most prominent Indian dance group *Namaste Israel* (discussed below). There is also a group of musicians and singers called *Lakat Haverim*. The women's association in Ashdod runs an active support network for themselves. Some second generation youth have created a website which allows them to correspond and to update the community and to interact among themselves.[25]

CULTURAL PROGRAMMES

The forty-odd cultural programmes which I attended between 2005–8, followed a standard pattern almost like a template. They were based on music and dance. They would be scheduled commonly on Thursday evenings—the beginning of the Israeli weekend and would start anytime between 7.30 and 8 p.m., usually some thirty minutes behind the time that was officially announced! The programmes whether they were held in Dimona, Kiryat Ata or the large city of Ashdod presented variations in scale, levels of performance, quality of stage production, size of audience, but little variety in content or plan. They all began with short introductory speeches by women comperes attired in elaborate Indian dresses and heavy make-up.[26] These women comperes were clearly modelled after Bollywood stars or the hosts of music shows on Indian TV channels. Local community leaders and the special invitees, the local mayor and the Indian Ambassador would be invited to the stage to address the audiences and this would be followed by a ritual of presenting plaques to distinguished members of the local community, including active volunteers of the organization, senior community members who had been among the earliest immigrants in that area or simply a family which is offered collective condolence for a tragic loss.[27] (See Plate 13.) Although when such stage rituals became too long, the audience would get restive for the song and dance to begin, it was clear that these gestures of recognition meant a lot for the individuals concerned. The concerts that followed were loud. Bollywood songs would blare from powerful sound systems in deafening volumes! They were also 'loud' in the choice of colours and stage effects. All performers wore heavily ornate Indian dresses and jewellery replicating the 'glitzy' look of mainstream Bollywood song sequences.[28]

LANGUAGE ASSERTION: *MAI BOLI* (MY MOTHER TONGUE)

In May 2005, I attended the first *Mai Boli* annual programme celebrating Marathi—the mother tongue of those who are from the western Indian state of Maharashtra, the Bene Israelis. Noah Massil, a resident of Jerusalem and a prominent member of the Indian community publishes the Marathi brochure-journal called *Mai Boli* (estd. 1985) which is a quarterly.[29] The committee of *Mai Boli* hold a conference once a year in Lod or Ramla early in May to synchronize with 1 May, celebrated as 'Maharashtra Day' in India.[30] A day-long event is planned from 9 a.m. to 4 p.m. and the Ambassador of India and the Mayor of the town are special invitees at the inauguration.[31] The conference has literary recitations, short skits prepared by members, poems and songs composed and presented by various Marathi-speaking members. (See Plates 7 and 8.) Performers from India are sometimes invited to do cultural shows. The entire proceedings are in Marathi thus limiting the audience not only to Bene Israelis but increasingly to the older generation. In 2005, the programme was attended by a packed hall of over 350 people. In 2008, the committee suffered losses as the numbers dropped to 150.

HODU YADA

The biggest Indian community bonanza I attended is the annual *Hodu Yada*—the mother of all song and dance programmes of the Indian Jewish community. I attended two consecutive ones in January 2006 and 2007 and the first time it was an amazing experience. In Israel, where a majority of Indians are tucked away in the peripheral regions, it requires effort to see the community collectively in significant numbers. *Hodu Yada* was a spectacle that defied that *invisibility*. It is traditionally held in Eilat, a port city and holiday resort, at the southern tip of Israel. As we drove to the gate of a large park which had been taken over by the Indian community, suddenly there were Indians everywhere. Inside the park area were about 2000 Indians, a few hundred seated on chairs watching the cultural performances, others loitering in the areas where stalls were selling Indian snacks, *namkeens*, bangles and such other Indian items. Others were strolling on the far edge of the park which blended with the sands of the beach on the gulf of Accaba. Older men and women just sat around in groups catching up and chatting while the music from the show blared on the speakers all around us. Three retiree women, all above sixty, whom I met at an adjoining table were enjoying themselves immensely because although they live in different cities in Israel, *Hodu Yada* is their opportunity to meet and have a weekend of fun. They come regardless of whether their grown-up children wish to join the celebrations or not. For many Indians this annual event is a welcome escape from the winter in the north or their routine lives elsewhere. Many pensioners commit to it months in advance and save for it. Although Israel is a small country where people do sometimes commute 40 or 50 km away for work, a number of the older generation Indians who were settled in remote towns and *moshavs* across Israel, in fact, hardly travel. *Hodu Yada*, then, becomes a way of reconnecting with other distant relatives or for renewing friendships from older days.

Over the years, *Hodu Yada* has snowballed into more than just a journey to a pleasant port town to attend a cultural day of Indian music and dance. The location and time of year for *Hodu Yada* have a special appeal. Eilat lies at the centre of the Gulf of Accaba flanked by Jordan in the east (about 200 meters away), and the Egyptian border in the west where the checkpoint is about 4 km away. It is a favourite holiday resort for Israelis and the economy of the city revolves around tourism, offering dozens of variously-priced hotels, restaurants and shopping centres in a radius of 3 or 4 km. Its warm and sunny weather in winter is a major draw. The event itself lasts a full day on a Friday and concludes before the Jewish *Shabbat* begins. While the cultural programme continues on the stage, stalls sell their wares. Local Indian entrepreneurs sell everything from Indian fashion jewellery, Indian dresses and typical Indian street-food like *bhelpuri*. Organizationally, it is the biggest event handled by the COIJI and has multiple organizational dimensions. The organization reserves 1000–1500 rooms in five-star hotels in Eilat and each hotel creates an atmosphere of festivity, giving special deals and facilities for a luxurious and fun weekend—a very attractive prospect for many who live middle-class existence all year round. Moshe Binyamin, a senior organizer from Dimona told me that in January 2007, that 90 per cent of the attendees were Bene Israeli Jews while 2–5 per cent were Cochinis. The programme is open to all regardless of ethnicity and now sometimes Moroccan Jews and Yemeni Jews also buy tickets to enjoy the Indian colourful songs, dance and music. It takes several months of organization on the part of the team to fine-tune everything from buses to pick up Indians from far off locations to bring to Eilat and also scouting for Indian artistes and performers to come and perform on an Israeli stage on the seaside at Eilat.

THE BOLLYWOOD APPEAL

Some remarks about the homogenizing appeal of Hindi Bollywood film music are in order. For the Indians Jews in Israel, Malayalam or Marathi may be the distinguishing vernacular languages they relate to. Indeed, the food in Bene Israeli families may use different spices from the Baghdadi or from the Cochini Jews, but the music and dance programmes reflect a definite shift away from the regional Cochini and Marathi songs to a much more homogenized Bollywood-inspired trend. Just as in India, Bollywood music has a pan-Indian appeal across regions in north, south and north-east India regardless of which vernacular language is spoken in the region, in Israel too, second- and third-generation Indian Jews dance and swing to songs in Hindi and mouth words they do not necessarily understand! Further, one cannot minimize the role of technology. Today, videos of Indian films, music albums and DVDs are all available in Israel soon after their release in

India, thus making it possible to replicate dance steps *exactly*. Indeed, some groups of young enthusiasts have emerged to become semi-professional groups which present carefully choreographed performances and are in great demand for the community programmes in different parts of Israel. The dancers are usually young students and hardly earn from these performances. But their enthusiasm to gather, rehearse and pay for expensive costumes reflects the need for community affiliation. These dancers consider it an honour to be invited to Indian Embassy-sponsored programmes. Different groups perform regularly on the Indian Independence Day and the Indian Republic Day celebrations when the Ambassador of India hosts a large reception for all people of Indian origin living in Israel. (See Plates 1, 2 and 12.)

There are numerous dance groups which have been formed by enthusiasts within the Indian Jewish community. Among the most well-established is *Namaste Israel* founded by David Negrekar of Ashdod whose parents and grandparents immigrated from Bombay. *Namaste Israel* dancers are second or third generation Indian-Israelis (mostly young women), in their late-teens or early twenties. They keep up with the latest Bollywood hits released in India and use playback songs to present the dance sequences. The shows are skilfully choreographed (by the founder himself) with dazzling stage-effects. *Namaste Israel* has staged its sophisticated productions at ticketed shows in Israel and at Embassy-sponsored programmes.[32] Other dance groups also exist in Beersheva, Kiryat Ata and elsewhere but their activities are not well-established. Commercially, the demand for dance groups is growing. Among the second and third generation Indian-Israeli families there is a popular trend to set up special dance coaching for young girls from the family who then perform the Hindi song-dances at a family wedding or special occasion. I must emphasize that this expertise is a Bene Israeli phenomenon. The main dancers and choreographers are Bene Israeli, although the groups are innovative and keep adding songs and dances from Moroccan music to their repertoire, hence widening their appeal for other audiences in Israel. (See Plate 12.)

NATIONALISM, POLITICS AND INDIA

If cultural programmes enthuse Indian community groups across generations as I witnessed several times, then community self-perceptions needed further investigation. How did Indian Jews perceive Israeli-ness and Indian-ness and how did they articulate being 'Israeli' and being 'Indian'? Alongside this, I wished to explore their relationship to India (imagined and real). How did they relate to the India they had left, and India in the millennium—a fast emerging global player to which investors are deeply attracted in the international business market.

Finally, to understand a sense of collective identity, I felt it important to raise some questions which would reveal the views of my respondents in the realm of politics. For instance, how did they perceive Israeli politics in terms of the protracted conflict in the region and the many wars in which they or their children have served? In Dimona and Ashdod I met several Indian Jews who were politically inclined and claimed support for Shas, a religious party. In the interviews some claimed to have belonged to the Shinui, which actively advocated that religion should not influence politics. But speaking more broadly, a large number of first-generation Indians Jews stated clearly in questionnaires and interviews that they were 'not actively interested in politics' and did not belong to a political party. Yet, when I engaged with individuals in longer conversations asking them about their views on how the conflict situation in Israel can be resolved, a vast majority responded to such questions with lines which faithfully echoed the mainstream Israeli media discourse about 'We want peace . . . Israel has been making efforts to make peace. . . .' And so forth. In a country like Israel where politics is shaped so overwhelmingly by religion, it was crucial to tease out sub-textual meanings and underlying complexities which shape citizenship, nationality and 'belonging'. I should emphasize that such questions were raised invariably in the last part of the interviews by which time, the respondents and I shared a high level of comfort. By that time, interviewees had discussed their struggles with downward social mobility or their brush with social exclusion and the 'colour-bias' in Israeli society, so discussing Israeli politics with a non-Israeli 'outsider' was no longer a sensitive issue.[33] The articulations on identity, nationalism and 'culture' which emerged through the interviews revealed fascinating ambivalences and complexities. Below I present a summation of this research quoting lavishly from the interviews.

Culturally, being 'Indian' and being 'Jewish' posed no conflict. However, being 'Israeli' and being 'Indian' was more vexed. This bears some analysis. For instance, respondents were comfortable in describing how their Jewish-ness had Indian legacies in its practice and personal preferences. Of course, the Bene Israelis and Baghdadis referred to the practices as *Indian* but Jews from Kerala preferred to use the narrow term *Cochini* rather than the regional (Kerala) or the national (Indian). Cooking regional Indian food or using Indian languages to communicate or wearing Indian dresses to Jewish ceremonies was a matter of personal preference and there were huge variations within the community (even from one family to another) in the degrees to which cultural practices were Indian. This was apparently not problematic. However, being 'Israeli' and being 'Indian' *was* problematic. Among the interviews, the educated ones were most articulate and went to great lengths explaining issues of culture, politics and nationality providing ample examples for me to see how (and in which context) they defined themselves as 'Indian' or 'Israeli'. In terms of self-description relating to national identity, respondents described themselves as 'Israeli' and many as proud Zionists saying: *ye hamara desh hai, Jews ka apna desh* (this is our country, the homeland for the Jews). Indeed, *all* my interviewees referred to their mandatory years in the Israeli military with great pride and were even prouder when they spoke of their sons and daughters who had served the Jewish nation similarly. This is of course, the widely prevalent Israeli position and serving in the IDF (the Israeli military) is seen by Jewish citizens as their duty to their Homeland. However, when discussing Israeli politics, things became more complex. There was a widespread echoing of the nationalist Israeli discourse. Indian Jews who had described living among Muslims in Bombay or Ahmedabad in India, just a few minutes earlier in their interviews, would emphatically state 'Israel wants peace, but what can we do, we can't trust the Arabs. . . .' This was a seamless, uncritical nationalist discourse in which there was little scope for self-critique. Indeed, it must be said that the majority of Jewish citizens of Israel have no contact with any Arab-Israeli town or the Arabs who live in those towns only a few miles away from their own Jewish cities and *moshavs*. The Indian Jews have partaken of this Jewish majoritarian ethos. Even those who lived in Jerusalem widely acknowledged that they had almost never gone to the Muslim-dominated areas of East Jerusalem, which are under Israeli occupation although these alleys and bazaars are a major attraction for international tourists. I also wish to note that although there are several left-wing activist groups in Israel who question Israeli occupation and volunteer at check-points and crossings between West Bank or occupied territories and Israel, I did not come across any Indian Jews in such organizations. In general, Indian Jews were not vociferous in expressing opinions on Israeli politics or the regional conflict which has raged for decades. And I did not hear any serious questioning of Israel's occupation of Palestinian territories.

On the other hand, about inter-personal relations or behavioural culture, many Indian Jews had a clear self-perception about being distinct. So when they spoke about personal etiquette in inter-personal relations or workplace behaviour, the majority of first generation Indian Jews had strong views about 'Indian' *vs.* 'Israeli' ways. In this, they clearly posited themselves as *outside* the Israeli norms often asserting that 'Indian' ways were *superior* (polite and respectful) compared to behavioural norms in the surrounding society (as 'rude' and 'pushy'). Thus, in observing etiquette or deference to elders in the family and so forth, there were sharp lines that were drawn to distinguish 'self' and 'other'. 'Indian' ways were proudly put forth as more 'cultured' as opposed to 'crude' behaviour which they had encountered in everyday life in Israel. Thus, when describing 'Israeli' ways, first-generation Indian Jews frequently dissociated themselves from certain norms of behaviour especially when they described how they wished (or did not wish) their children to be. For example, Rachel and

Sally, two Baghdadi women from Calcutta, who have married *Ashkenazi* men looked back on their child-raising years in Israel:

We demanded more respect, and propriety.... Our children's friends were not being taught the same values about respecting authority and respecting parents.... I often clashed with my teenage children and my husband because I found it difficult to accept 'what normal Israeli kids do'.... in particular, the late night going out at 11 p.m. and returning at 4 a.m. or 5 a.m. made me very uncomfortable.... When I would insist on the children phoning me to tell me where they were, they would say 'You are the only mother who does this.... You are not in India, Mom!'.... But they look back today with much appreciation and we have a mutually respectful relationship.

However, some parents were emphatic in stating that they had consciously tried to inculcate an 'Israeli' spirit in their kids, so they would 'push their way forward'. For example, Sharona Reuben who is an independent scientific consultant living in Herzliya and working for Israeli pharmaceutical companies said:

Of course our Indian culture plays a part in our parenting values, but we have to change with changing times ... we are not as conservative as our parents were yet we are still more conservative than our Israeli counterparts.... Our children are very much Israelis and not at all Indian.... We as Indians are very polite and considerate of the next person and this stopped us at several points in life from acquiring what we deserved, so we try to let our children not be influenced by this so that they may acquire much more than we did.

To collect data from a wider sweep within the community and to understand identity issues in the workplace, I also sought men and women entrepreneurs who were running successful businesses and who had connections with India. Such individuals who had attained professional achievement and social acceptance in mainstream Israeli society and whose struggles with marginalization were behind them, provided some lucid explanations of how 'Indianness' could work as a negative stereotype. With hindsight and experience, such men and women could now analyse these issues with far greater objectivity. Some of their formulations are immensely useful because they provide yet more layers of meaning in this discussion. The two individuals quoted below are successful entrepreneurs, who visit India regularly for work and pleasure and are not disconnected from the Indian community in Israel. Esther who came in 1978 as an educated, smart young woman raised in metropolitan Bombay in a well-connected upper middle class family of professionals, found her life as a wife and mother in the small town of Hadera quite 'traumatic'. 'After Bombay . . . their fastest city here was not fast enough for us!' Alongside raising children Esther gradually built herself a career in marketing for Israeli pharmaceutical companies who dealt with India and with European markets. She now has a successful independent consultancy and actively promotes business between Indian, Israeli and European pharmaceutical companies. Looking back on her struggles this woman entrepreneur remarked:

In Israel *dark* equals *Arab* . . . if you are coming from India, you have to be twice as good to succeed against your *Ashkenazi* competitor. . . . The perception is that Indians can be bullied around. . . . They are good workers but in inferior positions. . . . To some extent Indians have also internalized a racial inferiority from our colonial history. . . . We are seen as *nice, quiet people*.

A similar self-critique of 'Indian-ness' was presented by Jacob who came as a teenager from Bombay and grew up in Lod. Jacob remarked: 'Indians did'nt aggressively make demands for benefits from the Israeli State . . . we are a little timid . . . when there is a conflict or a confrontation we say *koi baat nahin* (never mind).'[34] Jacob believed that this 'lack of fight' and 'lack of push' is also responsible for Indian Jews being poorly represented even in the professions in Israel—a domain in which Indian-origin communities have excelled in many other diasporic situations in the Western world.

It was evident that as a community Indian Jews were very conscious of the negative stereotypes of 'Indian-ness'. In subtle ways, this has shaped the attitudes and self-perceptions of even those who had no direct experience with social exclusion or discrimination. For instance, during the interviews, several individuals chose to tell me that they did not fit the 'typical Indian' stereotype. Men who were successful made remarks like '... Eventually, at my workplace they realized that I knew the job I was doing.' Among women who had achieved upward mobility more than a few remarked proudly how 'In Israel, people say, I don't look Indian', which they took as an unequivocal compliment.

DESTINATION—INDIA!

When Indian Jews spoke about India, almost without exception there was a tone of warmth and appreciation mainly for its cultural and civilizational heritage and the fact that Jews in India did not face anti-semitism. This was a shared sentiment regardless of whether their origin had been in Kerala, Calcutta, Bombay, Ahmedabad or Poona. However, there were differences in the articulation. For instance, for many of the Baghdadis from Calcutta or Bombay who had no community left in India, the memory was frozen in time. For them, India was an imagined entity of colonial cities in which Baghdadi families had lived with other Westernized communities, always somewhat isolated from the surrounding Indian communities in Calcutta or Bombay. Many Baghdadis spoke of 'belonging' to India although many have never returned since they left.[35]

Among first generation interviewees there were others who had never returned to India. They either had no family left in India—like many of the Baghdadis from Calcutta or those from Kerala who over time had migrated almost in entirety (either to Israel or elsewhere). Some were those who came as infants or toddlers and had no active connecting memories of being there. In such cases, when I investigated I found that their older siblings who *did* have memories of their childhood or schooling had in fact been back as tourists. Others who had never returned were those whose economic hardships had prevented them from being able to afford trips to India. In terms of understanding issues of identity and culture an important feature that emerged was that dozens of men and women remarked that their first trip to India after emigration had been after several years—ten or fifteen years sometimes even more. Men and women from lower middle-class families who came to Israel in the 1950s and 1960s did not have the financial means to take vacations to India—or anywhere else.[36] It is important also to stress that Indian Jews who made *aliya* were leaving India *for good*. In that, they were unlike other diasporic Indian communities overseas because to return to India *they needed a visa*. This bears a further clarification. India and Israel did not have diplomatic relations in the years immediately following the establishment of Israel. In principle, India did not support the establishment of a nation on the basis of religion, given its own policy of supporting religious pluralism in domestic politics. Second, India supported Palestinian independence. In fact, in 1947 New Delhi proposed to the Special Committee of the United Nations on Palestine (UNSCOP) the creation of a federal Palestine with autonomous status for the Jewish population. These were hard years for Indian Jews in Israel. In this scenario, getting visas to India entailed contacting consular authorities at Indian embassies either in Europe or closer by for instance, in Turkey. However, after the late 1980s, this paradigm changed. Around 1989–90 some important developments like the dissolution of the USSR and the initiation of the Middle East Peace Process created a significant shift in India's international equations. This changed political framework led to the establishment of diplomatic relations between India and Israel in 1992. With the establishment of the Embassy of India in Tel Aviv, travel between the two countries became easy.

For the past fifteen years, travel to India figures very prominently in the lives of hundreds of Indian Jewish families. Typically, the Bene Israelis visit family and friends and the Baghdadis and Cochinis visit Kerala, Calcutta or Bombay, some taking their children to show them their old schools and childhood haunts combining the trip with visits to India's favourite tourist attractions like the Taj Mahal in Agra and Rajasthan. Bene Israeli families delight in going for shopping to India before family weddings if the budget permits.

Individuals offered different reasons for loving their visits to

India. For instance, Pearl who came in the early 1990s and earns a good salary working for one of the embassies in Tel Aviv, waits eagerly for her annual trip to India. Her sister still lives in Bombay and her vacation is about visiting old haunts, eating *paani-poori* (a kind of street food in India) and refurbishing her supplies of Indian clothes and accessories for her daughter's and her own 'fusion' wardrobe. She even prefers to get her special hair-styling jobs done in Bombay! Dan, a well-off retiree came as a young lad to Israel in 1964. When I met him in January 2008, he was at the Embassy of India Tel Aviv seeking a visa to visit India for six weeks. He has no family there but he goes regularly to catch up with friends. He has been to India fourteen times in the past few years. 'I go back and meet up with my school and college friends. . . . Most of them are scattered in India, in United States or Canada but we meet in India when they come back. . . . My friends don't let me stay at a hotel, I stay with them.' Dan's friends in India are all non-Jewish. He has known them since they were all in their twenties. Despite the passage of time, Dan is very enthusiastic about the friends he 'left behind'. He said another interesting thing: 'I am secular in Israel . . . and don't go to a synagogue. . . . But when I go back to India . . . to my home-city Poona, I go for Friday prayers to the synagogue where I used to go as a child. . . . I sit on the same seat that my grandfather used to sit. . . . I listen to the prayers in the same tunes in which I used to hear them. . . .' Dan's wife is an *Ashkenazi* of Norwegian origin and does not go to India with him. He explained, 'She went with me once. It was very difficult for her. . . . She can't see all the poverty and dirt. . . . She comes back and feels depressed for several days. . . . So now I go alone.'

It is important to note that 'Destination India' attracts not only the Indian Jews but also thousands of other Israelis every year. Nearly 40,000 Israelis visit India each year, many of them for extended stays of six months to a year. Although some of these are for businesses, there is a heavy flow of young Israeli tourists to India, most of whom are backpackers who like to spend several months trekking in Manali or lying on the beaches in Goa—a vacation they take soon after being released from the compulsory years of military service that Israelis are expected to do. For thousands of Israeli youth, India is a favoured destination. At Tel Aviv and Haifa universities and indeed, even in Tel Aviv restaurants and cafes (where many young Israelis work part-time before they complete university education or settle into careers), I struck conversations with many who had toured and backpacked for several months in India. They spoke warmly about their travels and everyday experiences with ordinary people in India. This is a long way from the stereotypes that Indian Jews have long lived with. As Hana, who came from Bombay and grew up in Ashdod said:

In the 1960s and 1970s, India was referred to as a 'dirty' and 'poor' . . . as children we would be teased that India is full of beggars. . . . Now its all changed. Even the newspapers and TV programmes show India in a different way. In the past ten years Israelis are much more curious about India. 'Now even my bosses talk about India, because many of their children have been to India for several months after their compulsory military service. . . . Now they find India exotic and attractive. . . .

My observations in Israel between 2005 and 2008, lead me to argue that various developments in bi-lateral trade and collaborations between India and Israel have shaped and given a significant boost to collective self-perceptions of the Indian Jewish community in Israel. The first-generation who are now active in community organizations express an unequivocal pride in their 'Indian cultural heritage'. Influential Israelis in the world of business, officialdom and defence forces are travelling to India many times a years and are receiving dozens of official delegations and private entrepreneurs from India. Media coverage of all these creates a heightened awareness of India in Israel. It is only fitting that this study of the Indian Jewish community conclude with an Epilogue which provides a summation of some key current developments in terms of Indo-Israeli bi-lateral relations and their impact on both the perceptions of India in Israel and also of the self-perceptions of Indian Jews whose 'home' Israel is.

NOTES

1. Sylvia returned to India first in 1972 with her *Ashkenazi* husband who she said, got 'a culture shock'.
2. As I attended Indian programmes, I interviewed founder-members of organizations, community leaders, mayors and Indian Embassy officials who were special guests at these programmes. From these sources, I collated information, often cross-referring various 'estimates'.
3. Local members of Indian organizations provided inputs about founding of organizations and their activities. Interviews had to be followed up with phone conversations and in rare cases, emails. Sometimes the information provided by different individuals in the same city was contradictory. Thus, I cross-referred and compared various inputs to reconstruct a balanced picture. Hence, the information presented is not necessarily exhaustive, but it is as comprehensive as possible.
4. The Rabbinate directed that Bene Israelis need to be 'converted' especially when it came to marriage with other ethnic groups—for instance, if an *Ashkenazi* wanted to marry a Bene Israeli. This controversy lasted from the late 1950s to about 1962–3.
5. This is ironic because in contemporary Israeli society, Jews from Iraq have done well and have risen to fairly higher positions in officialdom, politics and business.
6. The Indian synagogues are sustained by community donations and there is often a close connection between the synagogue and the association since the membership largely overlaps.
7. For instance, for the Indian community programmes that I attended in Ramla, Lod, Beersheva, Dimona and Kiryat Ata between 2005 and 2007, the hall or the community-centre space had been made available by the local municipality. Local councils also assist by covering transportation costs if a large group from the community wants to attend a Indian Embassy-sponsored programme or the annual Indian programme *Hodu Yada*.
8. Information about COIJI was provided in personal communication and interviews with Noah Massil who has been Secretary, and now President of COIJI for several years. Although I came across some internal criticism about the organizational running of COIJI, Massil's election as President has never been opposed.
9. It is common to hear complaints about the organizers/leaders, although it is less common to see enthusiasm to actually join in organizational capacities. The leadership of the COIJI is still occupied by the first-generation Indians in their mid-fifties or above.

10. I am grateful to the women at Lod, especially to Elizabeth David, the Secretary of the organization for many informative conversations and invitations to their programmes.
11. Information provided by Noah Massil, Chairman of Central Organisation of Indian Jews in Israel.
12. Information provided during interview with Elkana Satamker of Beersheva, 26 June 2008.
13. Information provided by Shahaf Nehemia, Director of River Authority and an active member of the Indian community.
14. An Indian couple has begun to do catering of Cochini food to supply business groups with pre-ordered meals. One couple has begun a small stud farm, maintaining riding-horses for short-stay visitors.
15. Situated in the Negev not far from Dimona, Kiryat Gat has few opportunities for upward mobility. Families who have been there since the mid-1960s have seen limited opportunities for economic empowerment.
16. These were the objectives stated in the introductory remarks to the Indian Cultural programme held at Kiryat Gat on 3 April 2008. Interestingly, from the Hebrew to English translations, the word folklore is used synonymously with the word 'culture', although the latter has strong connotations of exoticization of a culture, with strong echoes from eurocentric and imperial discourses in which non-Western traditions are seen as 'folk'.
17. At the programme held on 3 April 2008, I interviewed the mayor Abraham Dahri who had extended major support to the Indian community in this initiative by providing them funds to pay Indian singers and dancers from across Israel. By itself, the association could not have supported this on the basis of the modestly-priced tickets for the show.
18. A drop in the population of Dimona by the 1980s, reflected the out-migration among the young. Since the 1990s, new immigrants from Russia have been settled in large numbers in Dimona.
19. In March 2007, in Dimona, I interviewed Moshe Binyamin who had been deputy mayor before 2005 and Ofer Talker who has been deputy mayor since 2005. Both were born in Israel.
20. At present this is simply a large room which has been filled with articles from Indian families (from saris and bangles to utensils and paintings from India) to display aspects of material culture and the life of the Bene Israelis.
21. Information gathered from interviews. I am grateful to Eliahu Dekel, a

Cochini Jew whose parents came to the Rosh Pina area in 1950. Dekel continues to live in this area. He is a member of the Labor Party and active in the work of the Jewish Agency.
22. The deputy mayor in 2007–8, Moshe Pinchas is of Indian origin.
23. Information based on personal communication with Shmuel Pazarker, member of the Local Council and also affiliated to Likud party.
24. Many second-generation Indian Jews have chosen to live in nearby cities which are considered to have better economies and amenities like Rishon, Rehovot and Holon.
25. This information was provided by Shalom Ashtamker.
26. Among the audiences Indian dresses were rare—worn either by some of the older Bene Israeli women or women guests from the Indian Embassy.
27. I witnessed two such occasions. In December 2007 at Kiryat Ata, when Avrahamee (Mazgaonkar) Rahamim (b. 1922, Bombay) was presented a special plaque by the Ambassador of India. In April 2008 in Ashdod, when Miriam Peretz, was presented the 'Magen' to condole the tragic death of her daughter Alona Abraham in the Twin Towers tragedy. Her remains were finally brought to Israel in 2008.
28. Some programmes did have performers who sang the slower melodies from the 1960s without any energetic dancers on stage, but those pauses in the otherwise loud levels were few and far between. Indeed, the younger members in the audience were enthralled by the faster dance numbers and applause at the end of each dance would match the energy of the performance!
29. There are 500 subscribers to this quarterly from all over Israel. The cost is NIS 40 a year, which includes postage. This is not issued electronically as most of the elderly in the community are not computer literate. Information provided by Noah Massil, President, COIJI and founder-editor *Mai Boli* (interviewed in Jerusalem, March 2007).
30. 1 May, is celebrated in India as Maharashtra Day. On this day, the state of Maharashtra attained statehood and the Marathi and Gujarati linguistic areas of the former Bombay state were separated. Maharashtra is one of the largest states in India, both in terms of population and area. Its booming capital Mumbai, makes it not only one of the most important states, economically, but also a major gateway for overseas visitors. Annual parades are held at Shivaji Park, Mumbai on 1 May.
31. Tickets cost NIS 80–100 which includes lunch packets from the local Indian restaurant.
32. In 2008, they were the first Indian-Israeli group to perform for audi-

ences in major cities in India, as part of on-going celebrations to mark the sixtieth anniversaries of India and Israel.
33. Posing questions on Israeli politics in conversations with Israelis never fails to generate a lively debate—more often heated arguments. Aware of this, I kept questions on politics for the end of the interviews or for a second meeting if the interviewee was well-educated and articulate. Some respondents agreed to write their views and mail them to me.
34. Today, Jacob runs a successful tour and travel business and has moved out of Lod into a more upmarket neighbourhood.
35. Baghdadi Jewish families from India had a 'scattered migration' which has spread various branches of families between Israel, UK, USA and Canada.
36. Some individuals in their late sixties described some collaborative attempts that had been made to go in groups of ten which enabled them to get the eleventh ticket free! Thus, they would all share out the discount. Since Bene Israelis had relatives in the Bombay region, these initiatives worked well for them, and they could all travel to the same destination.

CHAPTER 7

Epilogue

I began this research to insert the Indian-Israelis into current scholarship and open spaces for comparative investigations of ethnicity and community bearing in mind this unique model of transnational migration. I wish to end this book with some final reflections on questions of identity which are current and relevant today. Given that Israel is not a widely accessible region for extended fieldwork (by international/non-Israeli scholars), I feel it appropriate to offer some thoughts that emerged as a result of my own three-year engagement with Israeli society and during subsequent months in 2009 when I analysed the fieldwork to evolve a comprehensive picture of Indian-Israeli identity and its articulations today in relation to India.

It is without doubt that an enhanced expression of ethnicity and Indian culture is widespread among Indian Jews in recent years. In 2007-8, I witnessed a surge in Indian community celebrations in Israel and there was a distinct sense of cultural pride expressed in all community programmes staged throughout 2008 to mark Israel's sixtieth anniversary.[1] Remote cities in the north (like Kiryat Ata and Kiryat Bialik) or in the south (like Kiryat Gat), where the Indian communities did not have the resources to stage such programmes for several years (if ever), staged cultural shows which became visible occasions for collective ethnic assertion. The excitement among the organizers and participants reflected the importance of these efforts to showcase the talent among the second and third generation Indians to the surrounding communities. It was quite apparent that the presence of the local mayor and the Ambassador of India meant a great deal as the 'official stamp' of status-enhancement.[2] Although the ethnic distinctiveness was being expressed with pride, I believe it is closely linked also to the growing relationship between India and Israel. In Israel, where Jews have migrated from many countries with which their Homeland either has no diplomatic relations or has an ambivalent relationship, the bi-lateral relationship between Indian and Israel today, is I believe crucial in shaping community self-perceptions and some degree of socially expressed ethnicity. Just as in the 1950s and 1960s, their Indian origin bestowed some negative stereotypes on them and thwarted for many, the recognition of their educational degrees, today, the changed global (and Israeli) perception of India, works in subtle ways to influence collective community identities. Thus, a few comments on recent trends in bi-lateral trade and business relations between India and Israel are in order.

Today, the arena for bi-lateral exchanges between India and Israel is wide and varied. Aside from the significant level of military-technical cooperation, the two countries are also building closer ties in the areas of nanotechnology, alternative fuels, agriculture, animal husbandry and space research. In 2005, the Ministry of Science and Technology, India signed an MoU with Israel for jointly funding industrial R&D projects.[3] The latest Israeli Radar Satellite, *Tecsar*, was launched by India on 22 January 2008. The world's first Jewish-Hindu interfaith leadership summit was held in New Delhi in February 2007. The biggest Israeli investors are increasingly getting into Indian markets taking on huge infrastructure projects. In 1992, when Indo-Israeli diplomatic relations were established, the bilateral trade was US $200 million.[4] In 2007, it had reached the level of US $3.3 billion. Israeli investment in India is on the rise. Initially, it was in the IT sector, telecom and pharmaceuticals. In virtually every major growth centre in India like Bangalore, Hyderabad, Pune, there is an Israeli investment presence. Over 2007–8 there have been significant investment flows estimated at billions of dollars, in real estate and infrastructure.[5] Another new trend has been that Indian companies have started investing in Israel. In 2007 for instance, one Indian company invested in a pharmaceutical plant in Israel, another Indian company bought over the largest tyre manufacturer (Alliance Tyres) in Israel, a third took a 50 per cent share in a major irrigation equipment manufacturing company. Media coverage in Israeli press of all these developments is significantly re-shaping the image of India from stereotypes of a 'poor', 'under-developed' country to one where hi-tech and business are booming.

Among the Indian-Israeli community, the majority of older immigrant retirees whom I interviewed, exude calm. As Elizabeth said, '*Vo din bahut tough the ... hamne himmat se nikale*' (Those days were very tough ... we somehow went through that phase with courage and fortitude). They have put behind their turbulent struggles for work and social acceptance. Over the decades, the dust seems to have settled on the turbulence of the early struggles. That generation has aged. Indeed, even among the few who had bitter stories to tell, there was no regret about the migration.

But what about the young Indian *sabras*—the 'Israeli-born children of the Jewish Homeland? What about second and third generations? During the interviews, I met them at their parental homes and I saw them sway to the Bollywood rhythms at the cultural programmes, both as dancers and as audience. They were born in the Jewish Homeland and grew up speaking (and teaching their parents) Hebrew. They are as varied as their parents were— in terms of economic status, educational levels and social class. Depending on the levels of acculturation of their parents and where they were raised in Israel, some understand an Indian vernacular like Malayalam or Marathi. But Hebrew is overwhelmingly their first language. While their parents sustain Indian organizations in Israel, the Indian *sabra* children are only tangentially involved. Some have visited India—the childhood home of their parents. Young Bene Israelis visit distant cousins in Bombay and more recently, Cochinis take their families to visit the coastal strip of Kerala where they grew up. The Embassy of India, Tel Aviv has also been successfully running the 'Know-India' programme sponsoring selected Indian Jewish youth for a month-long conducted tour of India. The response has been enthusiastic and dozens have been to India on Government of India sponsored trips to their 'ancestral homeland'. But it must be said that, a majority of young second-generation Indian Jews know little about current developments in the politics or the economy of

India, even if they watch an Indian cable television channel regularly. For the young Indian-Israelis, the land of their birth is the Jewish Homeland and their concerns are those of upward mobility and economic achievement. They are conscious of the 'peripheral' location of the community within local Israeli power structures. As Dan, a successful entrepreneur said: 'It's not easy for Indians to succeed . . . we need to have a Knesset member from the community. . . . We need to be more involved with Israeli politics. If any of our young people aspire to politics, they should join one of the existing political parties like Likud then work from the grassroots. . . . That is the way to strengthen ourselves and have a voice. . . .'

But how do *sabra* Indians deal with ethnicity in their personal lives? Does their Indian-*ness* influence inter-ethnic marriage patterns when they marry other Israelis of other ethnicities? What is the role of inter-generational cultural transmissions? Does the fact of their Jewish-*ness* dilute their sense of connection with their ethnicity and therefore, with India? Does the narrative of 'exile' and 'homecoming' diminish the connections that second-generation Indian-Israelis feel for their ethnic linkages? Do they relate to India in the ways that other second-generation Indians do in other diasporic communities around the world? What are the ambivalences in their articulations of 'Indian-*ness*' and Israeli-*ness*? Finally, how do all these intertwining strands shape identities?

These, however, are questions for *another* book. . . .

NOTES

1. The mayors of Kiryat Gat and Kiryat Bialik told me at the interviews that their offices had disbursed extra financial support to various community groups—and the Indian communities like some others had organized programmes.
2. Indeed, at some programmes in 2008, as I saw Jews of Morrocan, Iraqi or East European origin from surrounding neighbourhoods clapping enthusiastically to Indian beats in unison with their Indian cousins, the sense of ethnic pride among the Indian community was palpable.
3. The aim of the fund is to promote Indian and Israeli collaboration for

R&D with industrial application. Several awards have already been made under this.
4. This information below was from the website of Embassy of India, Tel Aviv, www.indembassy.co.il (July 2008).
5. One Israeli company ELBIT Imaging, has plans to build nearly 15 shopping malls, several hospitals, and major housing and industrial development sites near cities such as Bangalore and Pune.

APPENDIX 1: QUESTIONNAIRE

1. Name:
   Year/Place of birth:
   Where do you live in Israel now:

2. Year of migration:
   How did you decide to migrate/make *aliya*:
   Family status at the time of migration:
   Who did you come with? Describe your journey:

3. Israel
   Describe what you saw when you arrived:
   Describe the first few days/months: Your difficulties? Was Israel like you imagined it would be:

4. Education/Professional Work:
   Where did you study:
   Some of the jobs you did in Israel—in the first 3 years:
   Were the salaries good? Did you have to assert yourself in order to be given professional recognition:
   Were there (overt/covert) obstacles relating to your Indian identity that posed a challenge to attaining professional recognition:
   Describe where you work now:
   Your job description:
   Did you serve in the Israeli army ? What work did you do:

5. Family
   Year of marriage:

Is your spouse Indian:

Names/Year of Birth of Children:

Their education:

If married—are they married to Indians:

6. Religion:

Are you strict about *Shabbat*? Jewish dietary restrictions? Only *Kosher* food? How often do you visit the synagogue:

Were you more religious in India or are you more observant in Israel:

7. Community life

Are you part of an Indian community group or club:

What do you like about it:

If not, why do you prefer not to:

Do you think the Indian community is 'well-respected' in Israel:

Do you have any suggestions for improvement:

What do you think the Israeli government can do help the status of the community:

What can the Indian community do to enhance its status/image collectively:

8. Israel

What are your views about Israeli politics—Are you member of a political party:

9. India

In your personal life or family culture do you feel 'Indian':

Are you culturally different from other Israelis of other ethnic origins:

Give examples:

Appendix 1

Which of your activities/preferences would you describe as 'Indian'? (For example, What language do you speak in the family? Food? Movies? TV):

Connections with India—Year of first visit:

How frequent are your visits to India:

Do you still have family in India:

APPENDIX 2: MAP OF INDIA: ORIGINS OF INDIAN JEWS

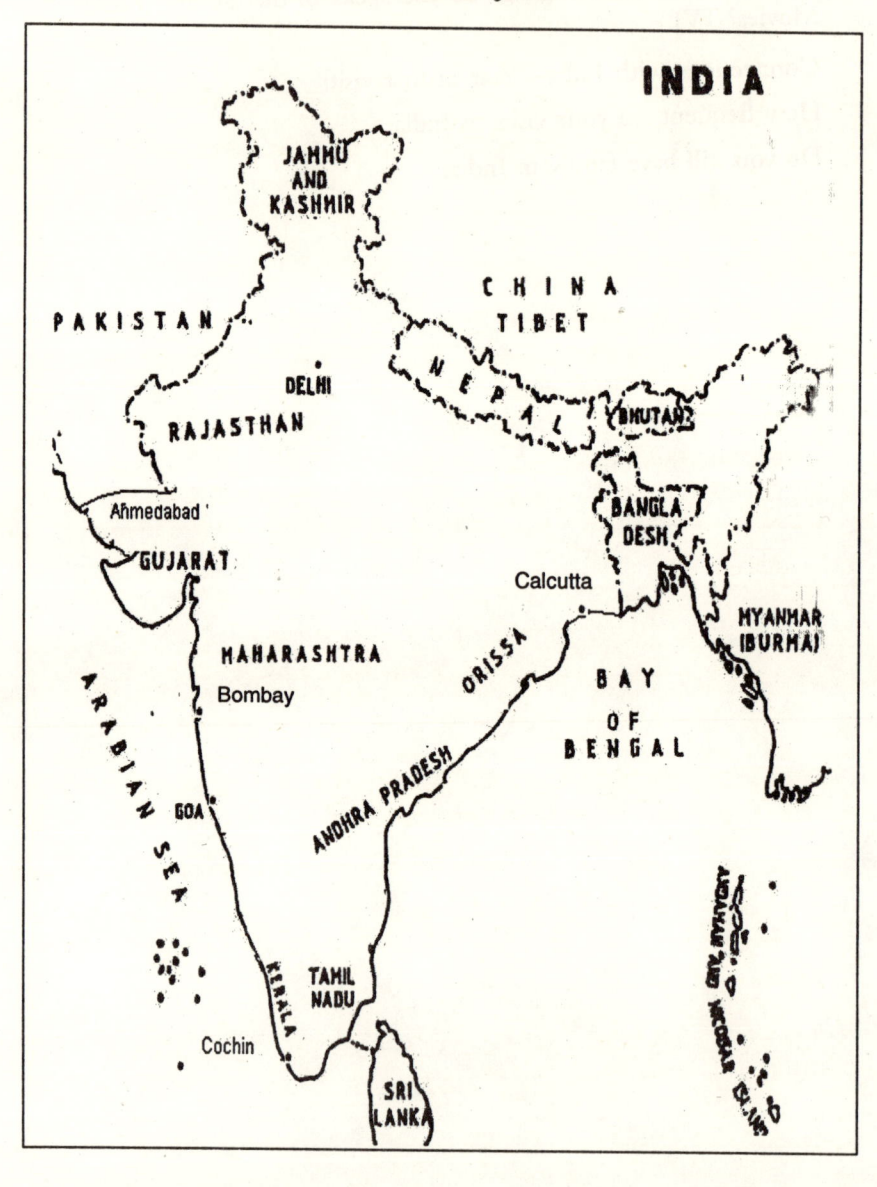

APPENDIX 3: MAP OF ISRAEL: CLUSTERS OF INDIAN JEWS

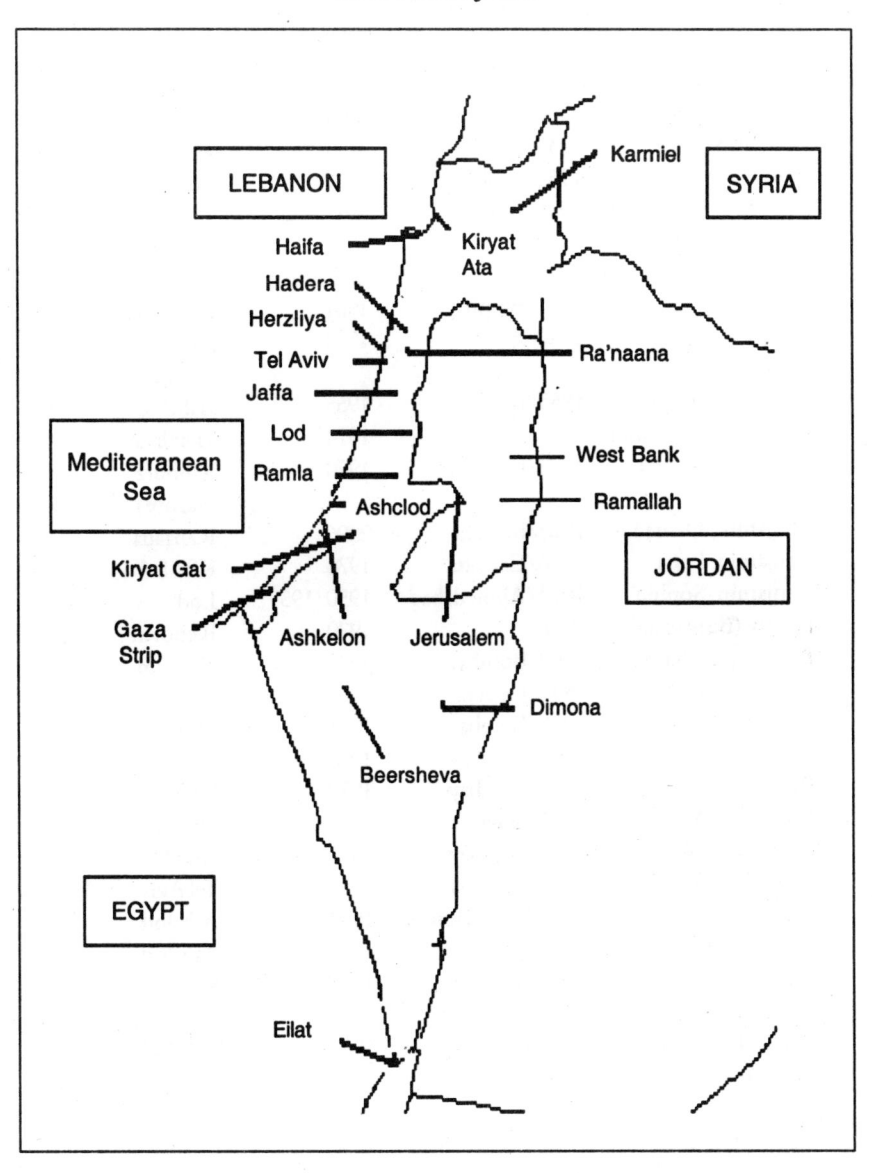

APPENDIX 4: SELECT LIST OF INTERVIEWEES/ RESPONDENTS WHO PARTICIPATED IN THIS RESEARCH

Name	Year/Place of birth	Year of migration	Place of residence in Israel
Apticar, Daniel	1930 /Ratlam	1971	Holon
Apticar, Sarah Daniel	1933	1971	Holon
Ashkenazy, Isaac	1955/Shillong	1977	Tel Aviv
Ashtamkar, Daniel	1958/Karachi	1971	Lod
Ashton, Jacob	1934/Bombay	1952	Petah-Tikwa
Ashton, Rosy Alfred	1950	unconfirmed	Dimona
Ashton, Sarah	1941/Bombay	1961	Petah-Tikwa
Avraham, Rigie	1940/Bombay	1954	Kibbutz Mayaan Tzvi
Bamnulkar, Hanan	1955/Bombay	1965	Ashdod
Benjamin, Ben-Sion	–	1974	Herzliya
Benjamin, Daniel	1952/Bombay	1970	Kibbutz Hazorea
Benjamin, Diana Lily	1928/Karachi	2006	Ranaana
Benjamin, Lena	1946/Calcutta	1976	Kfar Saba
Benjamin, Sophie	1924/Ahmedabad	1950/1957	Lod
Benny (Binyamin)	1957	1970	Rehovot
Benyamin, Sharona	1969/Bombay	1990	Shoham
Ben Yahuda, Rebecca	1944/Karachi	1967	Lod
Best, (Dr.) Lael	1951/Bombay	1979	Haifa
Best, Rebecca	1959/Bombay	1979	Haifa
Bhastikar, Rukhama	1944/Bombay	1972	Dimona
Binyamin, Moshe	1957/Israel	–	Dimona
Bromberg, Yvonne	1961/Bombay	1971	Kfar Saba
Chen, Rachel	1930/Calcutta	1950	Tel Aviv
Chincholikar, Hana	1955/Parel, Bombay	1964	Ashdod
Damiel, Limor	1979/Israel	–	Ashdod
David, Elizabeth	1942/Bombay	1970	Shoham
Dekel, Eliahu	1950/Israel	–	Rosh Pina
Dighorkar, Shlomo	1968/Bombay	1992	Ashdod
Eliyahu, Alon (Ellis Shalom)	1935/Karachi	1950	Haifa
Eliyahu, Betzion	1941/Mattancherry (Kerela)	1954	Moshav Shahar

Appendix 4

Name	Year/Place of birth	Year of migration	Place of residence in Israel
Eliyahu, Bezalel	1930/Jew Town (Cochin)	1955	Moshav Shahar
Eliyahu, Yerusha	1936/Karachi	1968	Dimona
Erulkar, Esther	1947	1959	Dimona
Erulkar, Mary	1945	1959	Dimona
Ezkiel, Sampson	1934/Bombay	1961	Haifa
Ezkiel, Sylvia	1933/Bombay	1961	Haifa
Gadker, Naomi (Shapurkar)	1958/Bombay	1971	Kiryat Ata
Gadker, Samson	1954/Bombay	1967	Kiryat Ata
Gershonovich, Jemima	1958/Bombay	1971	Nahariya
Gilad, Eti	1951/Parur, Kerala	1955	Rehovot
Greenfield, Ruth	1961/Delhi	1983	Ranaana
Gudlaezer, Esther (Judah)	1946/Calcutta	–	Tel Aviv
Guedj, Julie	1939/Bombay	1986	Karmiel
Hacco, Galia	1942/Kerala	1954	Tel Aviv
Isaac, Becky	1924/Karachi	1957	Lod
Israel, Aviva	1982/Bombay	1993	Gan Yavne
Israel, David	1951/Bombay	1993	Gan Yavne
Israel, Esther	1928/Bombay	1993	Gan Yavne
Israel, Shayela	1954/Bombay	1993	Gan Yavne
Jacob, Rebecca	Yeotmal (Madhya Pradesh)	1979	Nahariya
Jhirad, Diana	1941/Bombay	1975	Yehud
Jhirad, Ivy	1939/Bombay	1964	Lod
Joseph, Debora Isaac	1924/Bombay	1950/1957	Jerusalem
Joseph, Elizabeth	1928/Bombay	1954	Lod
Joseph, Esther	1841/Karachi	1966	Holon
Joseph, Rosemarie	1955/Bombay	1978	Hadera
Judah, Sophie	1949	1972	Kfar Saba
Koletkar, Naomi	1950/Bombay	1969	Yehud
Koren, Katie	1947/Calcutta	1950	Herzliya Pituach
Lane, Zippora (Venus)	1944/Cochin	1972	Tiberias

Appendix 4

Name	Year/Place of birth	Year of migration	Place of residence in Israel
Masil, Noah	1946/Tala (Maharashtra)	1970	Jerusalem
Masil, Sybia	1945/Karachi	1974	Jerusalem
Merci	Cochin	1991	Rishon Letzion
Miller, Aviva	1940/Raigad (Maharashtra)	1968	Moshav Mozliach
Moses, Naomi	1943/Bombay	1971	Modi'in
Moses, Sima	1955/Parur (Kerala)	1970	Rishon Letzion
Moshe	1945/Karachi	1962	Dimona
Mozelle (Meyer), Bruh	Calcutta	1967	Tel Aviv
Muttah, Judith	1955/Jabalpur	1976	Netanya
Pal, Sima Molly	1955/Parur (Kerala)	1970	Hadera
Pallivathikal, Miriam Arzi	1948/Parur	1971	Rehovot
Rappaport, Zvia	1953/Parur	1970	Gedera
Reuben, Caroline	1948/Bombay	1979	Herzliya
Reuben, Naomi	1932/Karachi	–	Lod
Reuben, Samson	1945	1979	Herzliya
Reymond, Sarah	1935/Cochin	1955	Rishon Letzion
Rohekar, Annie	Srivardhan Maharashtra	1964	Lod
Sanker, Ruth	1939/Bombay	1966	Tira Ata (Haifa)
Sassoon, (Dr.) Essie	1936/Cochin	1973	Ashkelon
Sassoon, Naomi	1950	1956	Dimona
Schwartz, Fleurette	1944/Calcutta	1964	–
Shallome, Reuben	1935/Karachi	1964	Herzliya
Shimoni, Flory	1945/Bombay	1968	Ashdod
Shirley	Bombay	Unconfirmed	Ashdod
Shoshana	1946	1961	Dimona
Solomon, Bina	1945/Bombay	1975	Lod
Solomon, Sarah	1935	1968	Haifa
Solomon, Uriella	1927/Bombay	Unconfirmed	North Israel
Tal, Ruby	1950	1968	Lod
Talker, Muzelle	1945/Bombay	1971	Lod

Appendix 4

Name	Year/Place of birth	Year of migration	Place of residence in Israel
Talker, Naomi	1966/Bombay	1996	Netanya
Talker, Nora	1947/Bombay	1965	Dimona
Talker, Ofer	1967/Beersheva	–	Dimona
Talker, Sampson	1964/Bombay	1996?	Netanya
Talker, Sara	–	1964	Dimona
Thifereth, (Dr.) Hemda	1943/Parur (Kerala)	1970	Rehovot
Wasker, Mozelle	1941/Bombay	1968	Tira Ata (Haifa)
Yehezkiel, Issac	Poona	1970	Zur Igal
Yehezkiel, Jeanette	1940/Bombay	1963	Haifa
Yehezkiel, Rebecca	1930/Poona	1970	Zur Yigal
Yosef, (Dr.) Reuven	1957/Poona	1994	Eilat
Zipora, Meir	1948/Ernakulam (Kerala)	1968	Ramla

Bibliography

PUBLISHED SOURCES ON ISRAELI SOCIETY

Al-Haj, M. and H. Rosenfeld (1990), *Arab Local Government in Israel*, (Westview Studies on the Middle East), Boulder: Colorado, Westview Press.

Ashkenazi, Michael and Alex Weingrod (eds.) (1987), *Ethiopian Jews and Israel*, New Brunswick: Transaction Publishers.

Azmon, Yael and Dafna N. Izraeli (1993), *Women in Israel*, New Brunswick: Transaction Publishers.

Ben-Zadok, E. (1993), 'Oriental Jews in the Development Towns: Ethnicity, Economic Development, Budgets and Politics', in E. Ben-Zadok (ed.), *Local Communities and the Israeli Polity: Conflict of Values and Interests*, New York: SUNY Press, pp. 91–122.

Bernstein, Deborah (1981), 'Immigrants Transit Camps: The Formation of Dependent Relations in Israeli Society', *Ethnic & Racial Studies*, 4 (1): pp. 26–44.

Bloom, Ann R. (1991), 'Women in the Defense Forces', in B. Swirski and M. Safir (eds.), *Calling the Equality Bluff*, New York: Pergamon Press, pp. 128–38.

Dahan-Kalev, Henriette (2001), 'Tensions in Israeli Feminism: The Mizrahi Ashkenazi Rift', *Women's Studies International Forum*, vol. 24: 1–16.

Dahan-Kalev, Henriette (2001), 'You Are So Pretty, You Don't Look Moroccan', *Israeli Studies*, vol. 6: 1–14.

Davis, Uri (1977), *Israel: Utopia Incorporated: A Study of Class, State, and Corporate Kin Control*, London: Zed Press.

Deshen, Shlomo (1981), 'Political Ethnicity and Cultural Ethnicity in Israel during the 1960s', in Ernest Krausz (ed.), *Studies of Israeli Society Migration, Ethnicity and Community*, New Brunswick: Transaction Publishers.

Deshen, Shlomo and Moshe Shokeid (1974), *The Predicament of Homecoming: Cultural and Social Life of North African Immigrants in Israel*, Ithaca: Cornell University Press.

Deshen, Shlomo, Charles S. Liebman and Moshe Shokeid (1995) (eds.), *Israeli Judaism: Studies in Israeli Society*, vol. VII, New Brunswick: Transaction Publishers.

Eisenstadt, S.N., Moshe Lissak and Yaacov Nahon (eds.), *Ethnic Communities in Israel—Socio Economic Status*, Jerusalem: Jerusalem Institute for Israel Studies, pp. 50–75 (Hebrew).

Gonen, A. (1985), 'The Changing Ethnic Geography of Israeli Cities', in A. Weingrod (ed.), *Studies in Israeli Ethnicity: After the Ingathering*, New York: Gordon and Breach Science Publishers, pp. 25–37.

Izraeli, Daphna N., 'Gendering Military Service in the Israeli Defense Forces', in Lewin-Epstein and Semyonov, *Studies in Israeli Society*, vol. 10. pp. 281–311.

Khazzoom, Aziza (2005), 'Did the Israeli State Engineer Segregation on the Placement of Jewish Immigrants in Development Towns in the 1950s?', *Social Forces*, 84 (1): 115–34.

―――― (2008), *Shifting Ethnic Boundaries and Inequalities in Israel*, Stanford, CA: Stanford University Press.

Kraus, V. and R. W. Hodge (1990), *Promises in the Promised Land: Mobility and Inequality in Israel*, New York: Greenwood Press.

Lewin-Epstein, Noah, Yuval Elmelech and Moshe Semyonov (1997), 'Ethnic Inequality in Home-ownership and the Value of Housing: The Case of Immigrants in Israel', *Social Forces*, 75 (4): 1439–62.

Lewin-Epstein, N. and M. Semyonov (1986), 'Ethnic Group Mobility in the Israeli Labor Market', *American Sociological Review*, 51: 342–51.

―――― (1992), 'Community of Residence, Community of Employment and Income Returns', *Israel Social Science Research* 7: 15–27.

Levy, Andre and Alex Weingrod (eds.) (2005), *Homelands and Diasporas: Holy Lands and Other Places*, Stanford: Stanford University Press.

Lu-Yon, Hubert, and Rachel Kalush (1994), *Housing in Israel: Policy and Inequality*, Tel Aviv. Adva Center (Hebrew).

Mark, Nili (1994), 'Ethnic Gaps in Earnings and Consumption in Israel', *Economic Quarterly* 41(1): 55-77 (Hebrew).

Matras, Judah (1973), 'Israel's New Frontiers: The Urban Periphery', in M. Curtis and M.S. Chertoff (eds.), *Israel: Social Structure and Social Change*, New Brunswick, NJ: Transaction Publishers, pp. 3-14.

Myers, Dowell and Seong Woo Lee (1998), 'Immigrant Trajectories into Home-ownership: A Temporal Analysis of Residential Assimilation', *International Migration Review*, 32: 593–625.

Motzafi-Haller, Pnina (2001), 'Scholarship, Identity, and Power: Mizrahi Women in Israel', *Signs*, 26: 697–734.

Nahon, Yaakov (1987), 'Education Levels and Employment Opportunities: The Ethnic Dimension', Jerusalem: Jerusalem Institute for the Study of Israel.

Neidert, L.J. and R. Farley (1985), 'Assimilation in the United States: An Analysis of Ethnic and Generation Differences in Status and Achievement', *American Sociological Review*, 50: 840-50.

Peres, Yochanan (1971), 'Ethnic Relations in Israel', *American Journal of Sociology* 76(5): 1021-47,

Raijman, Rebeca and Moshe Semyonov (1995), 'Modes of Labor Market Incorporation and Occupational Cost Among New Immigrants to Israel', *International Migration Review*, 29: 375-93.

Rebhun, U. and C. Waxman (eds.) (2004), *Jews in Israel: Contemporary Social and Cultural Patterns*, Lebanon, NH: University Press of New England.

Saunders, P. (1978), 'Domestic Property and Social Class', *International Journal of Urban and Regional Research*, 2: 233-51.

Schmettz, Uziel O., Sergio Della Pergola and Uri Avner (1991), *Ethnic Differences Among Israeli Jews: A New Look*, Jerusalem: The Herbrew University, Institute of Contemporary Jewry.

Semyonov, Moshe and Tamar Lerenthal (1991), 'Country of Origin, Gender, and the Attainment of Socioeconomic Status: A Study of Stratification in the Jewish Population of Israel', *Research in Social Stratification and Mobility*, 10: 327-45.

Semyonov, Moshe (1997), 'On the Cost of Being an Immigrant in Israel: The Effects of Tenure, Origin and Gender', *Research in Social Stratification and Mobility*, 15: 115-31.

Semyonov, M. and N. Lewin-Epstein (2000), 'Immigration and Ethnicity in Israel: Returning Diaspora and Nation Building', in Rainer Muentz (ed.), *Diasporas and Ethnic Migrants in 20th Century Europe*, London: Frank Cass.

Shavit, Yossi (2004), 'Segregation, Tracking, and the Educational Attainment of Minorities: Arabs and Oriental Jews in Israel', in Moshe Semyonov and N. Lewin-Epstein, *Stratification in Israel*, New Brunswick: Transaction Publishers, pp. 37-54.

Shohat, Ella (2001), 'Rupture and Return: The Shaping of Mizrahi Epistemology', *Hagar*, 2 (1): 61-92.

Sorensen, J. (1992), 'Locating Class Cleavages in Intergenerational Mobility: Cross-National Commonalities and Variations in Mobility Patterns', *European Sociological Review*, 8: 267-79.

Shuval, Judith T. (2000), 'Diaspora Migration: Definitional Ambiguities and a Theoretical Paradigm', *International Migration*, 38 (5): 41-57.

—— (1998), 'Migration to Israel: The Mythology of "Uniqueness"', *International Migration*, 36 (1): 3-24.

Smooha, Sammy (1978), *Israel: Pluralism and Conflict*, London: Routledge and Kegan Paul.

Smooha, Sammy and Yochanan Peres (1980), 'The Dynamics of Ethnic Inequalities: The Case of Israel', in Ernest Krausz (ed.) *Studies of Israeli Society Migration, Ethnicity and Community*, New Brunswick: Transaction Publishers.

Smooha, Sammy and Vered Kruas (1985), 'Ethnicity as a Factor in Status Attainment in Israel', *Research in Social Stratification and Mobility* 4: 151–75.

Spiegel, Erika (1966), *New Towns in Israel*, Stuttgart: Karl Kramer Verlag.

Spilerman, C. and J. Habib (1976), 'Development Towns in Israel: The Role of Community in Creating Ethnic Disparities in Labor Force Characteristics', *American Journal of Sociology*, 81: 781–812.

Spilerman, C. and J. Habib (1976), 'Development Towns in Israel: The Role of Community in Creating Ethnic Disparities in Labour Force Characteristics', *American Journal of Sociology*, 81: 781–812.

Swirski, B. and M. Safir (eds.) (1991), *Calling the Equality Bluff*, New York: Pergamon Press, 1991.

Toren, Nina (1980), 'Return to Zion: Characteristics and Motivations of Returning Emigrants', in Ernest Krausz, *Studies of Israeli Society Migration, Ethnicity and Community*, New Brunswick: Transaction Publishers.

Weiker, Walter F. (1988), *The Unseen Israelis: The Jews from Turkey in Israel*, Jerusalem: The Jerusalem Center for Public Affairs/Center for Jewish Community Studies.

Weingrod, Alex (1965), *Israel: Group Relations in New Society*, New York: Frederick A. Praeger Publishers.

—— (1966), *Reluctant Pioneers: Village Development in Israel*, Ithaca: Cornell University Press.

—— (ed.) (1985), *Studies in Israeli Society: After the Ingathering*, New York: London: Gordon and Breach Science Publishers.

Weintraub, D. and V. Kraus (1982) 'Social Differentiation and Locality of Residence: Spatial Distribution, Composition, and Stratification in Israel,' *Megamot* 27: 267–81 (Hebrew).

Willner, Dorothy, 'Politics and Change in Israel: The Case of Land Settlement', *Human Organization*, 24 (1): 65–72.

Yaakov, Nahon (1987), *Education Levels and Employment Opportunities: The Ethnic Dimension*, Jerusalem: Jerusalem Intitute for the Study of Israel (Hebrew).

Yogev, A. and R. Shapira (1987), 'Ethnicity, Meritocracy and Credentialism in Israel: Elaborating the Credential Society Thesis', *Research in Social Stratification and Mobility* 6: 187–212.

Yuchtman-Yaar, E. (1985), 'Difference in Ethnic Patterns of Socio-economic Achievements in Israel: A Neglected Aspect of Structure Inequality', *International Review of Modern Sociology*, 15: 99–116.

PRIMARY AND SECONDARY SOURCES: INDIAN JEWS

Abraham, Margaret (1995), 'Marginalization and Disintegration of Community Identity Among the Jews of India', in Nathan Katz (ed.), *Studies of Indian Jewish Identity*, New Delhi: Manohar.

Abraham, Margaret (2007), 'Ethnicity and Marginality: A Study of Indian Jewish Immigrants in Israel', in Prakash C. Jain (ed.), *Indian Diaspora in West Asia: A Reaqder*, New Delhi: Manohar.

Bammer, Angelika (1997), 'Mother Tongues and Other Strangers: Writing Family Across Cultural Divides', in Angelika Bammer (ed.), *Displacements; Esther David, Walled City*, Madras: Manas.

Cernea, Ruth Fredman (2007), *Almost Englishmen: Baghdadi Jews in British Burma*, Lanham: Lexington Books.

Chiara, Betta (2003), 'From Oriental to Imagined Britons: Baghdadi Jews in Shanghai', *Modern Asian Studies*, 37:4 (2003), 999–1023.

DeCosta, A., 'The "White" and "Black" Jews of Malabar', *India Church Quarterly Review*, April 1985, pp. 106–25.

Egorova, Yulia (2006), *Jews and India: Perceptions and Image*, London: Routledge.

Egorova, Y. (2003), 'The Home of One's Own: Indian Jewish, Fiction and the Problem of Bene-Israel Identity', *Journal of Indo-Judaic Studies* 6: 71–9.

Elias, F. and J.E. Cooper (1974), *The Jews of Calcutta: The Autobiography of a Community*, Calcutta: The Jewish Association of Calcutta.

Ezekiel, Joseph and Joseph Jacobs (1907), 'Cochin', *The Jewish Encyclopedia*, vol. IV, pp. 135–8.

Ezra, Esmond David (1986), *Turning Back the Pages: A Chronicle of Calcutta Jewry*, vols. I and II, London: Brookside Press.

Hallegua, Fiona (1984), 'The Jewish Community of Cochin: Its Twilight Years', M.A. thesis, University of Kerala, St. Theresa's College, Ernakulam.

Hallegua, I.S. (1988), 'The Paradesh Synagogue of Cochin and Its Dying Community of Jews', Cochin, photocopied MS. For private circulation by author.

Hyman, Mavis (1995), *Jews of the Raj*, London: Hyman Publishers.

Isenberg, Shirley Berry (1988), *India's Bene Israel: A Comprehensive Inquiry and*

Sourcebook, Bombay: Popular Prakashan; Berkeley: Judah L. Magnes Museum.

Jackson, Stanley (1968), *The Sassoons*, New York: E.P. Dutton.

Katz, Nathan and Ellen S. Goldberg (1993), *The Last Jews of Cochin: Jewish Identity in Hindu India*, Columbia: University of South Carolina Press.

Katz, Nathan (ed.) (1995), *Studies of Indian Jewish Identity*, New Delhi: Manohar.

Katz, Nathan and Ellen S. Goldberg (eds.) (2005), 'Kashrut, Caste and Kabbalah', *The Religious Life of the Jews of Cochin*, New Delhi: Manohar.

Kushner, Gilbert (1973), *Immigrants from India in Israel: Planned Change in an Administered Community*, Tucson: University of Arizona Press.

Mandalia, Sejal, 'Not welcome in the Holy Land' (4 October 2004). Source: http://www.newstatesman.com/200410040022

Mandelbaum, David G. (1986), 'Social Stratification Among the Jews of Cochin in India and in Israel', in *Jews in India*, ed. Thomas A. Timberg, New Delhi: Vikas, pp. 61-120.

Marenoff, Martha, 'The Black and White Jews of Cochin', MS, Folio 654, Jewish Historical General Archives, Hebrew University, Jerusalem.

Musleah, Ezekiel N. (1975), *On the Banks of the Ganga: The Sojourn of the Jews in Calcutta*, North Quincy, MA: Christopher Publishing House.

Ray, Nisith Ranjan (1986), *Calcutta: The Profile of a City*, Calcutta: K.P. Bagchi & Co.

Ray, Dalia (2001), *The Jewish Heritage of Calcutta*, Calcutta: Minerva Associates.

Roland, Joan G. (1989), *Jews in British India: Identity in a Colonial Era*, Hanover and London: University Press of New England, published for Brandeis University Press.

Ross, Israel J., 'Cross-Cultural Dynamics in Musical Traditions: The Music of the Jews of Cochin', *Musica Judaica*, 2(1) (1977-8), pp. 51–72.

Rushdie, Salman (1991), *Imaginary Homelands*, London: Granta Book.

Schermerhorn, R.A (1978), 'Jews: A Disappearing Minority', in *Ethnic Plurality in India*, Tucson: University of Arizona Press, Chapter 10, pp. 238-61.

Silliman, Jael, 'Crossing Borders, Maintaining Boundaries: The Life and Times of Farha, a Women of the Baghdadi Jewish Diaspora 1870–1958', in *Journal of Indo-Judaic Studies*, 57–59, vol. 1, April 1998, no. 1.

Silliman, Jael (2002), *Jewish Portraits, Indian Frames: Women's Narratives from a Diaspora of Hope*, Calcutta: Seagull.

Slapak, Orpa (ed.) (1995), *The Jews of India: A Story of Three Communities*, Jerusalem: The Israel Museum.

Spector, Johanna, 'Shingli Tunes of the Cochin Jews', *Asian Music*, vol. 3, no. 2, 1972, pp. 23–8.

_____ (1971), 'The Music of the Jews of Cochin with Special Reference to Shingli Tunes', in S.S. Koder (ed.), *Commemoration Volume: Cochin Synagogue Quater-centenary Celebrations*, Cochin: The Kerala History Association and the Cochin Synagogue Quatercentenary Celebration Committee, pp. 177–85.

Strizower, Schifra (1962), *Exotic Jewish Communities*, New York: Thomas Yoseloff.

Timberg, Thomas A. (ed.), (1986), *Jews in India*, New Delhi: Vikas; New York: Advent.

Walerstein, Marcia (1986), 'The Cochini Jewish Wedding of the Malabar Community in India and Israel: Change in Custom, Symbol and Meaning', in Thomas A. Timberg (ed.), *Jews in India*, New Delhi: Vikas, pp. 248–70.

Weiker, Walter F. (1988), *The Unseen Israelis: The Jews from Turkey in Israel*, Jerusalem: The Jerusalem Center for Public Affairs/Center for Jewish Community Studies.

Weil (Vail), Shalva (1977), 'Bene Israel Indian Jews in Lod, Israel: A Study in the Persistence of Ethnicity and Ethnic Identity' (unpublished Ph.D. thesis, 2 vols., in Haifa University Library.)

_____ (ed.) (2002), *India's Jewish Heritage: Ritual, Art & Life Cycle*, Delhi: Marg Publications.

SELECT PUBLISHED SOURCES: INDIAN DIASPORA

Bahri, Deepika and Mary Vasudeva (eds.) (1996), *Between the Lines: South Asians and Postcoloniality*, Philadelphia, PA: Temple University Press.

Brown, Judith, M. (2006), *Global South Asians: Introducing the Modern Diaspora*, Cambridge: Cambridge University Press.

Jain, K. Ravindra (1993), *Indian Communities Abroad: Themes and Literature*, New Delhi: Manohar.

Lee, Jennifer and Min Zhou (eds.) (2004), *Asian American Youth: Culture, Identity, and Ethnicity*, New York: Routledge, 2004.

Leonard, Karen I. (1992), *Making Ethnic Choices: California's Punjabi Mexican Americans*, Philadelphia: Temple University Press.

Luhrman, T.M. (1996), *The Good Parsi: The Fate of a Colonial Elite in a Postcolonial Society*, Cambridge: Harvard University Press.

Maira, Sunaina (1995), 'Making Room for Hybrid Space: Reconsidering Second-Generation Ethnic Identity', *Sanskriti*, 6:1.

Maira, Sunaina, and Rajini Srikanth (eds.) (1996), *Contours of the Heart: South Asians Map North America*, New York: Asian American Writers' Workshop.

Mishra, Vijay (1996), 'The Diasporic Imaginary: Theorizing the Indian Diaspora', in: *Textual Practice*, 10 (3): 421–47.

Petievich, Carla, (ed.) (1999), *The Expanding Landscape: South Asian and the Diaspora*, New Delhi: Manohar.

Sollors, Werner (1994), 'Who Is Ethnic?', in *The Post-Colonial Studies Reader*, 219–22.

Tatla, Darshan S. (1999), *The Sikh Diaspora: The Search for Statehood*, London: UCL.

Thampi, Madhavi (2005), *Indians in China 1800–1949*, New Delhi: Manohar.

Tuan, Mia (1999), 'Neither Real Americans nor Real Asians?: Multigenerational Asian Ethnics Navigating the Terrain of Authenticity, *Qualitative Sociology*, 22 (2): 105–25.

Index

Abraham, Margaret 39, 61, 217, 218
acculturation 27, 28, 34, 35, 39, 42, 45, 53–4, 68, 90, 96, 116–17, 153, 175, 181, 186, 198, 222 (*see* assimilation)
adaptation 34, 40, 125
Aharon Ovadiah 70
Ahmedabad 30, 73, 102, 106, 166, 208, 212
Aleppo 70
Algeria 30, 76, 171, 175
aliya 29, 69, 93–4, 97, 100–7, 111, 115, 122, 126, 129–38, 144, 146, 150–1, 157–8, 160, 162, 166, 167, 176–7, 183, 213
Amutat Tzedek 197
anglo-Indian 71, 87, 92, 93, 140
Arab communities 48, 78
arrival experiences 109
Ashdod 47–9, 54, 81, 85, 102, 106, 113, 115, 123, 128, 168, 170, 172–4, 180, 189, 190, 193–4, 201–2, 206, 207, 215, 218
Ashkelon Pipeline Company 145
Ashkenazis 30, 63, 137; *Ashkenazim* 43, 44, 74, 77
assimilation 28, 32, 35, 39, 46, 49, 54, 57, 58, 76, 184, 198, 32
Azmon, Yael 63

Baghdadis 30, 37, 39, 40, 51, 54, 66, 68, 70–1, 74–5, 87, 91, 101, 120–1, 129, 150–2, 172, 174, 191–2; 208, 212, 213; Baghdadi-Indian Jews 31
Bahri, Deepika 59
Bandra 93
Basra 37, 70

Be'er Ya'aqov 83, 186, 200
Bedek 84, 123, 147
Beersheva 51–2, 54, 58, 78, 81–2, 89, 97, 105–6, 112, 123, 132, 134–5, 145, 147, 161–2, 166, 194, 196, 206, 216–17
Ben Gurion University 81, 135
Bene Israel 60, 61, 72, 87, 96, 117; Bene Israeli /s 30, 32, 37, 38, 39, 40, 41, 47, 51, 54, 66, 68, 72, 73, 74, 75, 81, 82, 83, 86, 87, 92, 96, 97, 104, 107, 120, 121, 127, 130, 132, 133, 140, 145, 146, 147, 150, 151, 152, 156, 157, 164, 165, 166, 170, 171–2, 174-5, 178–80, 183–4, 186, 190–2, 197, 199, 200, 203, 205–6, 208, 213, 216, 217, 218–19, 222
Ben-Zadok, E. 62
Bharat Dance 201
bilateral trade (India-Israel) 221
Bnei Menashe 36–7, 60
Bollywood 175, 186–7, 200, 202–3, 205–6, 222
Bombay 28, 30–2, 37, 40, 47, 51–2, 60, 70, 73, 84, 87, 91–3, 94, 95, 98, 99, 100, 102–3, 105–14, 115, 118, 120, 122–3, 128, 131, 132–3, 138–40, 142–8, 150–2, 155, 157–8, 160–1, 162, 165–6, 172, 174, 176, 178, 183, 184, 191–2, 206, 208, 211–12, 213, 214, 215, 218–19, 222
British imperialism 44
British subjects 72, 101
Brown, Judith M. 59
buddhists 68
Bulgaria 30, 60, 153, 159

Index

Burma 60, 71

Calcutta Jews 30, 40, 70, 71, 75 (*see* Baghdadis)
Central Organization of Indian Jews in Israel (COIJI) 191, 193 (*see* community organizations)
Cernea, Ruth Fredman 60
Chendamanglam 69
Chiara, Betta 60
Christian /s 32, 40, 43, 68, 71, 80, 84, 87, 93, 100, 131, 140–1
citizenship 29, 76, 186–8, 207
class stratification 34, 49 (*see* social mobility; stratification)
cleavages within Israeli society 41
Cochini 30, 37–41, 47, 51, 54, 60–1, 66, 68–9, 70, 74–5, 81–2, 86, 89, 91, 103–4, 109, 111, 121, 123, 127, 141, 150–1, 157, 163–6, 170, 172–4, 183, 185–6, 191–2, 195–7, 199–200, 205, 208, 213, 217–18, 222
Cochini immigration to Israel 38
Cochini Jews 30, 39, 47, 60, 69–70, 74, 82, 86, 91, 103–4, 121, 166, 205
collective identity 207
colour-bias 56, 96, 110, 139, 208 (*see* discrimination)
community 28, 30–1, 33–4, 36–42, 44–6, 48–50, 53–5, 57–63, 67, 69, 71–5, 79–80, 85–7, 89, 92–3, 97–8, 100–1, 103–4, 106–7, 109, 111–12, 117–18, 121, 124, 126, 134–5, 144, 151, 154, 156, 162–3, 167, 169, 171, 173–5, 177–9, 181–3, 186, 188–99, 201–4, 206–7, 211–12, 215–18, 221–3
community networks 45, 57, 184; community organizations 189, 193, 195, 215
community self-perceptions 59, 221
conjugal relations 36; conjugality 48, 154, 164, 169
convent school 37

Cranganore 69
cultural challenges 55
cultural displacement 32, 153
cultural programmes 58, 186–9, 191, 195–7, 198, 202, 222
cultural symbols 73, 97

Dahan-Kalev, Henriette 42–3, 63
Dead Sea 82, 134, 151
Delhi 30, 59, 86, 102, 107, 144, 182, 213, 221
Deshen, Shlomo 60, 63, 114, 137, 138, 182
'Destination India' 53, 214
development towns 36, 42, 44, 48, 54, 62–3, 75, 78, 84–6, 88, 109–10, 124–5, 127, 134, 149–50, 153, 155, 157–9, 161, 164, 166, 170, 182–3 (*see* 'new towns'; periphery)
diaspora 27, 28–9, 31, 33, 35, 37, 39, 41, 43, 45, 47, 49, 50, 52, 53, 55, 57, 59, 61, 70
Dimona 42, 47–8, 54, 58, 81–2, 84–5, 97, 115, 124, 134–5, 139, 151, 157, 161–2, 167–8, 170–3, 175–6, 180, 182, 186, 189, 190, 193–4, 196, 198, 199, 201–2, 205, 207, 216–17
discrimination 43, 44, 86, 110–11, 113, 116, 191, 211 (*see* acculturation; colour-bias)
displacement 32–4, 56, 95, 98, 110, 125, 134, 149, 153, 170
Diwali 73
domestic ideologies 53 (*see* gender; family)

East Jerusalem 88, 209
Egorova, Yulia 61
Eilat 47, 49, 58, 119, 120, 135, 189–90, 198–99, 203–5
Eisenstadt, S.N. 42
El-Al 120
Elias, Cooper 37, 60, 87
Elly Kadoorie 99, 143

Index

Embassy of India 89, 189, 213–14, 222, 224
Emigration 28–9, 33–6, 39–40, 45–6, 54, 68, 71, 73, 86, 90, 91, 93–4, 95, 99, 101, 102, 103, 105, 127, 158, 212 (*see* migration)
English 30–1, 34, 41, 44–5, 51–2, 60, 63, 64, 70, 74, 93, 95, 101, 112, 116, 120, 125–30, 133–4, 140–9, 152, 159, 162, 167, 170, 173, 192, 217
English education 44, 170, 192
Ernakulam 61, 69, 86, 104 (*see* Cochini Jews)
ethnic stereotypes 44, 126
ethnicity/ethnic identities 29, 33–4, 36, 38, 40–6, 48, 49, 50, 52–4, 56–7, 59, 61–2, 65, 75, 95, 110, 117, 151, 154, 156, 173, 175, 182, 186–7, 189, 192, 195, 198, 205, 220, 221, 223
ethnography/ethnographic data 34, 42 (*see* fieldwork)
European colonialism 44
exile 28, 30, 35, 59, 95, 223
'exotic' Jewish diasporas 39

Ezra, Esmond David 61

family 36, 56, 57, 120, 126, 128, 134 (*see* gender; domestic ideologies)
fieldwork 38–9, 52, 119, 120, 128, 175, 187, 189, 220
food 31, 36, 39–40, 53, 57, 70, 73, 76, 96–7, 102, 111–12, 115, 127, 129, 131, 135, 137, 159, 170, 173–4, 175, 179, 181–2, 184, 196–7, 205, 208, 214, 217

Ganesh-Chaturthi 73
gender 29, 36–7, 41–6, 52–3, 56–7, 62–3, 106, 114, 120, 126, 136, 141, 143, 154–5, 157, 159, 164, 167, 168, 169, 181, 189, 190
Germany 30, 50
Goldberg, Ellen S. 60–1, 86, 182

Government of India 41, 102, 107, 222
Gujarat 72, 73, 84, 91–3, 101, 140; Gujarati 30, 73, 148, 218
Gulf of Aqaba 47

Habib, J. 62
Ha-Cohen 70
Hadera 102, 133, 185, 211
Hallegua, Fiona 61, 86
Hannukah 73
Hebrew 34, 41, 43, 50–3, 62–3, 84, 100, 116, 125, 127–30, 133–4, 136, 139, 143, 144, 146, 158, 160, 163, 172, 178, 181, 184, 185–7, 198, 217, 222 (*see* language)
Hebrew pronunciation 53
Herzliya 48, 52, 81, 89, 123, 184, 210
heterogeneity 40, 48
Hindi 30–1, 51–2, 73, 95, 133, 148, 151–2, 172, 175–7, 180, 184, 185, 187, 190, 192, 198, 205–6
Hindu-Muslims riots 92–3
Hindus 32, 40–1, 68, 71, 92, 110, 174, 179, 183
Hodu Yada 49, 58, 193, 203–4, 216
holocaust 31, 76, 98, 129, 171
Holy Land 76, 94
home 28, 31–5, 56–7, 70–1, 78–9, 81–2, 85, 93–4, 98, 100–2, 105–6, 115, 126, 129, 132, 134, 137, 139, 148, 152, 153, 154–6, 158–60, 163–5, 167, 172, 174, 178, 180–2, 185, 202, 215, 222
homecoming 29, 35–6, 63, 86, 110, 223
homeland 27, 28–30, 33–5, 39, 40, 43, 45, 53–6, 59, 66–7, 73, 76, 86, 90, 91, 94–5, 97, 101–4, 106, 111, 125, 127, 142, 150, 153, 155, 158, 162, 180, 188, 194, 208, 221, 222–3
Hong Kong 70, 92
hybridized identities 59
Rabbi Shlomo 60

Hyman, Mavis 87

identity 27, 28, 32, 34–7, 41–6, 48, 50–1, 53, 57, 59–61, 63, 65, 71, 73, 86–7, 96, 100–1, 117, 122, 151, 175, 180, 182, 184, 185–6, 188–9, 192, 196, 207–8, 210, 212
IDF (Israeli Defense Forces) 208
imagined community 36
immigrant 29, 30, 32–3, 35–6, 41–2, 44–8, 50–1, 53–5, 58, 60–3, 65, 66–7, 76–9, 81–6, 88–9, 95, 96–7, 99, 103, 105, 108–11, 113–18, 119, 120–1, 123–8, 130–1, 134–6, 138, 140, 141–2, 144, 149–52, 153, 154–5, 157–61, 163–4, 166–7, 169–70, 173, 175, 177, 181–2, 187, 191, 197, 199–200, 202, 217, 222; immigration 34, 38, 46, 54–5, 61, 65, 66, 69, 76–7, 88, 90, 95–9, 103, 112, 115–17, 122, 132, 153, 164, 169
immigrant towns 33, 54, 83, 85, 97, 113, 118, 159, 177 (*see* development towns)
India 27, 28–41, 47, 51, 52, 53–7, 58, 59–61, 63, 64, 66–76, 81, 84, 86–7, 89, 90, 91, 92, 93–4, 96–7, 99–100, 101, 102–13, 115–18, 119, 121–3, 126–8, 129, 133–4, 137–50, 152, 154–5, 157–65, 167, 170, 173–81, 184, 185–90, 191, 192, 194–5, 200, 203, 205–8, 210–16, 217, 218–19, 220, 221–4 (*see* home)
India's trade with Israel (*see* bilateral trade) 36
Indian-Israelis 31, 35, 41, 46, 65, 176, 182, 220, 206, 223; Indian-Israeli identity 34, 35, 57, 184; Indian-Jewish identity 35
Indian Embassy 41, 49, 58, 152, 186, 193, 206, 216, 218

Indian family names 87
Indian independence 41, 49, 206
Indian-Jewish migration 28
Indian Jewish Organizations 190
Indian Jewish women 56, 126, 153, 168
Indian jewry 35, 96
Indian neighbourhoods 48
Indian organizations 182, 190, 216, 222
Indian railways 73, 132
Indian synagogues 33, 49, 54, 156, 192, 195–7, 201, 216
Indian-Jewish practices 154
Indo-Israeli diplomatic relations 221
Inter-generational family ties 156
Inter-faith marriages 106
Iraqis 31
Isenberg, Shirley Berry 60, 87
Israeli backpackers 58
Israeli citizenship 29, 187
Israeli nation 36, 96
Israeli politics 188, 190, 207–9, 219, 223
Israeli scholarship 41, 45
Israeli society 33, 36, 41, 42, 43, 46, 48, 49, 53–5, 58, 61, 62, 63, 66, 76–7, 88, 95, 97, 157, 167, 168–70, 172, 178, 181–2, 184, 189, 208, 210, 216, 220
Israeli sociologists 30; Israeli sociology 41, 46, 157
Israeli state 44, 50, 55, 63, 76, 78–9, 96, 124, 196, 211
Izraeli, Dafina N. 63

Jabalpur 73
Jackson, Stanley 87
Jain, K. Ravindra 59
Jains 68
Jerusalem 38, 54, 60–1, 63, 78, 80–1, 83–4, 88–91, 97–8, 114, 117, 121, 130, 143, 158, 162–3, 168, 172, 180, 184, 191, 195, 203, 209, 218

Jew town 32, 47, 69 (see Cochini Jews)
Jewish Agency 29, 32, 48, 69, 70, 89, 94, 97–100, 103–6, 108, 111, 114, 127, 129, 135, 136, 139, 142, 144, 151, 155, 159, 166, 218
Jewish Baghdadi women 37, 71 (see Baghdadis/Calcutta Jews)
Jewish community in Delhi 144
Jewish diasporic communities 34, 37
Jewish history 32, 35, 71
Jewish homeland 27, 28–30, 33–5, 39, 54, 56, 59, 66–7, 76, 86, 90, 95, 97, 101–2, 104, 106, 142, 150, 153, 155, 158, 180, 188, 194, 222–3 (see home/homecoming)
Jewish-ness 29, 34–5, 40, 50, 56–7, 68, 73, 97, 108, 110, 116, 156, 176, 208, 223 (see Judaism)
Jewish studies 37
Jewish synagogue architecture 39
Judaism 30, 32, 60, 72–3, 80, 156, 165, 180, 182
Judeo-Arabic 70 (see Baghdadis/Calcutta Jews)

Kadima 112
Kamaag 162
Karachi / Karachi Jews 30, 47, 72–3, 84, 92–3, 122, 133–4, 136, 143, 155, 162, 171, 177 (see Bene Israel)
Kashruth 98, 156, 177, 180
Katz, Nathan 39, 60–1, 86, 182
Kedma 112
Kfar Hasidim 111
Kfar Yuval 42, 81, 83, 121, 167, 190, 199
Khazzoom, Aziza 44, 63
Kibbutz/ kibbutzim 42, 61, 67, 79, 88, 100, 104, 106–7, 111, 114, 126, 132–3, 135–6, 148
Kiryat Ata 42, 47, 54, 83, 124, 170, 172, 189, 199–200, 202, 206, 216, 218, 220

Kiryat Bialik 83, 172, 186, 189–91, 199–200, 220, 223
Kiryat Gat 82, 84–5, 132, 186, 189, 197, 217, 220, 223
Kiryat Haim 83, 199
Kiryat Motzkin 83
Kiryat Shmona 52, 111–12, 114, 124, 131, 158, 167, 170
Kiryat Yam 42, 83, 115, 118, 155, 160, 199
Konkan coast 72 (see Bene Israel)
Kosher 73, 97, 102, 176, 181, 195
Kupat Holim 161
'Kushi' 113
Kushner, Gilbert 38

Lakat Haverim 202
'Land of Milk and Honey' 54, 90, 98, 100, 105, 136 (see homecoming/ homeland)
language 29, 31, 33, 36, 40–1, 46, 50–2, 53, 56–8, 64, 70, 73–4, 76, 95, 102, 113, 116, 120, 125, 127–9, 134, 136, 141–4, 152, 156, 159, 169, 170, 172, 180–1, 187, 191–2, 195, 198, 203, 205, 208, 222 (see Hebrew)
Law of Nationality 29, 76
Law of Return 29, 76
Lee, Jennifer 59
Leonard, Karen 59
Lerenthal, Tamar 62
Lewin-Epstein, Noah 62
Libya 76
Liebman, Charles S. 182
life cycle rituals 34, 36, 39–40, 45, 49, 56–7, 153, 154, 156, 171–4, 182 (see gender; Jewish-ness)
Lissak, Moshe 61, 88
location (politics of location); see spatial location 27, 29, 33, 36–7, 43, 46–50, 65, 66–7, 77–81, 85–6, 95, 109, 114–15, 117, 119, 120, 122, 124, 128, 149, 169, 176, 178, 181, 189, 190, 193, 195–6, 201, 204–5, 223

Lod 38, 47–9, 54, 58, 61, 78, 80–1, 83–4, 88–9, 93, 109, 111, 123, 130, 139, 140, 143, 147, 151–2, 160, 168, 172–6, 189–90, 193–4, 196, 199–203, 211, 216–17, 219
Luhrman, T. M. 59

Maharashtra Day 203, 218
Mai Boli 58, 194, 195, 203, 218 (*see* Bene Israel)
Maira, Sunaina 59
Malayalam 30, 32, 41, 51, 205, 222 (*see* Cochini Jews)
Malida 57, 156, 178, 194
Mandate for Palestine 98
Mandelbaum, David G. 86
Mangal-Sutra 73 (*see* Bene Israeli)
Marathi 30, 32, 41, 51–2, 58, 73, 95, 105, 133–4, 148, 170, 172, 177, 184, 192, 194–5, 198, 203, 205, 218, 222 (*see* Bene Israeli)
Mark, Nili 62
marriage patterns 164, 223
Matras, Judah 61–2, 88
Mattencherry 69
Mehndi 57, 174–6 (*see* life cycle rituals)
methodology 46, 55, 188; methodological issue 40 (*see* fieldwork)
Middle Eastern Jews 44, 70, 76 (*see* Baghdadis; Iraqi; *Mizrahim*; Oriental Jews)
migration 27, 28–9, 30–3, 37, 39, 41, 43, 45–7, 49, 50–2, 53, 55, 56, 57, 59, 60, 61, 62, 63, 68, 70, 72, 74, 76–7, 85, 91, 94–5, 101, 102, 106–7, 119, 120, 121, 122, 124, 126, 139, 151, 153, 154–5, 157–8, 163–4, 166–7, 171, 173, 174, 179, 180, 181, 186, 187, 188, 192, 197, 219, 220, 222
migration studies 27, 52
mixed marriages (*see* inter-faith marriages) 74, 82, 89, 107
mixed neighbourhoods 32, 57, 87

Mizoram 37
Mizrahis 30–1; *mizrahim* 43–4, 77
moshav 38, 42, 47–8, 54, 61, 66–7, 75, 78, 79, 80, 81, 82–3, 85, 88, 112, 121, 153, 154, 159, 161, 163, 164, 166, 170, 172–4, 182, 189, 190–1, 193, 195–7, 199, 204, 209
Motzafi-Haller, Pnina 63
Mount Carmel 55
multi-ethnic/multi-ethnicity 30–1, 53–4, 66–7, 75–6, 154, 170
multi-cultural 41
music 130, 173–5, 177, 186–7, 192, 194, 196–7, 200, 202, 204–6
Musleah, Ezekiel N. 60, 87
Muslims 32, 40–1, 68, 71, 80, 92, 110, 174, 208

Naach 201
Nahon, Yaacov 178
Namaste Israel 202, 206
Naogaon 73
national politics 57
nationalism 188, 190, 207–8
Nazareth 145
Negev 47, 55, 81–2, 88, 103–4, 115, 119, 121, 123, 132, 163, 173, 190, 199, 217

Nevatim 42, 47, 48, 81–2, 121, 174, 189, 190–1, 196–7 (*see* Cochini Jews)
new immigrants 29, 35–6, 44–5, 48, 50, 55, 61–2, 66–7, 77, 81–2, 88, 99, 105, 108–9, 111, 114–15, 117, 120, 123–7, 131, 140, 144, 155, 157, 187, 199, 200, 217
'new towns' 42, 54, 61, 66, 78, 85, 88, 151 (*see* development towns; periphery)

Olim 187 (*see* migration; new immigrants)
Onam 185
oriental culture 31

Index

Oriental Jews 45, 62, 77
ORT India schools / ORT schools 98, 99, 118
Overseas Citizens of India (OCI) 41

Palestine 61, 76, 88, 98, 104, 213
Pali 73
parental expectations 53, 57, 156 (see family)
Parur 69, 111–12
Pen 73
periphery 61, 62, 67, 79–80, 82, 88, 124, 150; peripheral regions of Israel 33, 42 (see development towns; population dispersal)
persecution 31–3, 36, 69, 75, 86, 98, 188
personal stories 38, 90, 96, 120
Pesakh 52, 178
pluralism 32–3, 41, 45, 49, 62, 64, 213
pogroms 31–2
Poland 30, 50, 75, 170
Poona 73, 102, 134, 145, 212, 214
population dispersal 42, 54, 78, 124 (see periphery)
post-colonial 27, 141
professions 43, 53, 55–6, 109, 119, 120, 122, 124, 211

Ra'naana 48, 89, 167
racism 44, 111, 148 (see colour-bias; discrimination)
Raijman, Rebeca 62
Ramat Aviv 81
Ramla 47–9, 52, 54, 58, 78, 81, 83–4, 88, 112, 123, 139, 168, 171, 173, 178, 189, 193–4, 196, 199–201, 203, 216
Rangoon 70, 92
Ray, Dalia 60, 87
Ray, Nisith Ranjan 87
religion 28, 34, 37, 40, 44, 46, 50, 93, 106, 156, 176–7, 180–1, 188, 207, 213 (see Judaism)
religious persecution 31–2, 36, 86

religious practices 34, 36, 39–40, 56, 66, 67, 153, 154, 156, 171 (see Judaism)
Republic Day 41, 194, 206
Roland, Joan 60, 87
Romania 30, 137, 159, 171
Rosenfeld, H. 62
Rosh Ha Shana 178, 180
Rosh Pina 81, 83, 104, 118, 199, 218
Russia 30, 217

Sabras 186, 202, 222 (see second-generation)
Safir, M. 63
Schermerhorn, R.A. 61
second-generation 33, 85, 193, 200, 202, 218, 222–3
Semyonov, Moshe 62
sephardic rites 30
sephardim 43 (see Mizrahim; Oriental Jews; Middle-Eastern Jews)
Sha'haar 47, 81–2, 88
Shabbat 52, 72, 98, 156, 177, 180–1, 185, 204
Shenhav, Yehouda 43
Shiluv Asarteev 196
Shohat, Ella 42, 62
Shokeid, Moshe 63, 117, 182
Sikhs 68
Silliman, Jael 37, 61, 117–18
Singapore 70
Sitar 198
Smooha, Sammy 42, 62, 117
social mobility 34, 42, 55–6, 126, 132, 135, 139, 141, 207 (see class stratification)
sociological research 33–4, 43, 46, 49, 95–6 (see Israeli sociology)
South Asia 28, 40, 45, 59
spatial location (see location) 47, 66, 78, 80, 86, 117, 124
spellings (Hebrew/ English) 50, 52 (see language)
Spiegel, Erika 62, 88, 151
Spilerman, C. 62
Srikanth, Rajini 59

status attainment 42, 44, 55, 117, 120 (*see* class stratification; social mobility)
stereotype 44, 56, 86, 120–2, 126, 128, 170, 194, 210–12, 215, 221, 222; stereotypes of Indians 120, 211
stratification 33–4, 41–2, 46, 49, 55, 62, 66, 80 (*see* class stratification; social mobility)
Strizower, Schifra 38, 61
Surat 70
Swirski, B. 44, 63

Tatla, Darshan S. 59
Technion 102, 136, 151
Tel Aviv 41, 48–50, 54, 62–4, 78, 80–1, 83–5, 88–9, 97, 107, 118, 123, 125, 130–1, 135, 141–4, 146, 148, 152, 158, 167, 177, 180, 185, 189, 191, 195, 213–15, 222, 224
Thampi, Madhavi 59
Tiberias 112
Tifferet Yehoshua 196
Tuan, Mia 59
Tunisia 30, 76, 100
Turkey 30, 60, 63, 213

Ulpan 52, 114, 128, 142–3, 145, 158, 167, 170
Urdu 134, 180 (*see* language)
Veteran immigrants 76

Waxman, C. 62
Weiker, Walter F. 60, 63
Weil (Vail), Shalva 61, 151
Weingrod, Alex 42, 61, 63, 88, 117, 118
Weintraub, D. 61, 88
Weiss, Rivka 104, 112, 141–2, 166
West Bank 209
Willner, Dorothy 61, 88
work and professions 55, 109, 119, 124
work-place stereotypes 56
World War II 71, 74, 75

Yarukham 42, 81, 97, 114, 123, 151, 155, 161, 170, 190, 199
Yemen 30, 50, 76, 112, 141, 159
Yeshiva 178
Yom Kippur 178–9
Youth Aliya 69, 94, 101, 104–5, 122, 126, 134–6, 157, 162, 166, 177

Zhou, Min 59
Zionism 28, 76, 94, 98, 110, 111, 158, 188
Zionists 28, 99, 102, 208